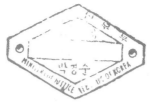

IMMIGRATION SERVICE
− 4 OCT 1988
DEPARTED
(1095)
HONG KONG

DEPARTMENT OF IMMIGRATION
PERMITTED TO ENTER
AUSTRALIA,
on 24 APR 1997
For stay of 12 Month
SYDNEY AIRPORT 54

IMMIGRATION DIVISION BANGKOK THAILAND
A 72
DEPARTED
− 9 FEB 1987
SIGNED

·············Person
30 OCT 1997
DEPARTED
AUSTRALIA
SYDNEY 32

T R A V E L E R ' S
AUSTRALIA
C O M P A N I O N

上陸許可
ADMITTED
15. FEB. 1986
Status: 4-1- 4
Duration: 90 days
NARITA(N)
№ 011278 Immigration Inspector

ADMITTED
20 OCT. 1988
Status: 4-1-16
Duration 180 days
Port: HANEDA
Signature

THE UNITED STATES
OF AMERICA
NONIMMIGRANT VISA
ISSUED AT
PASSED
Air Port

U.S. IMMIGRATION
170 HHW 1710
JUL 20 1998

HONG KONG
(1038)
− 7 JUN 1987
IMMIGRATION
OFFICER

The 1998–1999 Traveler's Companions
ARGENTINA • AUSTRALIA • BALI • CALIFORNIA • CANADA EAST • CANADA WEST • CANADA •
CHINA • COSTA RICA • CUBA • EQUADOR • FLORIDA • HAWAII • HONG KONG • INDIA • INDONESIA •
JAPAN • KENYA • MALAYSIA & SINGAPORE • MEDITERRANEAN FRANCE • MEXICO • NEPAL •
NEW ENGLAND • NEW ZEALAND • PERU • PHILIPPINES • PORTUGAL • RUSSIA • SPAIN •
THAILAND • TURKEY • VENEZUELA • VIETNAM, LAOS AND CAMBODIA

Traveler's AUSTRALIA Companion
First Published 1998
The Globe Pequot Press
6 Business Park Road, P.O. Box 833,
Old Saybrook, CT 06475-0833
http://www.globe.pequot.com

ISBN: 0 7627 0235 4

By arrangement with Kümmerly+Frey, AG, Switzerland
© 1998 Kümmerly+Frey, AG, Switzerland

Created, edited and produced by
Allan Amsel Publishing, 53 rue Beaudouin,
27700 Les Andelys, France. E-mail: aamsel@aol.com
Editor in Chief: Allan Amsel
Editor: Laura Purdom
Original design concept: Hon Bing-wah
Picture editor and designer: David Henry

Printed by Samhwa Printing Co. Ltd., Seoul, Korea

TRAVELER'S AUSTRALIA COMPANION

by Harry Blutstein

Kümmerly+Frey

The
Globe
Pequot
Press

Old Saybrook

Contents

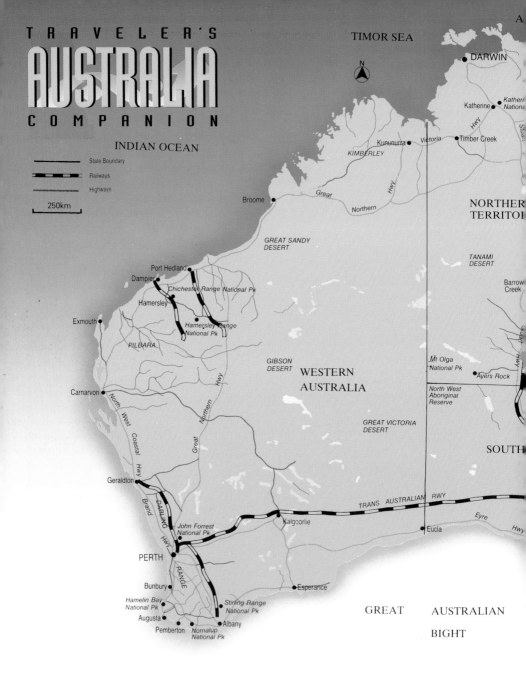

TRAVELER'S

AUSTRALIA

COMPANION

INDIAN OCEAN

State Boundary

Railways

Highways

250km

TIMOR SEA

N

●DARWIN

Katherine ● Katheri
Nationa

Kununurra ● Victoria ● Timber Creek

KIMBERLEY

Broome ●

Great

Northern

Hwy

NORTHER
TERRITOI

GREAT SANDY
DESERT

TANAMI
DESERT

Barrow
Creek

Port Hedland ●
Dampier ●
Chichester Range National Pk
Hamersley ●
Exmouth ●
Hamersley Range
National Pk

PILBARA

GIBSON
DESERT

WESTERN
AUSTRALIA

Mt Olga
National Pk

● Ayers Rock

North West
Aboriginal
Reserve

Carnarvon ●

North West Coastal Hwy

Northern Hwy

Great Hwy

GREAT VICTORIA
DESERT

SOUTH

Geraldton ●

Brand Hwy

DARLING RANGE

John Forrest
National Pk

Kalgoorlie ●

TRANS AUSTRALIAN RWY

Eucla ●

Eyre
Hwy

PERTH ●

Bunbury ●

Hamelin Bay
National Pk

Augusta ●

Pemberton ●

Stirling Range
National Pk

● Esperance

● Albany

Nornalup
National Pk

GREAT   AUSTRALIAN

BIGHT

TOP SPOTS

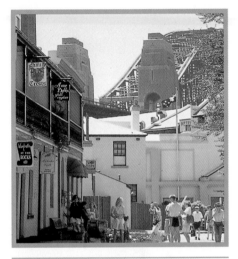

Ferry Across Sydney Harbour

WHY NOT SEE ONE OF THE GREAT NATURAL WONDERS OF THE WORLD, SYDNEY HARBOUR the way the locals see this stunning body of water, on a commuter ferry. The harbor divides Sydney in two, and commuters wishing to avoid the traffic chaos of the roads take a trip on one of the many ferries connecting the northern and southern suburbs. The trip is more relaxing and often much quicker than by car, and the views are breathtaking.

Hop onto one of the lumbering green and gold-colored **Sydney Ferries** ((02) 131-500, which every day make hundreds of trips around the harbor. They all depart from Circular Quay, and timetables and routes can be obtained from the office opposite Wharf 4.

The first ferry, the Rose Hill Packer, started in 1789, only a few years after Sydney was founded, delivering colonists and cargo to Parramatta. While the first ferries were no more than large rowing boats, by 1909, 51 steam-powered ferries were carrying over 40 million passengers a year.

Combining a ferry trip with a walking tour around the foreshore means you get great views of the harbor both on the water and from the beach. The Sydney Ferries information booth provides free brochures containing maps and information on recommended tours, and John Gunter's book *Sydney by Ferry and Foot* (Kangaroo Press, AU$14.95) provides an excellent selection of scenic tours around the foreshore.

My favorite is a trip on the Mosman Ferry, departing from Wharf 4 every 30 minutes, across to Cremorne. From Circular Quay the ferry skirts around the **Opera House**, providing views of this most remarkable building from various angles, the best way to view the sculptural brilliance of its "sails", and on your left is the majestic **Sydney Harbour Bridge**.

Not far offshore is **Fort Denison**, which was built in 1857 as a response to the Crimea War, although the chance of a Russian frigate straying from the Black Sea to Australia, I would have thought

OPPOSITE: Commuter ferries provide an inexpensive means of exploring landmarks on the shores of Sydney Harbour. ABOVE: The historic Rocks area sits at the foot of Sydney Harbour Bridge.

was quite remote. Before serving as a gun battery, it had been used as a place of temporary exile for convicts, at which time it was colloquially known as Pinchgut Island. It earned this name because prisoners sent to the island were left with only a meager supply of bread and water. There are tours to Fort Denison at 10 AM, noon and 2 PM, and bookings are made through the **National Parks and Wildlife Service** ((02) 9206-1166 weekdays and ((02) 9206-1167 weekends.

Alight at the twee Cremorne Point Wharf, and take the path up to the end of the peninsula. Below you stands a small lighthouse built in 1904, and some of the best views of the inner harbor. Back through the park, you will find a pathway through the scenic bushland along the foreshore. The route takes you past some million dollar mansions, many built in the first half of the twentieth century. There are numerous grassy knolls along the track, which are perfect for a picnic or just for sitting and watching the bird life, which includes rainbow lorikeets, sulfur-crested cockatoos and kookaburras. In winter the coral trees along the path are full of red blooms, providing additional color to the walk.

The track circles Mosman Bay to Mosman Wharf, and then continues through some suburban streets to Sirius Cove, where the secluded Whiting Beach provides another stop and an opportunity for a quick dip. The walk ends at **Tooronga Zoo** ((02) 9969-2777, Bradley Head Road, Mosman, which deserves a visit in its own right. Take a ferry from the Tooronga Zoo Wharf to return to Circular Quay.

There are also organized tours of Sydney Harbour. **Captain Cook's Harbour Explorer** ((02) 9206-1111, offers trips which include meals and take in many of the major attractions. Departures are daily from Jetty 6 at Circular Quay.

The Maidenbush Trail OPPOSITE loops through the towering karri forests in southwest Western Australia, dwarfing man and beast. Near Pemberton ABOVE the forest can also be accessed by car.

Tram through the Tall Timber

IN WESTERN AUSTRALIA EVERYTHING APPEARS LARGER THAN LIFE, and nowhere is this more obvious than in its southern forests, where the trees dwarf every other specimen in the country.

The karri is the tallest tree in Australia and the third tallest in the world. These massive trees measure up to 75 m (200 ft) in height, weigh about 200 tons fully grown and are only found in the southwest corner of Western Australia. They have long slender trunks, whitish grey in color, and take up to 200 years to reach full size.

There is no better way to see the tall timber forests than by tram. A rail line built in the Depression now operates as a tourist tram between **Pemberton** and **Northcliffe**, and the trip among the towering karri, and the shorter but still impressive jarrah and marri trees is astonishingly lovely. The tram travels through the heart of karri country, traversing streams on wooden trestle bridges, passing ancient forests and winding its way through pretty countryside along its 36-km (22-mile) route. The best time to see the forest is in early summer, when it is a colorful blaze of wildflowers.

These trees are impressive when viewed from the ground, but the view is spectacular from near the top. Three kilometers (two miles) from Pemberton, visitors can climb 61 m (180 ft) up a fire lookout tree called the **Gloucester Tree**, by means of a spiral ladder made out of wooden karri pegs and steel spikes. If that's not high enough for you, in the Warren National Park, 17 km (10 miles) north of Pemberton, you can climb the 68-m (200-ft) **Bicentennial Tree**. Once 30 karri trees were used as bushfire lookouts during the dry hot summer, permanently manned by fire control officers who were perched in cabins built in the uppermost branches. This task is now done by spotter planes, but some of these trees have survived the ax.

Karri trees only flower once every three years, and the honey produced from their nectar is quite delicious. Jars can be bought from the **Lavender and Berry Farm** (/FAX (08) 9776-1661, on Browns Road, two kilometers (one mile) north of Pemberton. Cozy café and cottage accommodation is also available here. In Jamieson Street, Pemberton, you will find the studio of world renowned wood craftsman **Peter Kovacsy** (/FAX (08) 9776-1265. Local timber is used for his beautiful handcrafted furniture and turned-wood products.

Swim with the Crocodiles at Kakadu

EVERY FIVE-YEAR-OLD IN AUSTRALIA KNOWS THAT SWIMMING IN CROCODILE-INFESTED WATERS IS A VERY DANGEROUS PURSUIT. Just ask Captain Hook. When swimming in Northern Territory make sure that the place is clear of the dangerous saltwater crocs who are large and mean, and apt to snack on just about anything — and anyone! Less often seen are freshwater crocs, which, being smaller and very shy, pose little risk to people.

To see freshwater crocodiles at close quarters visit the inland waters of the **Kakadu National Park**. Several tour companies offer four-wheel drive day tours around the waterfalls in the park. You can tour the park in your own vehicle (four-wheel drive only), but the track is very rough and a good command of off-road driving skills is essential. If you want to see crocodiles at close

quarters, I recommend going with an experienced guide who knows his reptiles well.

Freshwater crocodiles can be seen at **Twin Falls**. This spectacular permanent waterfall lies deep within a steep gorge, and is only accessible by swimming or paddling an inflatable raft (provided by the tour company) upstream from the banks of the lower reaches of the creek. The trip is great fun and a high level of physical fitness is not required. If you are lucky you may get a glimpse of one of the freshwater crocs gliding past on your way. The narrow stream finally widens into a large pool, fringed by white, sandy beaches and pockets of monsoonal forest, palms and ferns. Have lunch on the shore, before the easy trip back downstream. Tours are provided by **Lord of Kakadu Tours** ((08) 8979-2567, and **Park Connections** ((08) 8979-0111.

If you want to see crocs who are not fussy in their eating habits, visit the saltwater variety on the floodplains of Kakadu's **Yellow Waters**, near the town

of Cooinda. Several cruises are run per day, each lasting approximately two hours, with an informative commentary by one of the park rangers who will accompany you. This area is on the Upper South Alligator River, and is renowned for the richness and variety of its wildlife. The cool, clear, still waters of the lagoon may tempt you to dive in for a quick and refreshing swim, but once you have seen your first salty at close quarters, and taken note of its huge, powerful jaws, strong teeth and hungry grin, your enthusiasm will quickly disappear. As well as the crocodiles, you will see an abundance of waterbirds, including the majestic and graceful jabiru, after which Kakadu's main town is named. Take the sunrise or sunset cruises to see the bird life at its most plentiful, and to avoid the hot midday sun.

OPPOSITE: A salty or saltwater crocodile waits patiently for a passing snack, such as a slow moving fish... or perhaps a nice plump tourist who doesn't bother to read the warning signs! ABOVE: In the wet season low lying areas of Kakadu form ephemeral wetlands lit up by colorful water lilies.

Take in a Bird's Eye View

CANBERRA IS THE HOME OF AUSTRALIA'S POLITICIANS and is, therefore, not lacking in hot air. Seldom appreciated by long-suffering taxpayers, the hot air has been put to good use to inflate balloons that take visitors drifting across the quiet morning skies, providing a bird's eye view of the nation's capital.

Mornings in Canberra are crisp and clear, and floating across the landscape provides a unique perspective on the city and surrounding countryside. From above, the care with which its planners have married the layout of the city with the surrounding topography becomes evident. **Balloon Aloft** ((02) 6285-1540 FAX (02) 6282-1054, takes small parties up at sunrise.

Floating through the cool air, gently moving wherever the prevailing wind takes it — the balloon will cover anything from five to 30 km (three to 20 miles), depending on the strength of the wind. Below you will see Lake Burley Griffin, bisected by the main thoroughfare which links Parliament House on Capital Hill, decked by gardens and topped by a gigantic flag pole, with the Civic Circle on the other side. Most of the city's major public buildings can be seen along the lakeshore.

Take advantage of the excellent vantage point that the supremely steady balloon basket provides for aerial photography. At sunrise the nation's capital sparkles with freshness and its monuments and buildings are quite stunning in the glow of early morning. Without a politician or public servant in sight, the place is quite serene.

Walk with the Animals

THERE ARE PLENTY OF ANIMALS TO KEEP YOU COMPANY on **Kangaroo Island**, which is teeming with Australian wildlife; it is the place to go to get a close look at them *au naturale*.

Kangaroo is the dominant island off the South Australia coastline, and Australia's third largest and is located 15 km (nine miles) off the tip of the Fleurieu Peninsula. Isolated from the mainland, and largely undeveloped, this island provides a haven for furry and feathered beasts. It's a natural gem offering an enormous amount for visitors to see and do, but the great pity is that it is seldom visited by overseas tourists.

At Kangaroo Island's **Seal Bay**, rare Australian sea lions sun themselves, oblivious to people wandering among them. While it is possible to enter the beach without supervision, I much prefer to go on a guided tour with a park ranger, who can explain the local etiquette. One thing to remember is to keep your distance. Invading the personal space of a bull seal could result in a chase down the beach, and these awkward-looking creatures can show a good turn of speed. Guided tours can

OPPOSITE: A glass of champagne awaits intrepid balloonists on their return to earth after a sunrise float across the Canberra countryside. ABOVE: Sociable kangaroos are always ready to share a meal with children.

be booked through **Tourism Kangaroo Island** ((08) 8553-1185, in Penneshaw.

At the other end of Kangaroo Island is the **Flinders Chase National Park**, a perfect place for nature lovers. At **Cape du Couedic** fur seals take a breather on the rocks from fishing expeditions, which can take them far out to sea. Fur seals are not as tolerant of humans as the sea lions, but you can watch them at a safe distance from the viewing platform on the cliff above their beach.

There are many koalas on the island, with the largest colony around **Rocky River**. If you are very lucky you may also catch a glimpse of a shy duck-billed platypus in streams in this area.

There are numerous picnic grounds around Flinders Chase National Park, but be prepared to have some of the curious kangaroos and greedy emus that wander freely in the area, wanting to join you for lunch.

Also found on Kangaroo Island are fairy penguins, cute flightless waterbirds standing approximately 35 cm (14 inches) high. After a day out fishing, they return to land at dusk, which is the best time to see them. The National Parks and Wildlife Service ((08) 8553-2381, conducts guided tours of penguin colonies at Penneshaw and Kingscote each evening; tours aside, don't be surprised to see penguins waddle across the main street on their way to the beach.

Visit the Oldest Art Gallery

THE MOST ANCIENT ART GALLERIES IN THE WORLD, estimated to be 20,000 to 65,000 years old (predating even the Paleolithic paintings found in France), showcase the artistic geniuses of prehistoric Australia. Found in caves and rocky overhangs in various sacred sites throughout the country, the oldest of these galleries is in **Arnhem Land**, in Northern Territory.

These priceless pictures are the everlasting heritage of the original inhabitants of the continent, depicting Aboriginal hunting stories, history and

Dreamtime myths. There are thousands of open-air galleries in Australia, and many are secret because they are sacred to the local Aboriginal clan.

Manifesting their fundamental connection with the natural world, Aboriginal artists covered the stone walls with pictures that speak of the earth, using natural pigments made from red and yellow ochre, white clay and black charcoal.

There are a number of different styles of Aboriginal art. The best known is the highly stylized "x-ray" art, so called because the organs and skeletons of the animals portrayed can be seen. Some of the galleries show animals long extinct — further testament to the age of these paintings. There are also "contact" paintings of the eighteenth and nineteenth century depicting Western sailing boats, rifles and white men, easily identified by their hats, pipes, and hands in their pockets, a stance that obviously intrigued the Aboriginal artists. The paintings were used by the Aborigines as a record of their history, and represent the longest continuous stream of artistic expression on the planet.

In the Outback vast tracts of land are still owned by clans who have maintained many parts of their traditional way of life, and are wary of hordes of tourists overrunning their unique piece of Australia. However, small groups of visitors are allowed in provided they are sensitive and respect the local culture. Few tourists come away from the experience untouched, feeling privileged to have had the opportunity to share some time with people so in tune with their environment.

Umorrduk Safaris ((08) 8948-1306 FAX (08) 8948-1305, of Bass Strait Island, is run by Brian Rooke who is of Aboriginal descent and Phyllis Williams from the Gummulkbun Aboriginal clan. The safari's main camp, 365 km (230 miles)

Traditional rock art (top) has been used as the inspiration of modern Aboriginal artists, who have produced highly stylized contemporary art (bottom) based on traditional motifs.

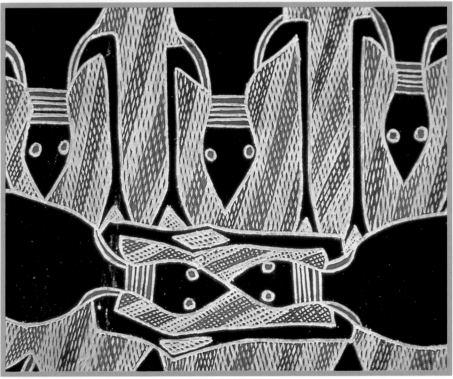

north of Darwin, on land belonging to the Gummulkbun, accommodates small groups of visitors. Tour guides are often Gummulkbun clan members who happily explain what the ancient images mean to them, and tell some of the traditional legends represented in the works of art. **Davidson's Arnhemland Safaris (** (08) 8927-5240 FAX (08) 8945-0919, runs similar tours in the Mount Borradaile area just across the East Alligator River from Kakadu National Park. Max Davidson, former buffalo hunter turned guide, has access to sites that date from the end of the last Ice Age. On his tour you can also see later pictures of the contact period, depicting vessels from Macassar, fifteenth-century traders from the Indonesia archipelago and English sailing ships.

Watch the Big Men Fly

IT'S TRIBAL. IT'S A RELIGIOUS EXPERIENCE. It's addictive. It's Australian Rules Football.

As winter approaches a mania takes over Australia, as men, women and children don scarves and woolen caps, grab flags in club colors and make a pilgrimage to the local oval to watch Australian Rules Football, referred to as just "footy". This unique code of football was born in the inner suburbs of Melbourne and spread to all other states except New South Wales, the home of rugby, where Australian Rules is disparagingly referred to as "aerial ballet".

Australian Rules Football grew out of Gaelic football, which was brought to Melbourne in the mid-nineteenth century, but it has developed into a distinct code that hardly resembles the original. It is a fast running game in which large mobile men launch themselves high above the pack to pluck the ball out of the air, or kick it on the run over 60 m (180 ft), with ease. It is also a game in which its combatants engage in bone-crushing physical encounters, and all without padding (take note, gridiron fans). During winter, league games are played in most capital cities, and a team

has even been established in Sydney, where it is gaining in popularity in this traditional home of rugby.

Even without fully understanding the rules, the excitement is infectious. I well remember an Austrian tourist I took to a game who found herself on her feet screaming madly, without quite understanding why!

To tourists who have never seen the game, it can be quite incomprehensible, and the best way to be initiated into its mysteries is to ask a local sitting next to you. In exchange for barracking for their team, they will generously explain the games finer points.

To learn more about the history of Australian Rules visit the **Australian Gallery of Sport (** (03) 9657-8894, in Jolimont Street Melbourne where memorabilia, videos and exhibits can be viewed. The tour costs AU$8 for adults and AU$5 for children.

It is possible to take in a match at a local footy field, free of charge, while for about AU$12 you can go to a major league game. Venues and times are

advertised in the sports pages of Friday's newspapers.

The ultimate experience is to watch an Australian Football League Grand Final, during which over 100,000 fanatics cram into the MCG oval in September for the climax of the year, to see which team is the best. Tickets are almost impossible to get, although some travel agents may be able to secure them for you if you make your request early enough.

North Queensland's Great Barrier Reef

QUEENSLAND'S WORLD HERITAGE-LISTED GREAT BARRIER REEF IS A WATER-LOVER'S PARADISE. The reef is a veritable underwater Garden of Eden, with over 500 different species of brightly-colored coral and 2,000 species of fish. It is a submarine world waiting to be experienced.

To best explore this wonderland at close quarters you obviously need to be prepared to get wet. Snorkeling can provide you with great views of the shallower parts of the reef, and requires no special skill or training. The only equipment necessary is mask, flippers and a snorkel, and these are usually provided free-of-charge by reef tours and at many resorts. Wetsuits are not needed in North Queensland's warm tropical water, and the underwater visibility is excellent.

SCUBA diving allows you to see the reef at its dazzling best. For those who have never dived before, a range of learn-to-dive courses is available. **Down Under Dive** ((07) 4031-1288, in Sheridan Street, Cairns, is Australia's largest training center. Courses begin with two days of pool and classroom training, followed by two or three days on their 45-m (140-ft) sailing vessel. If your time is limited, brief, supervised dives for novices are offered as an extra on many of the day trips which visit the reef, such as those

ABOVE: A Grand Final football match between Carlton and Hawthorn, in which over 100,000 fanatical supporters cheer on their side.

run by **Ocean Spirit Cruises** ((07) 4031-2920, out of Cairns. Underwater cameras are also available for hire, so that you can record your exploits and make the folks back home jealous.

While the reef can only be accessed by boat from the mainland, on some of North Queensland's coral cays and islands you can literally walk off the beach into a coral wonderland. A fascinating variety of marine life awaits you, as you swim amongst the colorful corals and giant clams, in the quiet company of shoals of exotic tropical fish.

The Unforgettable Port Arthur

PORT ARTHUR IS A PLACE OF MENACE. Two hundred years ago it was a hell-hole jail, into which Great Britain dumped its poor, some of whose only crime was stealing a loaf of bread to feed their hungry children. The last prisoners left Port Arthur in 1877 but ghosts remain of men sentenced to the hideous conditions, from which many died and some went insane. Restored, this attraction is a grim reminder of the dark history of Australia.

The penal settlement was founded on a peninsula called **Eaglehawk Neck**. Across its narrowest point a line of ferocious dogs was chained to discourage prisoners from escaping. The dogs did their job well, and only a handful of convicts ever got away.

The only contact the prisoners had with the outside world was the icy blast of wind from the Antarctic. Despite the cold there was no doubt in the minds of the some 12,500 convicts who served time at Port Arthur that they had come to hell.

No amount of landscaping decreases the evil of the **Penitentiary,** which dominates the site. Discipline was severe and misbehavior punished by placing the prisoner in solitary confinement in the **Model Prison**, which has also been restored. Prisoners were subjected to a form of sensory deprivation, as the cells were soundproof and dark. Wardens even wore felt slippers to mute their footfalls. The silence was complete. Disobedience resulted in more extreme deprivation, as transgressors were thrown into dumb cells that were separated from the world by a meter of solid rock and four doors. Many prisoners went mad and ended up in the **Lunatic Asylum**. Its very existence is a stark reminder of the degradation to which Port Arthur subjected its inmates. The Asylum has been turned into a visitor center and museum with displays on how the inmates lived.

In the middle of the bay is the forbidding **Isle of the Dead**, where 1,769 convicts and 180 freemen lie buried. The headstones for the freemen, carved by the convicts (complete with spelling mistakes), can still be seen.

Port Arthur Historic Site ((03) 6250-2363 FAX (03) 6250-2765, is located 100 km (62 miles) southeast of Hobart, on the Tasman Peninsula. Visitors can explore the ruins, restored buildings, cottages and gardens, join historical walks and take ferry cruises. Admission prices are AU$13 for adults and AU$6.50 for children, or AU$32.50 for a family including two adults and up to six children. Reduced rates are available for seniors and students.

Noodle for Opals in the Outback

FOR THE AUTHENTIC AUSTRALIAN OUTBACK EXPERIENCE IT IS NECESSARY TO TRAVEL LONG DISTANCES; and then some more. There are few places more remote than the town of Coober Pedy, which is 850 km (530 miles) north of Adelaide and 687 km (430 miles) south of Alice Springs.

There is no reason for the existence of Coober Pedy in the middle of the desert... except that opals were discovered there in 1915. And so a frontier town grew up around 70 fields where miners went in search of "fire" opal, colored with beautiful reds, greens, and blues on a white or light background.

Opals were mined, and are still mined within a 50 km (30 mile) radius of Coober Pedy, and discarded mullock heaps still containing opals missed by miners can be noodled (or fossicked) by visitors. Permission must be first obtained if you want to noodle a mullock heap next to a miners claim, and some miners reserve this right for themselves.

Opals are composed of silica and water. Ninety percent of all opals, called "potch", are without fiery colors and are considered worthless. Colored opals on the other had can fetch good prices. The most valuable is the black opal with its dark base. The crystal opal which is almost transparent displays colors ranging from fire-red — the rarest and therefore most prized — to the less preferred green and blue gems. Swirls of color in the opal are more valuable that pinfire opals where the color is in small specks.

While it is possible to noodle without a guide, the best way to undertake the full Outback experience is on a **Coober Pedy Discovery Tour** ((08) 8672-5028. As well as tips on where to noodle, the tour includes visits to an underground house and church, and for the less than successful a free opal gift.

Noodling is hot work with temperatures hovering above 40°C (100°F), but the hope of uncovering a valuable opal makes this a popular activity. If you come away empty-handed, then drop into the **Umoona Opal Mine and Museum** in the center of town where you can see how hard the miners toil to extract these sublime stones from the earth, and drool over displays of the finest opals.

Coober Pedy is a corruption of the Aboriginal words "Kupa Piti", meaning white man's burrow; the name is apt as about half the population live in underground buildings to escape the searing heat. Stay in an underground hotel, and visit the underground shops or houses that are on show to get an idea how miners have adapted to the hostile environment.

Port Arthur, which once housed convicts under inhuman and cruel conditions, is now a popular tourist attraction.

YOUR CHOICE

The Great Outdoors

Australia's landscape has so many diverse areas of natural beauty that there is something for every taste and interest. However, remember that there are large distances between attractions, and you need to be prepared to undertake some long trips. But the rewards are more than ample compensation.

Colorful reefs invite divers to explore the coral and exotic aquatic life. Wilderness areas include deserts, alpine high-country and rain forest, all prized by walkers. Wonderful beaches lure fishermen and surfers, while offshore every sort of watercraft can be seen.

Australia values highly its natural heritage, and has over 800 national parks.

In recognition of the significance, natural value and uniqueness of some areas in Australia, World Heritage listings have been given to Kakadu National Park, the Willandra Lakes, the Tasmanian Wilderness, Uluru-Kata National Park, the Great Barrier Reef, the Wet Tropics of Queensland and Shark Bay in Western Australia. National parks are managed by the states, other than the Great Barrier Reef which is managed by the Commonwealth Government. Information and maps can be obtained from local national parks offices — telephone numbers for which can be found throughout this book under each park's respective region.

It has been described as one of the seven wonders of the natural world, a claim endorsed enthusiastically by anyone who has visited the **Great Barrier Reef**. This diverse ecosystem has the largest collection of coral in the world, 500 species in all, and living off the coral are 2,000 fish species of every shape and color imaginable. The water is warm, averaging about 18°C (64°F), which is ideal for the maintenance of this natural wonderland, and provides a comfortable environment for exploring the reef either using SCUBA gear or snorkel. The waters around the reef are clear, with visibility on the order of 50 m (150 ft) not uncommon.

OPPOSITE: A coral garden is at your fingertips when SCUBA diving off the Great Barrier Reef.
ABOVE: Clownfish flit among the tentacles of sea anemone, where they graze.

It is difficult to comprehend the size of the Great Barrier Reef, which stretches over 2,000 km (1,200 miles), covers an area of 350,000 sq km (130,000 sq miles), and is visible from space. The composition of the reef varies over its length, and in fact it is not one structure but a series of 2,900 individual reefs.

Port Douglas, in far north Queensland is one of the closest towns to the reef. **Quicksilver Connections** ((07) 4099-5500, has two vessels that leave daily for Agincourt Reef, the only ribbon reef accessible for day trips. A platform at the back of the boat provides access to the crystal clear, warm water for swimmers of all abilities and ages. Snorkeling gear and life jackets are supplied. The company also organizes dives, which vary according to your experience. Those who don't want to get wet can view the coral from a glass-sided submarine.

One advantage of using Port Douglas as a base is that it is near the **Daintree Rainforest**, another World Heritage area. The Daintree consists of rugged wet tropical terrain, with spectacular waterfalls cascading off steep escarpments. The rain forest is populated by colorful butterflies and tropical birds. The lowland rain forest can be explored along the lower reaches of the Mossman Gorge, 15 km (10 miles) from Port Douglas. However to visit the less accessible sections of the rain forest it is advisable to hire a four-wheel drive vehicle or take an organized tour.

At the other end of the country, the Tasmanian wilderness provides a contrast, with **Cradle Mountain** rated as one of the great walking areas in the world. For the fit, the six-day **Overland Track** takes you past jagged peaks, winding its way through heathland and dense beech forests, past high alpine moorlands and over fast flowing streams. This area provides the best example of pristine, cool, temperate rain forest in Australia, if not the world. There are catered tours run by experienced guides, such as those run by **Cradle Huts** ((03) 6260-4094. The best part of this trip is that you are only expected to carry a light backpack with

your sleeping bag, lunch, and the bare minimum of clothes. Accommodation is provided in comfortable cabins along the route, which are well-stocked with food and complete with hot and cold running water, showers and toilets. Walking the track without a guide is much cheaper, but you need to carry tents, plenty of warm clothes and enough food for the whole trip. You should report to the ranger's office before you leave, and beware of unpredictable weather. There are also easy day trips from Cradle Mountain Lodge or Lake St. Clair.

For a sensational walk through the center of South Australia take the **Heysen Trail**. Crossing 1,500 km (932 miles) of wilderness, the trail goes from the coastal beaches of **Cape Jervis** where sea eagles soar overhead, through the **Mount Lofty Ranges**, to the spectacular **Parachilna Gorge** in the northern **Flinders Ranges**. The trail is well-marked with red blazes, and accommodation is available in numerous huts, and YHA hostels. You can also camp. Winter is the best time to tackle the Heysen Trail, and maps can be obtained from Friends of the Heysen Trail ((08) 8212-6299.

For some of the best scenery in Western Australia try the 650-km (404-mile) **Bibbulmun Track** that runs between **Kalamundra** and **Walpole**. The track passes through jarrah and karri forests, often winding along old logging tracks and disused rail lines. The best time to do this walk is in spring when the countryside comes alive with a kaleidoscope of wildflowers.

Sporting Spree

Australians are passionate about sports, and at any time of the year you will find men, women and children at ovals and playing fields all over the country enthusiastically taking part in

OPPOSITE: A glacial lake reflects the grandeur of Cradle mountain, locaqred in the untouched wilderness of western Tasmania. OVERLEAF: Fields awash in color roll through a valley of the Flinders Ranges.

a variety of sporting activities. For a tourist, the best way to learn the finer points of a game you may be unfamiliar with, such as cricket or Australian Rules Football, is to take a seat at a suburban field, and seek instruction from a local, who will be only too pleased to induct you into their "religion".

The weather is good all year round for most sports, and top quality facilities are available.

Living in a country surrounded by water, it is not surprising that many Australians enjoy a wide variety of water sports. For yachting enthusiasts, the annual Sydney-to-Hobart race, which takes place between Christmas and New Year is one not to be missed. Most seaside towns and resorts will have a yacht club, and it is always possible to find someone looking for crew members for the day. For more information on what is available contact the **Australian Yachting Federation** ((02) 9922-4333.

At beach resorts it is usually easy to hire sail boards, jet skis or power boats. There are special sections of beach for these activities, to segregate them from swimmers, and the hire company should be able to fill you in on the local rules. As well, tour operators at the more popular beaches will take you water-skiing or parasailing.

If your thing is shooting the curl, then you are likely to be impressed at the number of good **surfing** beaches. An amazing experience is to surf at Bondi Beach, which is fringed by an inner suburb of Sydney. Victoria's Bell's Beach, off the Great Ocean Road, is the world's only Surfing Recreation Reserve, and each year hosts the International Bell's Beach Surf Classic. Other top surf beaches are at Noosa Heads in Queensland, Byron Bay in New South Wales and Margaret River in Western Australia. Experienced surfers who want the thrill of the big wave should try the area around Port Campbell in Victoria, justifiably called the Awesome Coast. For more information about surfing in Australia contact the Surf Life Saving Association ((02) 9597-5588.

Inland there are still some wild rivers for **white-water rafting**. The best places are in the Tasmanian highlands, with the Franklin River being an exciting ride through some truly magnificent scenery. Rivers in the higher regions of the Great Dividing Range along the eastern coast, such as the Snowy and Mitta Mitta Rivers provide scintillating white-water rafting. Peregrine Adventures ((03) 9663-8611, runs rafting expeditions on all these rivers.

Surrounded by so much water, luxurious reefs, rich sealife and with its fair share of wrecks, Australian off-shore areas are ideal for **scuba diving**. There are a few special treats for those in the know. Get a close look at whalesharks, 12-m (36-ft) gentle giants of the sea at Ningaloo Reef off the Western Australian coast. The Exmouth Diving Centre ((08) 9949-1201, organizes dives between April and June, when these fish frequent the reef. The greatest underwater sex show in the world occurs at the Great Barrier Reef in November when the coral spawn *en masse* producing an explosion of color.

Tusa Dive ((07) 4031-1248, runs night dives out of Cairns to watch this wonder of nature. Good dive sites in this area are listed in Neville Coleman's book *The Dive Sites of the Great Barrier Reef* (AU$33.95). Drop into Fish Rock Cave, located at the mid-north coast of New South Wales, which is one of the largest ocean caverns in the southern hemisphere. Fish and crayfish can be seen scuttling around the rocks. These caves provide an amazing diving experience. Tours are available from Fish Rock Dive Centre ((02) 6566-6614, at 332 Gregory Street, South West Rocks. The area west of Port Campbell in Victoria is know as the Shipwreck Coast. Here it is possible to reach the *Fiji*, wrecked in 1891 near Cats Reef, worth a visit in itself. Schomberg Diving Services ((03) 5598-6499, organizes dives to the wreck, Ryan's Den an underwater cave system and Cats Reef.

Deep sea fishing trips are available at many towns along the eastern coast, and fighting fish such as marlin, mackerel, barracuda and sailfish can be caught. The Great Barrier Reef is a popular destination, and there are organized fishing trips out of Cairns for giant black marlin (see FAR NORTH QUEENSLAND, page 159). No fishing license is required, provided your catch is for your own consumption.

There are some world-class spots for **freshwater fishing** in Australia. In Central North Tasmania, the Land of Three Thousand Lakes (see UP THE MIDDLE in TASMANIA, pages 218–220) is stocked with wild brown trout and around Darwin barramundi run from June to November. Fishing licenses may be required; ask at the local angler's shop or contact the State Fisheries Department.

Not many people would associate Australia with **skiing**, but there are popular ski fields in New South Wales and Victoria. While there are some reasonable downhill runs, it is the cross-

OPPOSITE: The Grampian Mountains offer serious rock climbers varied and challenging faces to scale. BELOW: Cycling along quiet country roads offers a leisurely way of seeing the countryside.

An intricate network of pebbly creeks, a vast array of grass bunkers and hollows, and a total of 90 sand traps, provide quite a challenge to players of all standards. In Western Australia, the three courses at Joondalup Country Club (9400-8888, at Connolly, just north of Perth, are of international renown. Each course has nine holes, and their names — Lake, Dune and Quarry — reveal how different each is from the other. They all have their share of breathtaking shots across stony ravines, precipitous drops and sudden climbs in the fairways, crater-like bunkers and hidden hollows. Enjoy!

In Victoria's high country the horsemanship of the mountain cattlemen is famous, and a number of **horseback riding** tours are organized by them. Out of Mansfield, Stoney's Bluff & Beyond Trail Rides ((03) 5775-2212, offers day and overnight rides in the Howqua Valley, and through the Bogong and Dargo High Plains. For something different, you can join the cattle muster and become a real cowboy or cowgirl.

If you prefer a smoother ride, then **bicycling** is a better bet. Many major cities now have extensive cycle tracks and some highways include bike lanes. To get off the main roads it is essential to have a mountain bike, while a touring bike is best for paved roads. Note that in many states it is compulsory to wear an approved helmet.

For tourists, it is possible to hire bikes in all capital cities and many tourist destinations. Most capital cities are reasonably flat, except for Sydney which presents cyclists with numerous challenging hills to traverse. Canberra provides the most extensive cycle tracks of any major city, with a network that covers 130 km (81 miles). A popular ride is around Lake Burley Griffin, which takes about two hours.

Outside the major cities there are a number of favorite routes, selected because of their lack of hills and good sightseeing. The wine-producing areas of Rutherglen, in Victoria, Barossa Valley, in South Australia, and the Hunter Valley

country ski touring that is world-class. In winter Kosciusko National Park has better snow cover than Switzerland, and is much safer because there is no threat of being caught in an avalanche or falling down a crevice. The ski season starts on the Queen's Birthday long weekend in early June, and lasts till October.

Australia has produced more than its fair share of **tennis** greats, and the temperate climate means that it is possible to have a game all through the year. There are courts that can be hired out in all cities and towns, and the local phone book should be consulted for contact details.

There is no lack of open space in Australia, so it's no surprise that **golf** courses are plentiful. Many are found in very attractive settings. Victoria's Cape Schank Golf Course ((03) 5950-8100, with its awe-inspiring views, is surrounded by rocky cliffs overlooking the foaming ocean waves below. Balls hit over the edge are beyond retrieval. The Paradise Palms Golf Course (4059-1166, near Cairns, between Clifton Beach and the rain forests of the Great Dividing Range, is a tough course of incredible beauty.

in New South Wales are popular destinations, and it is possible to reach them by train, which takes bikes for a small extra charge. There are a number of fairly flat islands which are popular cycling destinations. They are Rottnest Island in Western Australia, Kangaroo Island in South Australia and King Island in Tasmania

Rock climbing and **abseiling** off the plateau or cliffs of the Blue Mountains provide both an adrenaline rush as well as spectacular views of the plain below. The Australian School of Mountaineering ((02) 4782-2014, in Katoomba, runs tours catering for both beginners and the more experienced. Transport, food, and specialist clothing and equipment are provided. For experienced rock climbers challenging cliff faces can be found in the Grampian Mountains in Victoria, Moonarie in the Flinders Ranges in South Australia, Bobs Hollow near Margaret River in Western Australia and Frog Buttress in Queensland. If you want to look death in the eye, and have good bowel control, then try Nowra in New South Wales for the best crags in Australia, some of which were not conquered until 1989.

SPECTATOR SPORTS

In all states but New South Wales, **Australian Rules Football** is a national obsession. This game is over a hundred years old, and unique to Australia. It combines long kicking, fierce tackling and high leaps as the ball is plucked out of the air. Aussie Rules is a winter game, with the season lasting from March to September. There are national league games in Melbourne every week, and in the other capitals at least once every two weeks. Games are advertised on the sports pages of Friday's newspapers, and entrance costs about AU$12.

Rugby union and **league** are also played in Australia, mainly in New South Wales and Queensland. These two traditional rivals put aside May and June to play three **State of Origin** test matches, where fanaticism is at its height and state pride is at stake.

Soccer is one of four football codes played in Australia, and is gaining in popularity since the national side

OPPOSITE: Soldiers and spectators relax on Melbourne Cup Day which is a public holiday in November. ABOVE: A close finish at Sydney's Rosehill course.

Socceroos have had some international success in the World Cup. It is played mainly in Melbourne, Sydney and Adelaide.

There is **horse racing** most of the year, but spring and autumn are the main seasons. During these times the calendar is full in the capital cities, with racing events on most weekends and sometimes during the week. Australians' obsession with horse racing reaches a peak with the running of the **Melbourne Cup** at Flemington, on the first Tuesday of November. It must be the only place in the world where a public holiday is declared for a horse race, and the nation stops for three minutes as the best horses in Australia and New Zealand race for the coveted cup. You don't have to be a horse racing fanatic to enjoy the Melbourne Cup; many people spend most of the day in the car park drinking champagne and enjoying themselves. Some don't even get to the race track, but nevertheless seem to have a great time.

Over two weeks in January the **Australian Open Tennis Championship** is played at Melbourne Park in Batman Avenue. The world's top players compete in this Grand Slam event. Day passes for the earlier matches can be purchased at the venue, are relatively inexpensive and allow you access to all games except those on center court. For the finals, you need to book in advance ((03) 9286-1234.

In summer **cricket** takes over from football, and one or two cricketing nations visit for a round of test matches and one-day tournaments. If you are not accustomed to the game, it can seem slow and uneventful. For the novice the one-day games provide more excitement, but for the connoisseur there is no substitute for a five-day test match, particularly if England is in town for an Ashes series.

Motor racing in Australia enjoys a high profile. The Grand Prix is raced in Melbourne in March, around the course at Albert Park Lake. This is the first event in the FIA Formula One World Championship and attracts the world's best drivers. It's incredibly popular, and early reservations are essential ((03) 9258-

7100. The race coincides with Moomba, and there are lots of sporting and entertainment events held during the same week, for those looking for a break from mainlining on petrol fumes. In September petrol-heads go to Bathurst, 221 km (137 miles) west of Sydney on the Great Western Highway, for the **Bathurst 1000 Road Races** which feature production cars and motorbike racing.

Australia has some of the best surf beaches in the world, and a lifestyle that centers on the sea. Two international events are held that are musts for surfers. In March towering waves challenge the world's best at the **Margaret River Masters**. The event draws a crowd of approximately 20,000 people to Margaret River, 227 km (141 miles) south of Perth. At Easter the **International Bell's Beach Surf Classic** attracts the world's greatest board riders to Southern Victoria.

The Open Road

Driving in Australia often means long distances, but fortunately most regions have excellent roads. For the adventurous and those who long to get off the beaten track, a four-wheel drive vehicle is essential. As there can be large distances between towns, particularly in the Outback, it is essential to take adequate provisions, particularly drinking water.

Gregory's and UBD produce a series of excellent fold-out road maps of all capital cities and popular tourist regions. If you plan on doing a lot of touring a better option is Robinson's *Road Atlas of Australia*. While off-the-road touring by four-wheel drive, consult the two-volume Gregory's *4WD Escapes*, which provides detailed maps of treks and GPS readings on all major routes across Australia. There is also useful travel information on the Internet at http://www.finalword .com/Touring_Australia/gtaframe.htm.

Driving the Australian Outback presents its own unique hazards. A fast moving kangaroo can do a lot of damage, so care should be taken on the open road, particularly at dawn and dusk when 'roos are more likely to be out and about.

While it is possible to make short trips out of the capital cities, the truly great routes can take days to complete and cover a thousand kilometers or more.

The following suggestions take in some quite different scenery, providing a good sample of what is on offer.

The **Great Ocean Road** stretches about 300 km (180 miles) from just past Geelong, an hour's drive southwest of Melbourne, to Warrnambool. Construction of the road started in 1919, as employment for Australian servicemen returned from the First World War, and was completed in 1932. Often using picks and shovels, the workmen carved the road into cliffs and mountains along Victoria's southwest coast.

The Great Ocean Road hugs the coastline, overlooking sheer cliffs, and takes in some breathtaking coastal scenery. It plunges down to empty bays and passes through small seaside holiday towns. Occasionally the road takes a turn inland, passing through virtually untouched remnants of dense rain forest, providing contrast to the ocean views.

The Great Ocean Road starts at **Torquay**, and heads southwest through **Anglesea**, **Aireys Inlet**, **Lorne** and **Apollo Bay**, which are popular seaside resorts situated on clean sandy beaches and separated by rocky headlands. There are good surf beaches along this stretch of coastline, and hardy surfers can be seen in their wetsuits riding a wave even in the depths of winter.

Just after Apollo Bay the road turns inland, climbing up the Otway Ranges, providing memorable views of the ocean and rugged cliffs. Lorne is a good base for exploring the **Otway National Park**. Walk through a rain forest of towering mountain ash and gullies of myrtle, beech, mosses and ferns. Take in the beauty of waterfalls that tumble down mountain sides. The Great Ocean Road Visitor Information Centre ℂ (03) 5237-6529, in Apollo Bay, can give you advice and maps on the best walks.

After cutting the corner at Cape Otway, the road returns towards the coast at **Princetown**, which is at the eastern end of **Port Campbell National Park**. This is the place I like to stop, camping at Port Campbell and getting up early in the morning to watch the rising sun reflect off the **Twelve Apostles**, rock formations carved by the crashing sea and the winds that whip this part of the coast. There are in fact only eight rock outcrops still standing, the other Apostles having been claimed by the sea.

At this point, the road follows the tops of sheer cliffs which have been cut away by the raging sea below. It is not difficult to see why this section of coast is called the **Shipwreck Coast**, as over 30 ships foundered here. Some can still be seen today between Warrnambool and Port Fairy.

The most mysterious wreck is one that has yet to be found. A grounded mahogany ship was seen in the sand dunes in 1880. It has been suggested that

To get off the beaten track in the Outback a sturdy four-wheel drive vehicle is essential.

it is a Portuguese ship that made its way to the east coast in 1522 only to founder on this treacherous coastline. The sand dunes in this part of the coastline are constantly moving, and the boat has been buried again. If found, this wreck would rewrite the history books on the discovery of the east coast by Europeans. To resolve this mystery, the Victorian Government offered a reward for the discovery of Mahogany Ship. The reward is still unclaimed so you might want to take a stop here and do a little beachcombing along Armstrong Bay, the last sighting of the phantom wreck.

Take a short detour in Warrnambool, and prepare to see one of the great creatures of the sea. From the lookout it is often possible to see great southern whales, which frequent this part of the coast between June and October.

Driving across the **Nullarbor Plain** is a test of endurance, but an experience you will not soon forget. Nullarbor, is from the Latin "no trees" and is an apt name for this arid limestone plain where nothing but low-lying bushes grow. The Nullarbor Plain runs along the Great Australian Bight, between Ceduna in South Australia and the mining town of Norseman in Western Australia. Covering 200,000 sq km (77,400 sq miles), similar in area to the British Isles, the Nullarbor Plain was an old seabed that rose about 100 million years ago. The road, however, is south of the true plain, so you will see trees on the route. Further north the railway line runs through the center of the plain in a dead straight line.

Traversing the Nullarbor is a similar experience to crossing the tundra along the route of the trans-Siberian — if you are excited by featureless expanses of flat terrain, then a 1,300-km (800-mile) drive along the Eyre Highway through parts of the Nullarbor Plain should be on your agenda. The almost barren rust-colored plain, tinged grey-green by bluebush and saltbush, is broken up by small towns that exist solely to service the train and passing traffic. Crossing the Nullarbor is the most direct route by land from Adelaide to Perth.

Ooldea, at the eastern end of the Nullarbor Plain, has a special place in Australian history. From 1919 until 1935 Daisy Bates camped on this site, caring for the Aborigines in what must be one of the most inhospitable places on Earth. Occasional passengers on the transcontinental train were astonished by the sight of an Edwardian lady in dark ankle-length skirts, black stockings, stiff collar, white gloves and parasol, traveling across the flat expanse in a camel buggy. In 1938, Bates wrote in *The Passing of the Aborigines:* "The Australian native can withstand all the reverses of nature, fiendish droughts and sweeping floods, horrors of thirst and enforced starvation — but he cannot withstand civilization". She believed her mission was to arrest civilization's contamination of the Aboriginal people, but as the title of her book suggests, in the end she had to admit defeat.

Underground, carved out of limestone, are subterranean rivers, cathedral caves and large lakes. The Nullarbor is a treasure trove for archaeologists, and the earliest human footprints, 5,500 years old, have been discovered there. A well preserved 4,600-year-old specimen of the now extinct Tasmanian tiger was discovered in a cave called Thylacine Hole, and is on show at the West Australian Museum in Perth. As the Eyre Highway is never far from the Great Australian Bight, sightings of southern right whales add interest to the crossing. The whales come to this area to breed, and 20-m (60-ft) whales and their calves can be seen off the coast, between June and October. The lookouts are off the highway on Aboriginal land and permits, costing AU$2 per person, can be obtained from Yalata Roadhouse ((08) 8625-6807, and Nullarbor Hotel-Motel Inn ((08) 8625-6271. Occasional sightings of an albino whale may be made in these waters.

If you want to get off the main road, then look no further than **Queensland's Fraser Island**, the largest sand island in the world at around 120 km (75 miles) long and up to 50 km (30 miles) wide.

There are no paved roads on the island, and the beach provides a driving track like no other. Buses and four-wheel drive wagons whip around the island along the hardened sand of the wide beaches that make up its perimeter. The beach is an official road, and although it may not have a white line painted down the middle all the usual road rules apply.

Looking in from the road it is possible to observe cliffs of colored sands, and behind them the tall trees of the largely unspoiled rain forest that make up the hinterland.

There is a car ferry from the mainland at Hervey Bay, but remember that to navigate the interior a four-wheel drive is essential. You can hire one from Island Explorers 4WD Hire ((07) 41254-3770, in Hervey Bay, or if you wish to camp on the island, Fraser Island Backpacking Safaris ((07) 4125-3933, organizes very popular trips, and supplies both vehicle and camping gear.

Inland, there are over 40 freshwater lakes, which have formed in depressions in the sand dunes on a bed of decaying and hardened organic litter dropped from trees and plants of the surrounding rain forest. Elsewhere crystal clear streams bubbling over sandy bottoms invite a refreshing dip. Fraser Island has a large community of dingos, or native Australian dogs, which roam the beach. While they are generally harmless, they have become persistent in begging for food, having been spoiled by generations of tourists feeding them. The lakes are also home to thousands of water birds.

Backpacking

The large number of young people holidaying in Australia on the cheap has resulted in an explosion in inexpensive backpacking accommodation in all the capital cities and favorite tourist destinations, particular around the beautiful beaches of Queensland, where major destinations include Surfers' Paradise, Magnetic Island, Airlie Beach, Cairns and Fraser Island.

An area that backpackers have recently discovered is Tasmania, because it is relatively uncrowded, and has good, inexpensive hostels over the whole island. While it is small compared with the mainland, there's still lots to see and do.

A number of free newspapers and magazines are produced for backpackers. *TNT Magazine* is a small quarterly booklet, which has lots of useful information, while the *Aussie Backpacker*, a bimonthly newspaper, has information on tours, special deals, travel information and accommodation, and its classified pages contain job advertisements for casual work. Both publications are readily available from hostels and bus terminals.

Another source of information is the **Backpacker Travel Centres** ((03) 9654-8477, located in three states: at Shop 19, Centre Place, 258 Flinders Lane in Melbourne; Shop P33 ((02) 9231 3699, Pitt Street Level, Imperial Arcade in Sydney; and Balcony Level ((07) 3221-2225, Brisbane Arcade, Queen Street Mall in Brisbane.

The most extensive accommodation network is offered by **Youth Hostels of Australia (YHA)**, where beds are about AU$12 to AU$18 per night, as well as a small annual membership fee. Information and reservations are available through YHA offices in each capital city, or from the larger hostels in the network. The standard at YHA hostels is consistently good. If you intend to use YHA extensively then it is worth getting one of their accommodation packages, either 20 nights at one of their hostels for AU$250, valid for six months, or 10 nights for AU$130, valid for two months. There are also cut-price tickets to the movies, bike hire and some excellent tours arranged out of YHA hostels.

In addition to YHA, there are many private backpacker hostels, particularly in the main cities, which charge between AU$12 and AU$20 a night, depending on the locality and level of competition.

They tend to be in the seedier parts of town, situated in converted older houses or motels. These disadvantages are offset by their central location and proximity to good public transport. In the capital cities, if you don't mind staying outside the main backpacker areas, you can find cheaper hostels in the suburbs. Each capital has an area where hostels concentrate. In Sydney it is Kings Cross, in Melbourne backpackers head for the inner suburbs of St. Kilda or North Melbourne, in Perth the areas are Northbridge and Scarborough while in the other capitals hostels are located on the edge of the central city area.

Standards at private hostels vary widely, from clean and comfortable to dingy and dirty. Some places can be very noisy, and may even advertise the fact — their claim to fame will be that there is always a party going on. If you like to sleep quietly, look elsewhere. Private hostels are advertised at interstate and intercity bus terminals and the most reliable information on which are the best ones can usually be obtained on the road by asking other backpackers.

A number of independent hostels have banded together to form the **VIP Backpackers Association** ((07) 3268-5733. For a membership fee of AU$25, discount cards are provided, which can be used to secure AU$1 per night off accommodation. It is worthwhile joining if you will stay in hostels often. Information on VIP Backpackers can be obtained on its web site, http://www.backpackers.com.au, or by requesting a copy of its *Little Yellow Book* which lists backpacker accommodation throughout Australia. Another backpacker organization is **Nomads** TOLL-FREE 1800-819-883, which provides a hostel discount card to members.

During the summer holidays some universities open up their dormitories for lodging. There are universities in all the capital cities, and you should contact their accommodation department to see if they have rooms available.

Backpackers planning to stay in a city for several months will find that they can get a room in a student household for about AU$60 to AU$100 a week. Advertisements are usually posted on notice boards in the university and in bookshops and cafés frequented by students.

In the countryside most major towns and tourist areas will have a caravan park and campground. For about AU$5 a night it is possible to camp with access to toilets and showers, while caravans can be hired for about AU$20 to AU$40 a night. During summer, Easter and school holidays these places fill up quickly, so book ahead if you intend to travel during these periods.

If you don't mind getting your hands dirty, then try "WWOOFing". The Willing Workers on Organic Farms (WWOOF) program gives travelers interested in permaculture and environmentally sensitive agricultural practices an opportunity to work on an organic farm. In exchange for a few hours work a day they are provided with free board. To join, contact Lionel Pollard ((03) 5155-0218 E-MAIL NH@b150 .aone.net.au, Mount Murrindal Coop, Buchan, Victoria, 3885. Joining costs AU$30 for single people and AU$35 for a couple. If you would like to relax at an organic farm, and prefer not to work for your board, Lionel Pollard also produces the *Organic Farm Bed and Breakfast Guide*, which can be purchased for AU$5 by writing to the above address.

If you come to Australia for a working holiday, it is essential that you have a working visa before seeking employment (see TRAVEL DOCUMENTS in TRAVELERS' TIPS). Casual work is fairly easy to find in major cities, and on farms and orchards during the picking seasons. Popular locations are Mildura, Bundaberg, Kununurra, and the grape growing areas of South Australia and Victoria.

The six-day hike along the Overland Track in Tasmania, which is considered one of the world's top walking tracks, passes glacial lakes and heathland teaming with wildlife.

For long trips, buses are the cheapest means of transport, and it is possible to travel from, say, Sydney to Darwin, a distance of 4,060 km (2,540 miles) for about AU$300. The cost of plying the more popular routes, such as between Melbourne and Sydney, is significantly cheaper because of the competition, and fares can be as low as AU$30. The two largest coach companies, Greyhound Pioneer and McCafferty's, offer special tourist passes, which allow unlimited travel for a fixed number of days through their network, which covers most tourist areas. There are also smaller regional operators that offer good deals on limited routes. Information for these are usually posted on bulletin boards of backpacker lodgings and YHA hostels.

In recent times governments have been closing down rail lines, and replacing them with bus coaches. While the range of destinations may be limited, travel by train is much faster and more comfortable than by bus. For the best deal on train travel, purchase an *Aussie Pass* — which can only be bought outside Australia. It offers unlimited travel for seven to 90 days.

For long stays in Australia, purchasing a car can be an economical option; a reasonable second-hand car can be bought for AU$2,000 to AU$5,000. Private sales are advertised through the Saturday newspapers, or you can buy from a second-hand car dealer. It helps to know something about cars to avoid buying a lemon, but in any case ensure that a Roadworthy Certificate is provided, which gives at least some level of assurance that the car is in reasonably good condition.

Generally, hitchhiking is not recommended in Australia. There have been some horror stories in the newspapers about abductions, and worse, of hitchhikers. On the other hand, getting a ride with other backpackers is fairly safe. You will find advertisements placed on hostel and university notice boards looking for people to share petrol costs for trips.

Living It Up

EXCEPTIONAL HOTELS

There are no hotels in Australia located in converted castles or historic mansions, and no earls or dukes who take in boarders to make ends meet. This does not mean, however that Australia is bereft of luxury hotels, which are defined by their excellence and location rather than their age or history.

Down south the choice spots tend to be in the mountains. My favorite in Victoria is the **Bentinck (** (03) 5427-2944, in Woodend. Set in one and a half hectares (three and a half acres) of delightful gardens and lawns, this English-style country house is a peaceful haven only an hour's drive from Melbourne. Inside there is a comfortable lounge for the guests, an open fire in winter provides a cozy atmosphere and a sumptuous dinner is served in the wood-paneled dining room. It combines old world charm, modern comfort and friendly hospitality. In New South Wales

there are similar places in the Blue Mountains, with million dollar views over sheer cliff faces into pretty valleys below. One of the most interesting is the **Hydro Majestic Hotel** ((02) 4788-1002, at Medlow Bath, with its striking domed front entrance inspired by *art nouveau*. Windows fill the wall facing the Megalong Valley, and the view is quite superb. The Hydro Majestic Hotel started out as a health resort, but when the promises of bowel kneading, enemas and centrifugal douching lost their attraction, the resort was turned over to vacationers and the inside remodeled to take on the appearance of a grand hotel.

Queenscliff, about 90 minutes' drive from Melbourne is an elegant Old World seaside town, that hasn't changed much from how it must have looked 100 years ago. **Mietta's** ((03) 5258-1066, at 16 Gellibrand Street, in the grand old-fashioned **Queenscliff Hotel** opposite the foreshore, is one of the best restaurants in Victoria.

The choicest luxury resorts are along the Queensland coast on pristine islands

or remote locations. They are totally self-contained, with gourmet restaurants, sporting activities, entertainment and shopping all provided within the complex. **Hayman Island Resort** TOLL-FREE 1800-075-175, is located in the middle section of the Great Barrier Reef, near Townsville, and offers palatial rooms overlooking tropical gardens. When you tire of spending your days dining at one of its six restaurants, parasailing over dazzling azure waters or snorkeling along dainty corals, it is possible to arrange a helicopter trip to a neighboring uninhabited island for a champagne lunch. They cater for families, and crèches, babysitting and activities for older kids are provided.

Further north between Cairns and Townsville is one of the most exclusive resorts in Australia, **Orpheus Island Resort** TOLL-FREE 1800-077-167. Orpheus is the archetypal desert island, with coral-fringed white beaches lined by

The Hayman Island Resort is an oasis of luxury in Queensland's Great Barrier Reef.

swaying palms. The resort has a limit of 74 guests at any one time, and to ensure that guests can enjoy the tranquillity of the island there are no televisions at the resort, and only overnight guests and children over the age of 15 are catered for. The food is gourmet, with the emphasis on seafood and tropical dishes, and all activities such as windsurfing, water-skiing, snorkeling and sailing are included in the tariff. The island is perhaps one of the best places to see the reef, with over 340 species of coral present, and the resort provides diving gear, and access to the outer reef by charter boat.

North of Cairns is Port Douglas. President Clinton visited here in 1996 when he wanted a break from it all, and film stars come for the laid-back atmosphere. As you would expect, there are some very nice top-of-the-range hotels in Port Douglas, such as the **Sheraton Mirage Hotel** ((07) 4099-5888, set in 120 hectares (300 acres) of tropical gardens dotted with saltwater lagoons. Another is the **Treetops Resort** ((07) 4030-4333, with its miniature waterfall and rock pools, a serene garden where you can swim, and a restaurant on stilts among the tree tops. Nearby is the Daintree Rainforest, and the rooms of the **Silky Lodge** ((07) 4098-1666, located in its midst, blend into the lush greenery.

EXCEPTIONAL RESTAURANTS

In Australia, while grand formal eating establishments can be found in the major cities, the majority of good restaurants have a relaxed and casual atmosphere. This does not mean, however, that the food is second rate. Great emphasis is placed on using the best and freshest ingredients, on careful preparation, elegantly simple presentation and on service of the highest standard.

Situated on one of the world's most beautiful harbors, it is not surprising that

Exclusive Orpheus Island Resort, in the Great Barrier Reef, is the playground for the rich and famous.

many of Sydney's top eating houses serve wonderful seafood. For a big night out, try **Rockpool** ((02) 9252-1888, at 107 George Street, The Rocks, where you will find some of Sydney's best food, as well as the city's most glamorous people. Of course, Sydney rock oysters are a special feature of the menu. Great seafood meals, as well as a wide range of innovative dishes are also available at **Restaurant Forty-One** ((02) 9221-2500, on the 41st floor of Chifley Square, in the heart of the city. Your dining experience is enhanced by superb views of the city and harbor. In the Blue Mountains, an hour and a half out of Sydney, you will find **Where Waters Meet** ((02) 4784-3022, on Mount Hay Road in Leura, a popular restaurant set in beautiful gardens, offering elegant dining and a spectacular bush setting.

In Melbourne the most luxurious (and most expensive) restaurant in town is **Paul Bocuse** ((03) 9660-6600, in the Melbourne Central shopping complex on La Trobe Street. It is a French restaurant of the "old school", providing grand comfort, the finest tableware, excellent service and of course, wonderful food. Don't miss the famous truffle soup when

available, or the delectable and wickedly rich desserts. The wine list is also impressive. Out of town, enjoy fine cuisine, a relaxed country-style ambiance at **Potter's Cottage** ((03) 9844-1222, on Jumping Creek Road, Warrandyte, in the Yarra Valley, northeast of Melbourne. The extensive and varied menu, as well as the excellent wine list, relies heavily on local produce. On Saturday nights they offer live jazz. I have only recently discovered one of Melbourne's newest and most exciting eateries, which is taking the town by storm: **Est Est Est** ((03) 9682-5688, at 440 Claredon Street, South Melbourne. This is where foodies in the know go, and the place is winning awards left, right and center. It has a fresh approach to preparing interesting and innovative food, and the presentation of their dishes is quite spectacular. Unfortunately this restaurant is one of the worst kept secrets in Australia. For weekends there is a four-month waiting list, while during the week you need to reserve a mere two to three weeks ahead for a table.

Fine dining opportunities in the nation's capital have improved markedly in recent years. **The Oak Room** ((02) 6270-8977, at the Hyatt Hotel on Commonwealth Avenue, remains the "grand old lady" of Canberra restaurants, and both the food and the formal atmosphere of the place are something quite special. For food with a view, try **The Boathouse by the Lake** ((02) 6273-5500, in Grevillea Park, Minindee Drive, Barton. Lake Burley Griffin looks absolutely wonderful from a window table at this popular waterside eatery.

In Hobart, Jill and George Mure have been running highly regarded seafood restaurants for many years. Their latest venture is **Mure's Upper Deck** ((03) 6231-1999, at Victoria Dock.

Up north in Queensland, **Artis Restaurant** ((07) 5447-2300, at 8 Noosa Drive, Noosa Heads, a recent winner of the Good Food Awards, serves stylish and beautifully presented French food

with a finesse usually found only in a high-flying, big-city establishment. And in Adelaide, renowned chef Cheong Liew blends fine cuisine from a range of cultures at **The Grange Restaurant** ((08) 8217-071, at the Hilton International Hotel on Victoria Square.

NIGHTLIFE

There is nightlife to appeal to every taste in all capital cities, and the major tourist locations.

There is a vibrant band scene, centered around pubs. Details can be obtained from gig guides in the local newspapers. The sounds are often raw and fresh, and it is possible to hear some great music at these venues.

Nightclubs are usually concentrated along major streets or inner suburbs of the capital cities, such as Kings Cross in Sydney, Northbridge in Perth, Hindle Street in Adelaide or King Street in Melbourne. These are lively strips, with dancing until all hours of the morning, either to live or recorded music.

For some less frenetic entertainment into the wee hours, major hotels have piano bars and live shows, while the casinos put on cabaret shows.

Family Fun

Most Australians travel with their families, so there is no lack of attractions and activities to keep children entertained. The best time to travel is in the school holidays when extra events and activities are put on for kids of all ages. Holiday dates can be obtained from any tourist bureau. The down side is that it is necessary to book well ahead for popular places that cater for children as they are usually packed at these times.

KID'S PARADISE

There is no better place for children than Queensland's Gold Coast with its numerous theme and amusement parks (see GOLD COAST in QUEENSLAND, pages 148–151). At **Dreamworld**, the rides are guaranteed to elicit delighted screams from children, while making their less adventurous parents face their mortality and question their sanity. On this

OPPOSITE: Sand crabs are one of the many fresh seafoods available in Australian restaurants. ABOVE: Mietta's offers elegant dining with an excellent selection of Victorian wines, in the restored nineteenth-century Queenscliff Hotel.

produced for films such as *Mission Impossible*, *Twenty Thousand Leagues under the Sea* and *Flipper*. Children can see how stunt men ply their trade or have the mysteries of special effects unraveled. For the smaller children, Tweety Pie, Bugs Bunny, and a host of other Warner Brothers cartoon characters can be seen wandering the streets, larger than life. Across the road, **Wet 'n' Wild** at Oxenford is a paradise for kids who like getting wet. There are water slides and pools of all varieties, including a wave pool and a film pool, where children and parents can watch their favorite movies from the comfort of a floating air mattress.

24-hectare (60-acre) site kids can enter the world of the Eureka gold rushes, take a cruise on Captain Sturt's paddle steamer, or see koalas at close range in Gum Tree Gully. They will be enthralled by the spectacular Coca-Cola IMAX Theatre with its six-story screen, where the visual effects make viewers feel part of the picture. Nearby is **Seaworld** at Surfers' Paradise, where children can see dolphins being fed, whales performing and sea lions lounging around on rocks. There are also numerous rides, with a nautical theme. **Warner Bros. Movie World**, 20 minutes north of Surfers' Paradise is based on studios that have been established in Australia to service its burgeoning film industry. It is also the place where special effects have been

Outside Queensland there are also special places for children. At Manly, a 30-minute ferry ride from Circular Quay in Sydney, is **Ocean World** ((02) 9949-2644, at West Esplanade, where children can walk through a clear plastic tunnel to view all sorts of Australian fish, including stingrays, grey nurse sharks up to three and a half meters (10 ft) long, and a giant cuttlefish with three hearts and green blood! For the more adventurous parents, it is possible to SCUBA dive with the sharks, an activity which is (fortunately) held after feeding time. More popular with children is the seal area, where Australian and New Zealand fur seals can be seen at play through viewing windows, and the touch pools in which children can handle a number of harmless sea creatures.

SCENIC TRAIN RIDE
Puffing Billy is a lovingly restored steam train that is just made for children. It winds around the hills of the Dandenong Ranges, just outside Melbourne, and the view from its windows is quite pretty. One reason the trip is a hit with children is that they are allowed to sit on the carriage window sills, dangling their feet outside the train. This brave little train starts its journey at Belgrave and passes through cool and peaceful fern groves and spectacular mountain ash forests before arriving at Emerald Lake about an hour later. This is a popular picnic spot,

THE BIGGER THE BETTER

and is furnished with gas barbecues and picnic tables. After lunch, check out one of the many scenic walking tracks or hire a rowboat on the lake.

THE BIGGER THE BETTER
They are big, some would say crass, but to children irresistible. In many tourist areas children can delight at the sight of gigantic animals, vegetables, fruit and other objects from Australian life and myth, made out of concrete, fiberglass and plaster.

Many people, when traveling around southern Queensland are not surprised to see groves of pineapples growing. If they happen to stray to Nambour, just one hour's drive from Brisbane they will be confronted by the **Big Pineapple**, which is five and a half meters (16 ft) tall. Inside the fiberglass pineapple are displays illustrating interesting facts about this spiky fruit. Once the novelty of walking inside a giant pineapple wears off the little ones can retire to the cafeteria where they can indulge in pineapple drinks and sweets, and afterwards ride a miniature train through the plantation where smaller, edible versions of this tropical fruit can be observed. Adjacent to the Big

Pineapple is the **Big Macadamia**, which is part of the same complex. Macadamia nuts are native to Australia, and taste delicious but their hard shell make them difficult to extract.

Coffs Harbour in northern New South Wales is banana capital of Australia, and to celebrate the fact the **Big Banana**, which is 13m (40 ft) long, is located just outside town. It is possible to walk through the Big Banana which has a photographic exhibition that deals with all aspects of banana growing. It is worth noting that the nickname for Queenslanders is "banana-benders", but you'll have to ask a local to explain it to you.

Out of Aboriginal mythology comes the bunyip. The bunyip used to chastise generations of Australian children when they misbehave. At Murray Bridge in South Australia you can see the **Big Bunyip**, which is located in Sturt Reserve. Bunyips are said to inhabit

OPPOSITE: Kids have a ball at Seaworld (top), scooting down the flume. Australian children such as this boy (bottom) like nothing better than to be outdoors. ABOVE: Children enjoy the thrill of a downriver ride in an inner tube. OVERLEAF: Stupendous promotion in the banana growing region of northern New South Wales.

billabongs, or waterholes and there have been sightings reported by Europeans since the early nineteenth century of these ugly amphibious creatures, which were believed to emerge from the billabong and feast on people foolish enough to camp nearby. While now acknowledged as a legend, it has been suggested that the bunyip is an ancient memory of an animal that existed in Australia when the Aboriginal people colonized the country 40,000 years ago. The **Big Bunyip** at Murray Bridge is not nearly as scary as the one of myth, although as it emerges from its cave it does emit a roar. The local tale told by the Aboriginal men of the area is that when one of them returned from an unsuccessful hunting expedition, he would claim that the fish he had caught had been taken off by the bunyip. While at Murray Bridge take time to visit the **Children's Zoo** ((08) 8532-3666, in Jervois Street, which has a walk-through butterfly house and bird aviary where the children can feed blue, green, orange and yellow lorikeets. There is also a nursery where children can pet baby farmyard animals. For the adventurous child who wishes to touch a snake, ask one of the keepers, who, provided they have time, will get out a python which can be safely handled.

MUSEUMS
All of Australia's capital cities have good museums, with wholesome educational displays for the children. But, if your children are anything like the ones I know, such phrases are the best way to elicit yawns and exclamations of boredom. There are, however, at least two museums that are guaranteed to please. **Scienceworks**, at Two Booker Street, Spotswood, an inner suburb of Melbourne, provides hands-on displays where children can learn about science and technology while having fun. There are touch-screen interactive computers, scientific puzzles to solve and displays that they can manipulate. **Powerhouse**, at 500 Harris Street, Ultimo, on the edge of the central Sydney area, is a large

hangar-like building — a space that is used to its fullest to surprise and enthrall the most jaded kid brought up on video special effects and computer games. The exhibits are interactive, designed to teach while amusing or intriguing children of all ages — adults, too. There is also respite for weary parents in the coffee shop, which has been colorfully decorated by well-known Sydney artist Ken Done.

In the Tasmanian town of Claremont, 18 km (12 miles) out of Hobart, is the **Cadbury Factory** where the intricacies of chocolate making are explained and demonstrated in tours conducted every weekday morning, except Christmas. While all very interesting, it is not surprising that looking at all that chocolate stimulates not only the mind but also the taste buds. Fortunately the tour ends with a sampling.

Cultural Kicks

ARCHITECTURE
The streets and suburbs of Australia showcase of a wide range of distinctive architecture that has adapted European forms to the local environment and climate. The earliest example of such an adaptation is the verandah of Governor Phillip's Georgian residence, added in 1793.

The verandah is where early settlers sat to catch the occasional breeze that relieved the persistent Australian heat. This structure became incorporated into an architectural style uniquely Australian called the *Queenslander* where verandahs wrap around the outside of houses on every floor, and the building is raised on stilts to allow efficient air circulation. These can still be seen in many country towns on houses and hotels, particularly in Queensland, and remain a very sensible response to the heat of the northern climes of Australia.

In Sydney and Melbourne, and to a lesser extent in Hobart, the financial boom of the 1880s and 1890s led to the construction of elegant Victorian houses, with their ornate metalwork decoration and stained-glass windows. Rows of Victorian workingmen's cottages can be seen in the inner suburbs or Melbourne and Sydney, while Victorian mansions, with their grand verandahs laced with ornate ironwork can be seen in the well-heeled suburbs of Toorak and Vaucluse. Some of these houses are now owned by the National Trust and open to the public.

The final period of distinctive Australian architecture is the Federation Period, in which Gothic turrets and lofts extended living space in houses constructed around the end of the 1800s. Decorative stained-glass windows reveal the influence of *art nouveau*. Gothic touches include ornaments such as dragons and even terracotta kangaroos and emus on roof ridges. Examples of this style can be seen in the middle class suburbs.

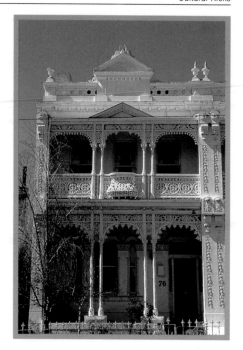

THE PERFORMING ARTS

As late as the 1960s the major theater companies in Melbourne and Sydney would ration themselves to one Australian play a year. For the rest of the year theater-goers were fed a steady diet of Bernard Shaw, Shakespeare and Oscar Wilde.

The renaissance in Australian drama happened in small fringe theaters such as **La Mama** in Melbourne and the **Nimrod Theatre** in Sydney. It was in these places that the twang of the Australian accent was heard and robust slang used to wake up the audience to the richness of their language and confront them with contemporary problems of everyday Australian life. These local plays had an exuberance and energy that was refreshing. Some, like Jack Hibberd's *Stretch of the Imagination* and David Williamson's *The Removalist*, have become modern classics, and now have entered the mainstream.

In Melbourne La Mama is still going, and has been joined by the **Courthouse** and **Budinsky**, while Sydney's Nimrod has competition from the **New Theatre** and **Stables Theatre** where the latest plays, often premiers, are showing.

All the capital cities have opera seasons, during which all the old favorite Italian, German and French operas are performed. There are also some Australian operas joining the repertoire, such as *Voss*, based on the novel by Nobel-prize winner Patrick White, *Summer of the Seventeenth Doll,* and an opera about the construction of the Sydney Opera House called *The Eighth Wonder*, which was, naturally, premiered there.

There are dance and ballet troupes that tour the country, but the best time to see many of them all in one place is during arts festivals. The most exciting groups currently performing are Chunky Moves, The Sydney Dance Company and The Australian Ballet Company.

For outstanding adult puppetry watch for performances by *Handspan*.

To find out the latest arts information access Internet address http://www .stateart.com.au, which reviews the latest in opera, dance, music, theater, film and visual arts.

ABOVE: Melbourne's 19th-century houses feature delicate ironwork.

Shop Till You Drop

MARKETS

Many country towns have markets, usually held monthly, which provide an opportunity for people from surrounding districts to come together. Fresh local fruit and vegetables, delicious homemade pickles and sauces, and exquisite handicrafts are all on offer. Market day is often an important event on the regional social calendar.

One of the nicest markets I have been to is located inland from Queensland's Sunshine Coast. The **Eumundi Village Market** draws thousands of people every Saturday morning, as the town's streets and parks are turned into a marketplace. Many of the foodstuffs and handicrafts for sale are produced locally. Beautifully crafted turned-wood bowls and jewelry boxes are made from rain forest timber. Handmade pottery, glassware and needlework are among the items on offer.

Another country market that has a strong following is the **Red Hill Market**, which is 80 km (50 miles) south of Melbourne, and held the first Saturday of the month from October to May. The market circles a cricket oval — there's usually a game in progress — with the players oblivious to the bustle around them. Meanwhile, buskers entertain shoppers as they wander around the stalls. The market has a reputation for excellent locally produced foods, especially breads, pickles and sauces.

The major cities have weekly markets, each with its own character. Held every Saturday in Sydney is the **Paddington Village Bazaar** at Eastside Parish Church, on the corner of Oxford and Newcombe streets. There you will find everything from bric-a-brac to antiques, books, handicraft and homemade food. In Melbourne, on The Esplanade overlooking the **St. Kilda** foreshore is a Sunday market which mainly sells art, crafts and handmade furniture. It is possible to purchase Australian paintings or jewelry with an Australian motif

directly from the artist. Near Perth, the **Fremantle Market** on South Terrace, is held Friday to Sunday. Located in this historic precinct the market sells all manner of goods and crafts. **Darwin** market reflects the laid-back nature of the town. Held every Thursday night, it is as much a social meeting place as a market. It is the one night that many people eat out at one of the stalls set up along Mindil Beach. Asian food dominates, with delicacies from India, China, Thailand and Indonesia on offer. For a more local flavor try barbecued kebabs featuring emu and kangaroo meat, or famous Mindil Market croc-burgers. To do as the locals do, bring your own deck chair, and at sunset settle down along the beach to contemplate the scenery, before returning to the bustle of the market.

CRAFTS

There are many craft areas and artist's communities around the country, where the best local pottery, jewelry, woodwork or glassware can be bought. There is also a lot of craftwork sold in tourist shops. In general, these should be avoided, because few "serious" craftspeople exhibit in such places.

There are, however, some accessible places to buy high quality crafts. In Hobart at **Salamanca Place** there are some excellent galleries specializing in glassware, and woodwork using local timbers. In Melbourne, the **Meat Market** at the corner of Blackwood and Courtney streets has some very good craft shops with handmade items including clothing, jewelry and pottery by some of the best Victorian craftspeople. As well, frequent exhibitions are held there, where all works are for sale. **The Rocks** in Sydney has a number of good craft shops and galleries, which are a cut above what you might have expected in this tourist precinct. In Adelaide the Jam Factory has a good selection of local craft, and the complex includes studios where some of the works are created. **Fremantle Arts**

The Skygarden shopping complex in downtown Sydney is noted for its fashion boutiques.

Centre at One Finnerty Street sells some of the best works in Western Australia.

There are a number of craftsmen with international reputations, who only show their works in occasional exhibitions. Watch out for fanciful leather sculptures by the Tasmanian Gary Greenway, and pottery by Ted Secomb, Milton Moon or Col Levy. In Bendigo, Peter Minko's fine porcelain, painted with splendid Australian designs, is well worth the detour. Most of the work by these craftsmen is produced on commissions, both in Australia and overseas, so acquiring a piece can be difficult. The best chance is to buy from the artists themselves or during rare exhibitions.

ABORIGINAL ART

Traditional aboriginal art was painted or carved onto rocks, bark, sticks and in the sand. Highly stylistic, and deeply spiritual, it speaks directly about the relations of the Aboriginal people to the land. A new generation of Aboriginal artists have rendered traditional motifs and styles onto canvasses to produce a unique style of visual expression which is becoming highly prized among art lovers. Many of their themes are taken from the stories of the Dreamtime, although some subjects and images are restricted because of religious taboos on presenting them.

A number of talented Aboriginal artists have been recognized for developing this school of art, with its characteristic dot style, although their names are not well known other than by collectors and critics. Many of these artists remain on their traditional land, where they get their inspiration, although works are often exported south into galleries specializing in Aboriginal art. These galleries can usually provide information on different artists. Aboriginal art sold by tourists shops should be avoided if you want works by the finest artists.

ANTIQUES

There are areas in all the capital cities where antique shops concentrate, selling Australian colonial pieces as well as imported European antiques. One of my favorite shops is **Unley Road** in Adelaide, where I have always found top-class furniture and Victorian ornaments on offer. Try Artist's Market Antiques ((08) 8271-7305, at 190 Unley Road, for silverware, porcelain, glassware and jewelry. In the Melbourne district of Armadale, **High Street** has individual shops as well as a number of antique arcades, such as Park Lane Antiques Centre ((03) 9500-9723, at Nº 1170. The western end of High Street contains a number of interesting antiquarian bookshops which are a must for bibliophiles. In Sydney, Woollahra, especially around **Queen Street**, is the city's main antique precinct. The Woollahra Antiques Centre ((02) 9327-8840, opposite Centennial Park at 160 Oxford Street, houses over 50 dealers and is open seven days a week from 10 AM to 6 PM. Also in Sydney, the **Balmain** area contains a mixture of down-market antique and bric-a-brac shops that can sometimes yield some wonderful finds. For the serious antique shopper, there are a number of auction houses in the capital cities, where traders shop, which means that the prices are usually wholesale. In Melbourne and Sydney Sotheby's, Christie's and Joel's auction houses have major art auctions, often featuring first-class Australian paintings.

CLOTHING

While most Australians live in cities, bush "clobber" has become very trendy, particularly gear with the **R.M. Williams** label. An akubra hat, traditionally made out of rabbit pelts, Dri-az-a-bone waterproof jacket and stockman's boots will have you looking like an Outback character, but may set you back a cool AU$600 or more.

Coogi Connections make uniquely Australian knitwear from pure Merino wool. With their bright colors and chunky textures these garments are highly prized by locals and visitors alike, despite the rather hefty price-tags. You will find Coogi outlets at Melbourne's Australia

Arcade on Collins Street, in the Queen Victoria Building in Sydney, and in Cairns and Port Douglas in North Queensland.

Artist Ken Done and designer Judy Done are well known for their lively and bright multi-colored depictions of Australian scenery. Their work can be found on all manner of clothing, especially T-shirts and beachwear, as well as on goods as diverse as umbrellas, sheets and placemats. **Done Art and Design** shops can be found in most capital cities, as well as Surfers' Paradise and Cairns.

GEMS AND PRECIOUS METALS
In the Kimberley region of northwestern Australia are the Argyle diamond mines. Gems found here, particularly the "champagne" and "cognac" varieties, are much prized for their subtle colors and high quality. Further north, in Broome, pearl diving is an important industry, while at Kalgoorlie in the southwest, gold is mined. **Linney's Jewelers of Subiaco** ((08) 9382-4077, in Perth's inner suburbs, sells hand-crafted Western Australian pearls, diamonds and gold.

Australia has 95 percent of the world's supply of commercial opal and most of it comes from the 70 opal fields around Coober Pedy in the Outback of South Australia. The opal is Australia's official gemstone, and opal jewelry can be bought in most places. To get the best quality stones it is wise to shop in established jewelry shops rather than in souvenir or tourist shops. Not surprisingly, Coober Pedy's shops have more opals on display than anywhere else in the world. At **The Opal Cave** ((08) 8672-5028, you can tour Faye's **Underground House**, hand dug by three women over thirty years ago, before making a purchase from their extensive range of stones and jewelry.

Short Breaks

There are some wonderful spots in Australia within easy reach of the major cities, which are worth visiting for a few days to enjoy their unique atmosphere.

Northern New South Wales, near the Queensland border has a back-to-nature

This nursery rhyme-animated musical clock is a well-visited attraction at a Hobart shopping arcade.

feel, and is a place where many city folk escape to enjoy more temperate climes, perfect beaches and a laid-back approach to life. The center of this area is **Byron Bay**, while inland are communes, eco-farms and aging hippies that time has forgotten. Local markets are the best places to get a feel for this area. They are all within an hour's drive of Byron Bay, with the best being at **Murwillumbah, Mullumbindy, Bangalow** and **Nimbin**, where locals come to sell tropical fruit, homespun garments and handicraft. Nimbin is the home of the counterculture, where the shops are painted in psychedelic colors and the center of the town's social life is the Rainbow Café, where locals trade produce, gossip and occasionally share a joint. It is as if the town was permanently frozen in time in 1973, when an Aquarius Festival put Nimbin on the hippie map.

Just a 90-minute drive north of Melbourne you'll find the twin towns of **Daylesford** and **Hepburn Springs**, which combine indulgent living with good food, and the restorative powers of health-giving natural spa water. Located on two pretty lakes — Jubilee Lake and Lake Daylesford — this area is known as **Spa Country**, where for years people have come to "take the waters". A therapeutic bath in the local spring water was claimed to provide relief for all manner of ailments.

The water tastes of sulfur or iron, but the queues lining up behind the pumps attest that many people swear to its restorative and health-giving efficacy. In the center of the park, where the springs are, is the hydrotherapy center which provides spa baths, saunas and massages. Reservations are essential as they have over 100,000 visitor a year.

The **Hepburn Spa Complex** ((03) 5348-2034, offers a public heated indoor swimming pool or private spa baths (with air jets and aromatic oils) for one or two people. Alternatively, pamper yourself at a guesthouse that offers a room with your own spa and an in-house masseur. My favorite is the **Rose of**

Daylesford ((03) 5348-1482, at 58 Raglan Street, which is small and intimate and offers spas and accommodation as part of a package deal. You can float back to your room after a massage by its experienced in-house masseurs, and your host Tulku Rose is knowledgeable about the excellent restaurants and galleries worth visiting in Spa Country.

The lure of the Queensland Coast means that few people bother to discover the beauty of the hinterland, particularly inland from the Gold and Sunshine coasts.

Start north, and inland from Noosa is the Blackall Range. Rising gradually from the coastal strip, with avocado groves along the side of the highway, the range features pretty little towns such as **Mapleton, Montville** and **Flaxton**, with their many antique shops and cafés. Further south are the **Glasshouse Mountains**, strange granite shapes rising dramatically from the surrounding plain. They are not easy to climb, with their sheer rock faces, and present a spectacular sight at sunset, as the surrounding plain takes on a deep mauve color, with the mountains silhouetted against a red sky. Traveling south is

Tamborine Mountain, which offers many easy walking tracks within the nine small national parks that are dotted around its slopes. The township of **North Tamborine** is a good central base for exploring the hinterland. Finally, straddling the Queensland–New South Wales border is the **Lamington National Park**, where you can do some serious walking along the top of its plateau and through ancient eucalypt forests.

The towns of the **Adelaide Hills** are home to many of the descendants of the German emigrants who came to Australia in 1838, escaping religious persecution in Prussia. The area provides some pretty, scenic drives through mountain villages. Take the South-Eastern Freeway out of Adelaide and turn right at the Hahndorf turn-off, a trip taking about 30 minutes. The villages of this area, particularly **Hahndorf**, still retain a Teutonic appearances with their solid nineteenth century Lutheran churches and gabled houses. Delicatessens sell traditional German würsts and specialty cakes such as sacher torte, and the local pub offers authentically brewed pilsner. Johnson Road takes you to Onkaparinga Valley Road, which follows the pretty Onkaparinga River through Woodside. Turn left down Tiers Road to Lenswood and right along the Adelaide Lobethal Road through apple orchards back to Adelaide.

While most people who visit Alice Springs focus all their attention on traveling an additional 400 km (250 miles) to **Uluru (Ayers Rock)**, there is an equally interesting drive much closer to Alice, into the western MacDonnell Ranges. This route offers some lesser known, but equally spectacular scenery, with a series of deep gorges cutting through the hills. There's a lot to cover in one day so it's best to start early. Take Scenic Drive west out of Alice Springs into the **West MacDonnell National Park**, through forests of stately ghost gums, where you are likely to see plenty of rock wallabies. Take the turn-off to **Standley Chasm**, which is best seen at midday when its walls flame red.

Go back to the main road and take the right fork along Namatjira Drive for 82 km (50 miles) to the turn-off to **Ormiston Gorge**. The stream flowing through the gorge is fed from an underground spring; its near vertical cliff face shimmers red in the sun, punctuated by white ghost gums rising from ledges. The road curves round to the south to join Larapinta Drive. At Hermannsburg Mission there is a turn-off to Palm Valley, an oasis of ancient cycads that are part of the **Finke Gorge National Park.** The gorge can only be explored by foot, and after rain a series of rock pools form along its length. Return to Larapinta Drive, for the trip back to Alice Springs.

Tasmania is known as the *Apple Isle* because it was Australia's main producer of this fruit, and the slopes of the **Huon Valley**, south of Hobart, are covered with orchards. This backwater is ideal for a very short break, as the Huon River opens out into a wide estuary, with

OPPOSITE: A quiet watering hole at the foot of the Uluru monolith which is sacred to Aboriginal clans. ABOVE: A rare cabbage-tree palm grows in Palm Valley, an oasis of greenery in the Finke River National Park.

picturesque villages along its length. The Huon Highway out of Hobart winds its way through agricultural land which gives ways to apple orchards around **Huonville**. The most delightful time is during October when the trees are in blossom. While in town take an hour to visit the **Apple Industry Museum** where over 500 varieties of apple are on show. The museum is open daily from 9 AM to 5 PM, and an admission fee is charged. The highway goes through the pretty towns of **Geeveston** and **Dover** which lie sleepily along the Huon River estuary as it spills into D'Entrecasteaux Channel. By the roadside are quaint tea houses and craft shops in which to while away the hours.

Festive Flings

Australians look for any excuse for a party, and a multitude of festivals and special events are held throughout the year. They vary from the sublime, with festivals celebrating the cultural diversity of Australia, to the ridiculous, such as boat races along dry river beds. Whatever the excuse, the aim is simple: to have fun.

ART FESTIVALS
Australia has developed a strong and vigorous culture, with singers, actors and dancers of world quality. The talents of these mainstream performers are showcased in arts festivals, where the best from Australia can be seen in one place. Innovation is essential to ensure that the arts remains vital, and often major arts festivals are associated with fringe festivals, in which the experimental and off-beat can strut their stuff.

The **Adelaide Festival** is the oldest and best known festival of culture, performance and the arts in Australia. Much of the action takes place in the Festival Complex on the Torrens River. This festival is held biennially, every even year in March. In odd years, you can enjoy the **Adelaide Festival Fringe** with

avant-garde performers taking over the streets, small theaters and pubs. Their productions are often experimental and the results are, sometimes spectacular, sometimes atrocious, but never boring.

All of January is turned over to the **Festival of Sydney**. An estimated four million visitors come for a month of music, theater and dance, much of it outdoors to take advantage of Sydney's great weather. The festival is launched with a spectacular computer controlled fireworks display over Sydney Harbour, starting on the stroke of the New Year.

In September the **International Festival of the Arts** brings to Melbourne the best performances by local and overseas artists. The Arts Precinct just south of the Yarra River becomes the center of the festival. Events are not confined to indoors, and it is possible to enjoy the cafés and restaurants of Southbank, while being entertained by street performers. In the month preceding the International Festival of the Arts is the **Melbourne Fringe Festival**, where some of the best alternative theater and cabaret in Australia can be seen.

The **Festival of Arts** (August and September) has grown in stature since it opened at the Brisbane Cultural Centre and attracts leading performers from Australia and abroad in all spheres of the arts.

In Western Australia there are two major arts festivals. In February and March the **Festival of Perth** provides an extensive program of music, theater and dance at a variety of venues around the city. In November the **Fremantle Festival** turns the port city over to 10 days of culture, ending in a parade and party.

COMEDY FESTIVALS
In March the **Brisbane International Comedy Bonanza** allows comedians to test the first principle of comedy: you need to be able to laugh at yourself.

During the Sydney Gay Mardi Gras parade (top) feathers and flowers adorn the outrageous outfits of the "ladies"; while at the Floriade festival (bottom) millions of flowers adorning dignified Canberra's gardens are kept strictly to their beds.

On this basis alone, Queensland which has often been ruled by inarticulate politicians and is renowned for its parochialism should provide hilarious material. Melbourne has a strong tradition of creating great comedians, and their talents are showcased during the **Melbourne Comedy Festival** which starts on or near April Fool's Day and has the place in stitches for four weeks.

MARDI GRAS

In February Sydney becomes the sequin, frock and leather capital of Australia, as the **Gay and Lesbian Mardi Gras** swings into gear. For a month homosexuals get to show off their culture, with live theater, music, film, visual arts, street performance, sports and community events filling the calendar. When the Mardi Gras started in 1981 is was both shocking and outrageous, but it has since moved from the fringe to become a major feature of the festival calendar. Its climax is an all night street parade that blends imagination, exhibitionism, hedonism and humor, attracting over 600,000 people, who line Oxford Street to watch dykes on bikes, displays of men wearing dazzling and extravagant costumes and lavish floats displaying all aspects of the gay lifestyle in Australia. This event is not just for gays; everyone enjoys watching the parade, indeed, it has become a family event. Despite its popularity, every year, one prominent fundamentalist preacher or another denounces Mardi Gras and calls on God to rain on the parade. So far God has shown himself more tolerant than his clerics.

After the parade there is a party at the Royal Agricultural Showground. While the parade is for everyone, the party is restricted to the lesbian and gay community. About 20,000 lesbians, gay men and their friends dance, rock to live music from top performers and generally let their hair down. Tickets are available to gay men and lesbians, including those visiting from overseas or interstate, but it is necessary to book well ahead. Tickets can be purchased by e-mailing mardigras @geko.com.au with your address and fax

number, by writing to P.O. Box 557, Newtown NSW 2042, or FAX (02) 9516 4446. The cost is AU$10.

SPECIAL EVENTS

In late August or early September the **Henley-on-Todd Regatta** is held in Alice Springs and is a "don't miss" event. Teams race along the dry bed of the Todd River in bottomless boats. I understand that the organizers actually insure the race against wet weather which would make the boats useless.

Being denied a white Christmas (December usually means heat waves and salad on the beach), Australians gather in mountain resorts to celebrate Christmas in June, where, with luck, snow may fall. One of the most organized mid-year Christmas events is **Yuletide** held in the Blue Mountains, where the many guesthouses fill up in June with revelers who have waited six months to enjoy roast turkey and plum pud. Christmas trees are erected in the main street of Katoomba and a snow man is featured in Leura. The streets and hotels are decked out in tinsel, and the Bing Crosby records are dusted off for some Christmas music.

In late September or early October the Commonwealth Park in Canberra is transformed for the **Floriade**, when 2.3 hectares (5.6 acres) are planted with about half a million flowers in a floral display unmatched anywhere else in the country. Private gardens are opened up and there are talks and demonstrations on every aspect of gardening.

CALENDAR OF EVENTS
Here is sample of other festivals and sporting events held in Australia. With the good weather all year round, you can be sure your visit will coincide with major festivals, wherever you go. For a full list contact the local state tourist bureau.

January
Provided the hangover from New Year's Eve is not too bad, take a trip out to **Hanging Rock Picnic Country Races**, 78 km (49 miles) northwest of Melbourne, on January 1 for the annual picnic races.

The **Australian Country Music Festival** is held at Tamworth at the end of January. Tamworth, 440 km (275 miles) north of Sydney, is to Australian country music as Nashville is in the United States, and 600 events are programmed over 10 days. Every pub, street corner and shopping mall is full of young hopefuls strumming "good old country music".

To celebrate Australia Day on January 26, a race is held around the entire country: the competitors are cockroaches and the course is a replica of Australia with a race track around the edge. The **Cockroach Race** is held at the Darwin Sailing Club ((08) 8981-1700.

The German origins of Hahndorf, 30 km (19 miles) from Adelaide on the South-Eastern Freeway, are evident during **Founder's Day** that includes traditional food and music. On Saturday there are shooting competitions. The venue is in the Adelaide Hills, just outside the city.

The Festival of Sydney OPPOSITE and BELOW lasts all January. Hundreds of events are on the calendar, many of them informal occasions during which anyone can join in the fun.

February

During the last weekend of the month vintage bike enthusiasts gather for the **Village Fair and National Pennyfarthing Championships** at Evandale, 20 km (12 miles) south of Launceston in Tasmania. The festivities also include market and craft stalls, side-shows and street entertainment.

The **Food and Wine Festival** allows Melbourne's best chefs to show off. Tastings are arranged at advertised venues around Melbourne from late February through early March.

March

Over three days in the second weekend of March the **Myall Prawn Festival** takes place in Tea Gardens, 250 km (155 miles) north of Sydney, near the coast. Highlights are the World Prawn-Eating Competition, a parade and the Prawn Masquerade Ball.

Moomba in Melbourne usually starts in the first week of March, and includes water-skiing on the Yarra River, fireworks, food and entertainment.

The **Canberra Festival** is a 10-day party that features concerts in the parks and outdoor art exhibitions. A highlight of the festival is the Birdman Rally, where hopeful aviators try out their homemade human-powered flying machines over Lake Burley Griffin. The winner gets AU$20,000 prize money — the losers get wet as their creations plunge into the lake.

Learn all you need to know about brewing good beer at the **New Norfolk Hop Festival**, held in the Derwent Valley, 38 km (24 miles) from Hobart.

Easter
Sydney's **Royal Easter Show** is the foremost agricultural show in Australia. Lasting 10 days, it is an opportunity to see farming livestock, and displays of rural produce. Rodeo events, fireworks displays and rides make it a fun fair.

April
The **Barossa Valley Vintage Festival** is held biennially, every odd year. The major theme is winemaking, and combined with food and music, it provides an excellent place to spend Easter.

The **Opal Festival** in the South Australian Coober Pedy celebrates the town's claim to fame, and many of the events have a mining theme.

The **Festival of the Falling Leaf** celebrates the coming of autumn, during which Tumut's deciduous trees put on a brilliant show of color each year. Tumut, is 442 km (275 miles) southwest of Sydney, on the Snowy Mountain Highway. Visitors can enjoy a street parade, band recitals, a billycart derby and a canoe relay on the Tumut River.

May
The **McLaren Vale Gourmet Weekend** provides an ideal opportunity to taste over 100 local wines, with the added bonus of food stalls serving dishes that you would normally only see in fine restaurants. McLaren Vale is on the Fleurieu Peninsula 30 km (20 miles) south of Adelaide.

Perhaps it isn't the most relaxing way to see some of Sydney's tourist spots, but anyone can join the **Sydney Half Marathon**, which takes competitors through The Rocks, Farm Cove and Darling Harbour.

June
The **Wintersun Festival** is held in Coolangatta on the border of New South Wales and Queensland. It reminds southerners that there is somewhere in Australia that is warm in June. In 1993 Miss Wintersun was won by Mr. Damien Taylor, showing the world that Australia is not chauvinist.

July
The **King of the Mountain Festival** in Pomona 150 km (93 miles) north of Brisbane features country "sports" such as tug o' war, iron-man competitions and wood chopping. And in Alice Springs, the brave mount their camels for the **Camel Cup** held along the dry bed of the Todd River.

August
The **Merry Muster Rodeo** in the western Outback town of Cloncurry in Queensland tests the skills of Australia's best horsemen against bucking and rearing animals who would prefer to be quietly grazing in a field somewhere else.

As the weather improves, the annual **City to Surf** fun run attracts thousands of runners to battle the 14 km (nine miles) from Sydney Town Hall to Bondi Beach, with the famous Rose Bay Hill testing runners to their limit.

Northern Territorians have a reputation for beer drinking, and rather than just throw the empties away they are put to good use in the **Beer Can Regatta**, where vessels are made entirely out of beer cans. The race takes place on Mindil Beach in Darwin.

In Broome, the **Festival of Pearl** (or **Shinju Matsuri**) lasts nine days, beginning at the end of August, with its conclusion in September coinciding with the night of a full moon. A Chinese dragon leads off the main street parade and the program also includes a pearling lugger race, the Ball of the Full Moon, crowning of the Pearl Queen and the Sayonara Ball. Different ethnic groups put on displays and there is a beach carnival.

A boat race for locals who haven't see rain in years, as the annual Henley-on-Todd Regatta gets underway in a dry river bed near Alice Springs.

September

The **Birdsville Picnic Races** is a horse racing event well known throughout the country. Birdsville is 1,569 km (973 miles) west of Brisbane near the South Australian border, in the middle of nowhere. Each September this tiny town with a population of approximately 30 attracts over 3,000 race fans who fly in from all over Australia.

The **Royal Melbourne Show** at the Royal Melbourne Showgrounds provides farmers with an opportunity to show off animals and agricultural produce to city folks.

The **Tasmanian Tulip Festival** is held in the Royal Tasmanian Botanical Gardens where the theme is Dutch culture, with dancing and, of course, thousands upon thousand of beautiful blossoms.

October

Those who prefer their music cool should look no further than the **Manly Jazz Festival** when the best musicians from Australia and around the world arrive to perform at this bustling Sydney seaside suburb.

More than 60,000 tulips flower every spring in Bowral. The **Tulip Festival** offers a chance to see this pretty little town — one hour's drive away from Sydney along the Hume Highway — at its best.

There are no horse racing courses anywhere near Coober Pedy, but this doesn't stop them from holding the annual **Coober Pedy Races.** The meeting attracts locals from hundreds of miles around.

November

As the water warms up with the coming of Spring Mount Gambier's famous volcanic lake turns a vivid blue, and the town celebrates the **Blue Lake Festival**. Mount Gambier is in southeastern South Australia, near the Victorian border.

In Broome, during the **Mango Festival**, this delightful fruit is served in every conceivable way by the "great chefs of Broome" in the annual cook-off, which is happily followed by tastings.

December

Most cities and towns in Australia gather outdoors for **Carols by Candlelight.** In Melbourne it's held at the Myer Music Bowl and in Sydney on The Domain.

Be in Hobart at the end of December for the arrival of yachts competing in the **Sydney-to-Hobart Yacht Race**, when the town is given over to celebration.

PUBLIC HOLIDAYS

As well the as the following national holidays, each state has an additional two or three days, for such events as Melbourne Cup, Labor Day and bank holidays.

New Year's Day	January 1
Australia Day	January 26
Good Friday	Friday before Easter
Easter Monday	Monday after Easter
Anzac Day	April 25
Queen's Birthday	Second Monday in June
Christmas Day	December 25
Boxing Day	December 26

Galloping Gourmet

Australian cooking has come a long way since 1895 when the *Presbyterian Cooking Book* was first published. This classic was an essential text in kitchens of the time, and for the next half century or so. According to this cooking book, Australian culinary imagination encompassed such dishes as crumbed sausages, rabbit casserole and rice pudding. Condiments were no more exciting than tomato relish or Worcestershire sauce. It was all good honest Anglo-Saxon cooking.

The traditional Australian meal, until recently, was roasted or grilled meat, mashed potatoes and vegetables, with perhaps fish and chips on Friday night.

During summer people like nothing more than eating outside around a barbecue, where sausages and steaks are cooked over an open fire, and even the occasional shrimp is "thrown on the barbie". The meat is usually accompanied by green salad and bread, and washed down with beer or wine.

The post war immigration from Europe, and more recently from Southeast Asia, has resulted in the development of a rich and varied cuisine, which has taken the fresh produce from the countryside and developed dishes that combine the best from East and West to produce a gastronomy that is uniquely Australian.

Spices, sauces and herbs taken from the Mediterranean and Asia, sometimes combined with native foods and spices, are used to create dishes that are both exotic and different.

AUSTRALIAN CUISINE

If Australia can lay claim to having invented any new dishes it is in the category of desserts.

The pavlova is a cake with a meringue shell filled with cream and topped with passion fruit pulp. It was created by Perth chef Bert Sachse to honor the visit of the ballerina that gave the cake its name. Anna Pavlova had an ever-so-slight figure, and it is doubtful she would have risked more than a mouthful of this rich confection.

Lamingtons are another desert invented in Australia. They are made from sponge cake cubes coated in chocolate followed by grated coconut. Named after Lord Lamington, Governor

OPPOSITE: An Australian delicacy, yabbies (bottom) are freshwater crayfish with a distinctive flavor. The best seafood restaurant in Sydney, Doyles (top) serves its meals on the verandah. ABOVE: In Australia's coastal towns, many fine restaurants cater to hungry tourists.

of Queensland (1895 to 1901), the apocryphal story of their origin tells of a grazier's wife from the same part of Scotland as the Governor, who covered a sponge cake in chocolate to prevent it going stale. She served it to her husband's shearers as "Lamington's cake".

While there may not be a large number of recognizable Australian dishes, unique dishes are constantly being invented by chefs taking advantage of high quality fresh ingredients and innovative combinations of cooking styles and tastes. A few years ago **The Great Australian Bite** restaurant, in North Melbourne was awarded a prize at the Gourmet Olympics for its salt and sugar cured lamb smoked over gum leaves. (I tried it and it was delicious.) A new generation of chefs have eschewed the gimmicky and are creating dishes that are both subtle and characteristic of the country.

There are no distinct regional cuisines in Australia, although some regions have developed distinctive foods, which are unique to the area. King Island in the middle of Bass Strait is wet and windswept, and while on few people's travel itinerary, the island has developed an exceptional range of cheeses and salamis that are produced locally. Restaurants all over Australia feature King Island cream, while a cheese plate would not be complete without the inclusion of one of its bries.

AUSTRALIAN INGREDIENTS

Meat from kangaroos is edible and sold by a few butchers, but there is resistance to eating the country's national symbol. Yet the meat is lean and low in saturated fats. The taste is gamey and usually requires a light sauce, such as red currants, to balance its richness. Emu and crocodile meat are also becoming available in butcher shops, and while they may have strong flavors, they are wonderful grilled or barbecued.

As most of the population lives around the coastline, it is not surprising that local seafoods are popular. Sydney

rock oysters are among the best in the world, while Tasmanian oysters are also much prized. Adelaide has superb whiting and Queensland is known for its mud crabs and crab-like Moreton Bay bugs. Barramundi are caught in estuaries and rivers of the north, reach up to one and a half meters (five feet), and are considered excellent game fish. Good fish markets will stock barramundi, although these are likely to have been bred by aquaculture. Only in places such as Darwin will you get fresh barramundi caught in the wild. Every Australian child who has lived on a farm would know of the delights of fishing for yabbies, a freshwater crayfish the size of a shrimp, and then cooking up these delicacies in a can of boiling water. Marrons come from Western Australia, although I have noticed that they are starting to turn up in other states. This freshwater crayfish is considered one of the best in the world. All these seafoods are generally available in the better fish shops.

BUSH TUCKER

Tucker is the Australian word for food, and there is new interest in indigenous edibles that grow naturally in the bush.

When Captain Cook visited Australia in 1770, he wrote: "The Land naturally produces hardly anything fit for Man to eat." How wrong he was. The Aborigines' diet was composed of an estimated 10,000 locally grown and raised plants and animals. Unfortunately Australians have been very slow in using this wealth of ingredients in their cuisine, other than the macadamia nut, which has become a profitable export for Australia.

A series on television called *The Bush Tucker Man* made viewers aware of the rich food sources that exist around them, introducing such exotica as banya-banya nuts, wattleseeds, Illawarra plums and bush tomatoes. Qantas Australian has included bush tucker on its menu for international flights. First class and business class passengers are tempted with bread rolls baked with wattle

seeds, bush tomato chutney and lemon aspen curd tartlets. In Sydney, **Reds** ((02) 9247-1001, at 12 Argyle Street, The Rocks, offers kangaroo and emu dishes, as well as barbecued wild duckling salad and bunya nut risotto, and is located in a admirably restored historic building. In Adelaide, the **Red Ochre Grill** ((08) 8212-7266, at 129 Gouger Street, serves dishes based on native Australian ingredients. The ingredients are difficult to find in shops, but in New South Wales **Bush Tucker Supply** ((02) 9816-3381, at 29 The Strand, Boronia Park, and in South Australia **Australian Native Produce Industries** ((08) 8346-3387, at 87 Harrison Road, Dudley Park, sell bush tucker jams and spices.

FAST FOODS

While it may be stretching the topic to refer to fish and chips as gourmet food, this most traditional of all Australian dishes should not be missed. There are a number of gourmet fish and chip shops about that have taken this unassuming dish and made it special. One of the best places in Sydney for fish and chips is at the **Bottom-of-the-Harbour**, which is located on Balmoral

Beach, where the cook Hans Prodinger serves up fish he has caught himself, cooked in a beer batter, and served with either homemade tartar or sweet chili sauce. In Melbourne, there is **Jean-Jacques by the Sea** at St. Kilda. Wherever you buy your fish and chips, it is best eaten out of the paper wrapping, and the chips should be liberally sprinkled with salt and lashings of vinegar. Yum!

After the gold rushes, Chinese migrants set up restaurants that served both Australian and Chinese food. They also sold take-away food such as fried or streamed dumplings, called *dim sims*, and *chiko rolls*, which are large fried spring rolls. These snacks catered to what Australians thought Chinese food was like rather than the genuine article. Today you can still buy chiko rolls and dim sims from fast food outlets, but Chinese restaurants now cater for a more educated Australian palate, and the food is as good as that served in Hong Kong or Singapore.

The wine producing area of Barossa Valley has many excellent restaurants where a meal can be enjoyed with a bottle of the local vintage.

While the hamburger that you buy in most outlets is American in origin, some inventive folk in Sydney have given it a distinctive Australian flavor. Skippy was a kangaroo that featured in a popular children's television series thirty years ago. The **Skippyburger Café** at 25 South Steyne, overlooking Manly Beach, serves kangaroo and emu burgers together with bush tucker, such as Warrigal green pesto, bush tomatoes and New Zealand spinach. For better or worse, the original Skippy television series has not put people off eating this cute Australian marsupial.

CUISINES OF THE WORLD

The start of the post-war migration was the death-knell for bland Anglo-Saxon food. Over the years Australians have experimented with such unfamiliar flavors as garlic, yogurt and curry. Today these ingredients are used widely.

Cosmopolitan Australians are now adventurous with their food, and scores of ethnic restaurants have cropped up to meet this demand. Restaurants serving food from Burma (Myanmar), Thailand, Macedonia, Turkey, Japan, Malta, Argentina and Egypt are but a few examples of the contribution made by migrants to spice up the eating habits of Australians.

Many of these restaurants started out catering only to the local ethnic community, who were looking for

authentic home cooking. This tradition continues today, and the best ethnic food can usually be obtained in areas where migrants are concentrated. The best news is that most of these restaurants are inexpensive.

Each capital city has its areas for ethnic restaurants. Vietnamese migration has been strong in recent years, and good inexpensive restaurants can be found in Hansen Road in Adelaide, Darra in Brisbane, Footscray and Richmond in Melbourne and Cabramatta in Sydney. Good German food can be obtained in the Adelaide Hills, while North Sydney has more than its fair share of fine Japanese restaurants. Both Melbourne and Sydney have strong Jewish communities. Authentic chicken soup with matzo balls can be had in Acland Street, St. Kilda or Double Bay.

WINES

Every state and territory produces its own wine, although over half the country's total production is in South Australia. The large variation in climate and soil type across Australia means that there are many styles and types of wines produced, with distinct regional variations.

Australia started growing grapes in the mid-nineteenth century, but unfortunately this industry was almost wiped out by disease in the 1880s. The revival of the Australian wine industry started in the 1970s, and has been going from strength to strength. Australian wine is now exported throughout the world, and it receives international recognition and acclaim.

Australian wines are not as immediately recognizable as are those from the great wine-producing areas of Europe such as Beaujolais, Bordeaux or Chianti. Not yet. However the world is starting to learn what many Australians have known for some time; that Muscats and Tokays from Rutherglen and Chardonnays from Mornington Peninsula in Victoria, Merlot and Cabernet Sauvignon from Coonawarra in South Australia and big bodied Shiraz

and Hermitage wines from Hunter Valley in New South Wales are equal to the best in Europe or California.

A reasonably good bottle of wine costs between AU$10 and AU$20.

Many of the large wineries get their grapes from a number of places to achieve consistent quality, but they lose the regional differences which make wine tasting interesting. To find genuine regional wines, refer to the label which should indicate whether the grapes have been taken from a single vineyard. Also check the label for information on awards — another good indicator of the wine's quality.

While bottle shops sell wines from most regions throughout Australia, I prefer to shop at small family vineyards. Some small boutique wineries do not sell their wines through bottle shops, and it's fun to explore such vineyards in search of wines that have real regional character. And, unlike most shops, wineries allow you to taste the wine before buying it.

The leading wine-producing regions are in Coonawarra, Clare Valley, McLaren Vale and Barossa Valley in South Australia, Cowra and Hunter Valley in New South Wales, Rutherglen, Yarra Valley and Mornington Peninsula in Victoria, Margaret River in Western Australia and northeastern Tasmania.

Special Interests

CULINARY LESSONS

Australian cuisine may be in its infancy when compared with that of Europe or Asia, but it is developing exciting taste sensations by innovative combinations of ingredients and use of bush tucker. Some of the greatest Australian chefs are drawn to **Howqua Dale** ((03) 5777-3503 FAX (03) 5777-3896, in the foothills of the Victorian Alps. Teachers at the workshops are the who's who of the Australian chefs — Jacques Reymond, Stephanie Alexander and Janni Kyritsis, to name a few. Cooking workshops are also held at **Lilianfels** ((02) 4780-1200 TOLL-FREE 1800-024-452 FAX (02) 4780-1300, in the Blue Mountains overlooking the splendid gorge at Echo Point.

OPPOSITE (detail) and ABOVE: The Queen Victoria Building presents modern shopping and cafés in an arcade that features some of the best commercial architecture of the nineteenth century.

VISITING VINYARDS

Most vineyards are open to the public for tastings and sales. Just drop in and try the latest vintage. Door sales provide the opportunity to take home bottles not available for sale elsewhere, and often choice vintages can be picked up at a discount.

The grape growing areas are usually easily accessible from most Australian capital cities.

Organized bicycle tours of wineries in all states, which combine sampling of good wines with visits to the best regional restaurants are provided by **Gourmet Tours of Australia** ((03) 5777-3503. Organizers Sarah Stegley and Marieke Brugman ensure that exercise during the day is amply rewarded at night at choice restaurants in the Clare Valley in South Australia, Bellarine Peninsula in Victoria, Margaret River in Western Australia, Hunter Valley in New South Wales and Tasmania's Tamar Valley, where tour guides are able to talk as authoritatively about a suitable wine to have with your fish as they were during the day explaining front and rear sprocket gear ratios.

HOUSEBOATING

The best place for houseboating is the Murray River, the grand waterway of Australia and the fourth longest river system in the world. The Murray courses more than 2,000 km (1,200 miles), across one third of the continent from its source in the Snowy Mountains, in New South Wales to meet the Southern Ocean near Goolwa, in South Australia. The central stretch of the river is best suited to houseboating. The Murray's banks form protected lagoons for a myriad of bird and animal life including sulfur-crested cockatoos nesting high in towering sandstone cliffs and, high above, wedgetail eagles soar. Cruise past majestic red gum forests, stark box tree flats and massive white sandbars forming island retreats. Houseboat hires are available out of Murray Bridge in South Australia through **Liba-Liba Houseboats**

((08) 8586-5341 TOLL-FREE 1800-810-252 or do the river in style aboard the *P.S. Murray Princess* ((08) 8569-2511 TOLL-FREE 1800-804-843, or the *M.V. Proud Mary* ((08) 8231-9472 FAX (08) 8212-1520.

Just two hours drive from Melbourne is Lake Eildon, where a range of houseboats are for hire from **Lake Eildon Holiday Boats** ((03) 5774-2107. Cruise along the hundreds of secluded small bays or dangle a line over the side, and relax.

NUDIST COLONIES

If you like to enjoy the great outdoors in the buff, you'll find Australia has many great facilities for nudists, and lots of sunshine. Resorts and nudist camps, catering for couples and families, exist in all states.

The year-round good weather makes Queenland a nudist's Nirvana, and there are numerous excellent secluded resorts from which to choose. **Pacific Sun Friends** ((07) 5498-8333, in Quinn Road Donnybrook, close to the Sunshine Coast is a large resort. Its facilities are excellent with in-ground pool, communal kitchen and recreation pavilion. There are bush trails for walking and a tidal stream for swimming and boat trips. Sports include pétanque, Frisbee and golf. Further north is **Hidden Valley Country Retreat** ((07) 4959-1205, on the Devereux Creek, near Mackay, which is a clothing-optional resort set in the middle of a lush tropical rain forest.

Nudists looking for something just a bit different should visit the Cairns–Port Douglas area where special naturist cruises to the reef aboard the powerful 17-m (56-ft) luxury cruiser, *Phantom* include diving among the coral, where swimwear is optional but flippers and face mask obligatory. The naturist trip goes every Wednesday, weather permitting. For reservations dial (/FAX (07) 4094-1220.

Most capital cities have nudist beaches. Location can be obtained from the **Australian Nudist Federation** (/FAX (07) 3806-8833.

Taking a Tour

The range of tours available in Australia is mind-boggling. You can do anything from droving with cattlemen in the Outback to sailing around the Whitsunday Islands. There are bus tours across the country, covering great distances, or you can tackle the arduous Overland Track at Cradle Mountain on foot.

While the major companies provide tours that are comprehensive and varied, it is still worth searching further for some of the small, specialized operators who offer something beyond run of the mill.

MAINSTREAM TOURS

There are a number of companies that provide a range of traditional tours, as well as some trips that are a little out of the ordinary. Certainly for people who will be in Australia for a short period of time, organized tours are an ideal way to see large tracts of the country efficiently and in comfort. Tours are usually booked through travel agents.

The largest and oldest tour company is **AAT King's** TOLL-FREE 1800-334-009 FAX (03) 9274-7400, which operates a fleet of luxury buses, the length and breadth of Australia. Accommodation is included in packages and is usually in good quality hotels. Even its camping safaris include a few nice touches such as wine with dinner. Some tours include transport by planes and trains. A very special trip is on *The Ghan*, one of the great train journeys in Australia, from Adelaide to Alice Springs.

Australian Pacific Tours TOLL-FREE 1800-675-222 FAX 1800-655-220, offers fully accommodated coach tours, camping holiday safaris and four-wheel drive adventure tours, from half-day city tours to 38 round-Australia trips taking in the Outback and major tourist destinations. The company provides four-wheel adventure expeditions into the wilderness of Far North Queensland, often going off the beaten track to visit

remote Aboriginal settlements, deserted beaches and little known but spectacular national parks.

A more limited range of bus safaris and camping tours is provided by **Australian Scenic Tours.** The two airlines, **Qantas** (131-415, and **Ansett** (131-413, combine flights with bus, cruise and train trips.

ADVENTURE TOURS

One of the most experienced adventure tour companies is **Peregrine** ((03) 9662-2700 FAX (03) 9662-2422, at 258 Lonsdale Street in Melbourne, which offers a wide range of adventure tours including rafting down the Franklin River and trekking in the Flinders Ranges, to name just a few.

Raging Thunder ((07) 4030-7990 FAX (07) 4030-7911, guarantees an adrenaline rush as they take small groups down grade-4 rapids on the Tully River. Another option is white-water rafting on the North Johnson River which is so remote it is entered by helicopter. While

Delicate lotus lilies spring up in temporary water holes that form throughout Arnhem Land during the wet season. OVERLEAF: A favorite Broome adventure is a sunset camel ride across the white sands of Cable Beach.

the company specialty is rafting, they have expanded into a wide range of adventure tours in Queensland and Northern Territory, including sea kayaking along the Great Barrier Reef, or hot-air ballooning over the Atherton Tablelands, camel rides, diving in the Coral Sea and cross-country cycling.

TOURS OFF THE BEATEN TRACK

There are a number of tour companies that take you off the beaten track. They are usually local, and provide very special trips in an area that they know a lot about.

There are few places in Australia more remote than its northern tip, Cape York, which is known as **Quinkan Country**, after a figure from Aboriginal mythology. **Trezise Bush Guides** ((07) 4060-3236 FAX (07) 4058-1560, take tourists into the heart of this wilderness, in four-wheel drive vehicles. At night, camps are set up under the stars and by day there are hikes to see rare Aboriginal rock art galleries, luscious wetlands and crystal clear mountain streams which are perfect for a cooling dip.

Nevis Tedoldi has developed an impressive network among Aboriginal people and her **Cultural Connections** ((03) 9349-4233 FAX (03) 9349-4211, offers a wide range of cultural tours into remote parts of the country. She can organize visits to contemporary artists and galleries where remarkable indigenous paintings can be seen and bought, or wilderness experiences which involve interaction with local Aboriginal people. Their tours provide unique opportunities to get an insight into an ancient and rich culture.

Most adventure tours focus on the Outback areas of Queensland, Western Australia and Tasmania. This is a great pity, because there are treasures in southeast Australia that are little frequented. **Bogong Jack** ((08) 8383-7198 FAX (08) 8383-7377, is one of the few tour operators that has adventure tours into places such as the Flinders Ranges, Kangaroo Island, the wild

Snowy River and the alpine areas of Victoria. The mode of transport is varied, and tours include trekking, canoeing and cycling.

ORGANIZED BIKE TOURS

Cycling the great distances involved when touring Australia presents a formidable challenge. A number of small companies provide organized tours, with support vehicles should the effort become too arduous. **Remote Outback Cycles** ((08) 9244-4614 FAX (08) 9244-4615, provides mountain bikes which are up to the task of traversing wilderness areas such as the Great Victorian Desert, MacDonnell Ranges in Central Australia and Margaret River in Western Australia. Only small groups are taken out, and tours last five to fourteen days. More information can be obtained at their home page http://omen.com.au/~roc/tour.

There are bicycle clubs in most states, with regular rides organized every weekend; they welcome visitors. If you don't mind a crowd, then join 5000 cyclists on the **Great Victorian Bike Ride** in November/December each year, a 16-day tour that takes in some lovely countryside. The cycling ranges from easy to medium, and the tour cost includes campsite, most meals and, best of all, a support vehicle. Contact Bicycle Victoria ((03) 9328-3000 FAX (03) 9328-2288 or e-mail bicyclevic@bv.com.au, to book a tour. The **Great Tasmanian Bike Ride** in January, the **Great Queensland Bike Ride** in August/September and **Great South Australian Bike Ride** in September are run along similar lines, and reservations can also be made through Bicycle Victoria. Bicycle NSW organizes a nine-day, 500-km (310-mile) tour, the **Great New South Wales Bike Ride,** through country towns and inland countryside. Reservations can be made at ((02) 9283-5200.

Girls, guys and gulls flock to the endless beaches that stretch along Australia's coastline.

The Land Down Under

A SUNBURNT COUNTRY

There is a poem I learnt as a child, and it is an anthem to Australia. Written by Dorothea Mackellar it starts

I love a sunburnt country
A land of sweeping plains
Of ragged mountain ranges
Of drought and flooding rains
I love her far horizons
I love her jewel-sea
Her beauty and her terror
The wide brown land for me!

The poem spoke of the overwhelming vastness of Australia, that years of exploring would not exhaust. Trips I have taken to its far flung ends continue to surprise me with a variety and beauty that is hard to express. Nevertheless I have made an attempt in this book to share some of the places I have discovered over the years.

While Australia's natural splendor is often astonishing, a country is more than its landscape; it is also its people.

Australians — particularly under the harsh conditions of the Outback — are bred with a sense of humor as dry as the land, and are unmatched in generosity of spirit. Above all they enjoy meeting people from elsewhere and sharing with them the wonders of the land they live in. Take time to visit the pub of a country town and talk to the locals. You will be entertained for hours with local folklore and learn something of their life — a hard existence, but one they wouldn't swap for all the riches of the city.

There is a second Australia to be discovered. It is found in the cities and major provincial towns where approximately 90 percent of the population lives. Nevertheless the Outback, even unvisited, has shaped the Australian psyche. The idea that we are a nation of "urban bushmen" is widespread. There is a famous poem by "Banjo" Patterson, called "Clancy of the Overflow" where a clerk sits in his city office dreaming of droving sheep in the Outback. There are many Clancys in the cities of Australia.

Urban Australians may imagine ourselves as outdoor types, but this seldom goes further than sitting in a sidewalk café in Melbourne's Lygon Street watching the football, or surfing at Bondi Beach in Sydney.

This identification with the great outdoors is evident in the number of four-wheel drive vehicles on city streets, which are seldom used for anything more taxing than going shopping or picking up the kids from school.

As Australia has become a major tourist destination the idea that this country could have worthwhile attractions is beginning to dawn on the locals. It is not unusual now to see Australians eschewing the pleasures of Rome or Singapore for a trip to the Top End or the Great Barrier Reef; indeed, it has become the norm.

So traveling in Australia is a choice between seeing sprawling cities with their cosmopolitan lifestyle, or touring the Outback — with its vast spaces dotted with small towns full of fascinating characters. Given sufficient time, both Australias can and should be explored.

I have tried to strike a balance in this book between these two realities. It is worth lingering in the cities as a country cannot be appreciated unless its people are understood; fortunately Australians are forthright and ready to let the tourist share their lifestyle. The wonders of nature, such as Uluru (Ayers Rock), the Great Barrier Reef and Kakadu National Park are also described.

There is yet another Australia to be explored and known, another viewpoint to be had: that of the people who have lived on the continent for over 40,000 years. The Aboriginal people of Australia are opening up their culture and art, and sharing their

OPPOSITE: Wave-worn columns at sunset off the Victorian Coast. ABOVE: Arnhem Land Aborigine.

love of the hidden places in Australia with tourists, often through indigenously owned companies. They can show you a different Australia, if you are willing to be lead off the beaten track.

THE GREAT SOUTHERN TREASURE HUNT

In a country the size of Europe, or just a shade smaller than the United States, with so much to see and do how can one book suffice? Like Aladdin, I was faced with a cave full of treasure. He could only carry out an armful, while I have the unenviable task of distilling a country overflowing with scenic gems, exotic locations and one-of-a kind cultural experiences.

In Europe tourists can look in awe at 1,000-year-old cathedrals with their rose windows, soaring arches and formidable façades. Australia too has its cathedrals, but they are millions of years old and not fashioned by medieval architects, but rather by the majestic forces of nature. There are rain forests with giant eucalypts that would dwarf Notre Dame, and waterfalls that plunge down the Arnhem Land escarpment which will leave you breathless.

Australia has 665 national parks occupying nearly 410,000 sq km (160,000 sq miles), eight of which have been classified as World Heritage areas. In addition, there are more than 220 offshore areas protected by legislation because of their unique ecology, or historic importance, such as being the site of a shipwreck. These national parks also contain a wide variety of native animals not seen anywhere else in the world. For example, there are 48 species of kangaroo, from the Great Red that lives on the plains, growing to about two meters (six feet), to the tree kangaroos, whose habitat is the forests of Cape York in northern Queensland.

So many places deserved inclusion in this guide, but some had to be omitted. The easy way out would have been to provide an exhaustive list of places to see. This would have avoided letting some gem slip through, but travel by catalogue is unsatisfying. Rather than establish objective rules I have relied on my own reactions to places to guide my choices.

I have not confined myself to the traditional modes of seeing a place. Floating across the landscape on a balloon, a leisurely cycle through the countryside, exploring desert landscapes on a camel, or roaring down an empty road in the Outback on a Harley Davidson are some ways to make a visit more memorable. If you can't take a risk on a holiday, then it never will happen!

At a practical level, I recognize that tourists come with different budgets. Therefore, hotel prices are given for double or twin share rooms, which have been divided into **luxury** (over AU$130), **moderately priced** (AU$60 to AU$130) and **inexpensive** (under AU$60). I have taken prices from the high season; if you travel out-of-season prices may be lower than listed here.

There is an excellent range of good restaurants in Australia, from cheap-but-interesting cafés, to five-star restaurant with silver service. To help you choose, I have classified restaurants into **expensive** (over AU$50), **moderate** (AU$20 to AU$50) and **inexpensive** (under AU$20). These prices do not include the cost of wine which can quickly drive up the cost of a meal. Many moderate to inexpensive restaurants provide an attractive alternative, allowing diners to bring their own wine for a charge of AU$2.

The greatest burden a tourist has to bear is not how many suitcases he or she is willing to cart around (and is a hair drier really essential?) but how to spend a short time in a country that offers so much. I have tried to relieve some of this burden. However, for travelers with time on their hands I have provided a section at the end of the book with recommended reading about additional attractions.

See as much of the country as you can, photograph its mountains and national parks, but also pause to speak to the locals about what Australia means to them. The Aboriginal writer and University lecturer Eric Willmot said of Australia that "only those who can be possessed by her can know what secret beauty she holds." Come and find out.

OPPOSITE: A road train on the dusty Bourke Cobar Highway (top) and symmetry in sandstone (bottom) in Western Australia's Bungle Bungle Range.

An Ancient Continent

WHEN I WAS AT SCHOOL my history books started with the discovery of Australia by Europeans, the exploration of the eastern coastline by Captain Cook in 1770 and the establishment of a penal colony at Botany Bay in New South Wales.

Little thought was given to the original inhabitants, who have occupied Australia for between 40,000 to 60,000 years. The Aboriginal people were relegated to a footnote in Australian history.

Aboriginal history does exist; it spans many more years and is richer than the European exploration and settlement of Australia. Academic historians have not given due weight to it because of the absence of written records. It is a history that is told around the fire and passed on orally from one generation to the next.

THE DREAMTIME

Aboriginal history is the story of the Dreamtime; it recounts the origins of the land and the people who inhabited it for hundreds of generations — how every river, mountain and gorge came into existence, carved out of the terrain by ancestral mythical beings. These creators also made birds, animals, plants, and all other living creatures, including man, and the legends established inter-relationships between the Aborigines and every element of their environment. The creators of the Aboriginal world have since left, but they can be resurrected through ritual and dance.

Archaeological evidence indicates that the Aboriginal people migrated south either across a land bridge that linked Southeast Asia to Australia or using boats to traverse the relatively short distance, hopping across the numerous islands scattered between the two land masses: it is believed by some that the Aboriginal peoples originated in Sri Lanka. Once they arrived on the Australian continent, the Aborigines adapted to conditions and spread into every corner of the vast continent.

It is a fallacy that they lived in harmony with the soil, maintaining it as they found it. They learned to master it and controlled burning of the bush was used to encourage regrowth, which in turn attracted animals

that could be hunted. Aborigines modified their habitat in other ways to increase food supplies. Sophisticated weapons such as the boomerang were developed to hunt kangaroos and other wildlife, some to extinction. In Victoria, an area rich in wildlife and fish all year round, Aborigines established permanent stone settlements, and in coastal areas they built intricate structures to trap fish.

Before the arrival of the First Fleet, Aborigines had reached an equilibrium with the land. This balance was based on a pro-

found knowledge of the seasons and how to survive in a country that appeared to outsiders to be poor in natural resources.

EUROPEANS ARRIVE

Captain James Cook, on his voyage of discovery, wrote in his journal that the Aborigines "appear to be the most wretched people upon the Earth, but in reality they are far happier than we Europeans." Despite Cook's insight, it did not stop him basing his claim on the eastern seaboard of Australia on

OPPOSITE: Beautifully textured Aboriginal paintings at Obiri Rock in Arnhem Land, Northern Territory. ABOVE: An Aboriginal as portrayed by an early Western observer.

the legal fiction that he had discovered a *terra nullius* — a land without people.

At the time of Cook's visit the Aboriginal population was probably between 500,000 and one million. The subsequent interaction between white settlers and Aborigines almost turned Cook's legal fiction into fact. Disease, high child mortality rates and persecution of the local inhabitants dramatically reduced their numbers during the eighteenth and nineteenth centuries. At the beginning of the twentieth century the Aboriginal population was reduced to 50,000. Today it is estimated that there are about 230,000 people of Aboriginal descent in Australia.

Aborigines were displaced, often by force, by early white settlers who were spreading out from their first settlements to secure grazing land for sheep. In Tasmania dispossession turned to genocide; its Aborigines were almost entirely wiped out. Only a few survived on offshore islands.

The fight between the Aborigines and the white invaders was unequal, as Stone Age weapons were pitted against firearms. However, the Aborigines did not simply give up their land without a fight. The expansion of the colony, however, was not greatly hindered by Aboriginal resistance, much weakened by the diseases brought by Europeans. The introduction of alcohol further debilitated their society.

Ironically it was the government in Britain who tried to curb the excesses of the colonists but these efforts were largely ignored by the colonial administration.

During the nineteenth and first half of the twentieth centuries Aboriginal labor was cheap and it helped build wealthy grazing properties, but Aborigines were not really relevant as a factor in Australian economic development.

They first obtained the recognition and admiration of white Australia for their prowess in sports: in 1868 the first cricket team to go to England was an Aboriginal side. They acquitted themselves well, winning 14, losing 14 and drawing 19 matches during the tour. That did not mean that there was no racism in Australia at the time: in 1897 the Queensland Home Secretary sought to bar Aborigines from foot races — because they always won!

In 1905, the government adopted a policy of "protecting" the Aborigines by segregating them from the bad influences of European society which formalized and accelerated a movement initiated in the 1870s of putting the Aborigines on missions and reserves. While the intention behind these policy purported good, Aborigines were removed from their traditional territories and different tribes were moved onto the same reserves without any regard to kinship or relationships, and, most tragically, many Aboriginal children were taken away from their parents and placed in the foster care of white families as a way of encouraging assimilation.

In 1967, a referendum was held to give Aborigines and Torres Strait Islanders citizenship. This marked the end of institutionalized racism.

Today Aborigines have established themselves in many aspects of Australian life. Sir Doug Nicholls became the Governor of South Australia in 1976 and Neville Bonner took his seat in the federal Senate in 1971 as the first Aboriginal parliamentarian. Prominent Aboriginal artists' and writers' contributions have enriched Australia's cultural heritage.

There is a saying among Aborigines that he who loses his dreaming is lost. In the Outback and urban Aboriginal communities, elders are making every effort to ensure that their children are told the secrets of the Dreamtime so that they do not loose touch with their culture, with its rich religious and spiritual values.

A festering sore remains Aboriginals' claims to their traditional lands. A recent High Court decision overturned the legal concept that Australia was occupied as *terra nullius* and has opened the way for Aboriginal land rights.

The reconciliation between the Aboriginal people and the rest of the country has only just begun, and the government has said that it wants a formal treaty. There is a tentative optimism among Aborigines, but one tempered by two hundred years of accumulated disappointments.

There are other changes heralding a period of reconciliation: School books now include sections on Aboriginal history, con-

temporary Aboriginal art is shown in the best galleries and the relationship traditional Aborigines have with their land is starting to be appreciated by a world that has shown itself incapable of reaching a balance with nature.

WHITE SETTLEMENT

DISCOVERY OF AUSTRALIA

There is evidence that the first visitor to Australia after the original migration of the Aboriginal people was the Chinese admiral Cheng Ho, who explored waters south of the Indian Ocean between 1405 and 1432. A Chinese statuette and sandstone carving have been discovered near Darwin, confirming other evidence of visits by northern fishermen.

Subsequent visits were by European sailors — Dutch, English and French — blown off course on their way to the Spice Islands. Other explorers went in search of *Terra Australis*, "the land to the south", which might offer similar riches to those discovered in the nearby East Indies. What they saw disappointed them, and the great southern land was left alone.

With these adverse reports, it is not surprising that the only justification to settle this newly discovered land was to establish a penal colony on its shores. In 1787, King George III instructed Captain Phillip to found a colony at Botany Bay.

THE FIRST SETTLEMENT

On January 26, 1788, Captain Arthur Phillip established the penal colony at Port Jackson

on what he described as "one of the finest harbors in the world," Sydney Harbour, finding Botany Bay unsuitable.

The First Fleet consisted of 443 seamen, 568 male and 191 female convicts, 160 marines and 51 officers. The expedition cost the government £84,000, which they judged less expensive and less troublesome than keeping convicts locked in hulks moored on the River Thames.

While it may be that Australians suffer a stigma from having convict forebears, today tracing one's family tree back to the First or Second Fleet is cause for pride. Convicts sent to Australia were mostly nothing more than petty criminals, victims of an ethic which harshly punished all attacks on society.

New penal colonies were established for recidivist offenders in godforsaken places such as Port Arthur in 1830, Norfolk Island in 1824 and Moreton Bay in 1824, where the treatment of convicts was inhuman. On Norfolk Island prisoners were known to draw lots to decide who would kill whom, because murder meant a trial in Sydney and some hope of escape.

It is little wonder that many of the tourist attractions relating to Australia's early history are prisons, and barracks for the troops who guarded them.

Transportation of convicts ended in 1864. It is estimated that more than 160,000 convicts were sent to Australia, and their presence touched every colony except South Australia, which was founded by free settlers.

Sandhurst (Bendigo) as it appeared in 1857, the gold rush period. Illustration by S.T. Gill from Victoria Illustrated, *first published in 1857.*

As the colonists came to terms with the new country, they began to appreciate that they were better off than if had they stayed in England. The first generation of Australian-born citizens established an indigenous culture based on solidarity to overcome the hostile environments — and a distaste for authority. They were called "currency" lads and lasses. The name was originally coined as a put-down: a pound in local currency was not worth as much as a pound Sterling. For the locals this name was worn as a badge of pride. Having adjusted to their new environment, they thrived.

THE GOLD RUSHES

The colonies obtained a major boost to their economies when gold was found first in New South Wales in 1851 and then in prodigious quantities in Victoria. The gold rush that followed had a dramtic effect on the economy as men left the land and crews jumped ship to seek riches on the goldfields. Fortune-seekers came from all corners of the globe, arriving in overcrowded ships. At its peak during the year 1852, over 86,000 people arrived in Australia from the British Isles.

The goldfields were roisterous. Untamed shanty towns were populated by men who worked hard during the day and dreamed of having great fortunes at night, as they sat around the campfires or huddled in pubs to discuss their day with the other diggers. It was on the goldfields that the Australian notion of mateship developed. Many of the gold mining towns are now tourist attractions.

The Victorian gold mining town of Ballarat is famous because it is the site of the only armed insurrection against authority in Australia (to use grand language). To discourage laborers leaving the land for the goldfields the government set a license fee for each claim and diggers without licenses were harassed by government troopers. On November 29, 1854, they had had enough, and a blue flag with the Southern Cross constellation was raised in defiance of the authorities. Licenses were publicly burned and the police attacked what has become known as the Eureka Stockade, swiftly put-

ting down the rebellion by killing 22 and arresting 114 diggers. This action by the government was not popular and most of the men of the Eureka Stockade were eventually freed; their leader, Peter Lalor, later became a member of the Victorian Parliament. The Eureka Stockade quickly caught the public's imagination.

Australians admire anyone willing to defy authority, so it is little wonder that bush-rangers were among the first "heroes" of colonial Australia. The term was coined in 1805 to describe escaped convicts who had turned to robbery to survive in the bush. Many poor farmers and laborers also tried their hand at bush-ranging. Some with colorful names such as "Yankee" Jack Ellis, Captain Moonlight and "Mad Dog" Morgan

became household names, while songs celebrating their exploits became popular. Governor George Gipps forbade a ballad that praised "Bold" Jack Donohoe because he was worried that others would follow "Bold" Jack's example.

The best known bush-ranger was Ned Kelly who, after his mother was wrongfully arrested, ambushed and killed three troopers. Outlawed in 1878, he and his gang held up banks and successfully evaded the police for two years. Ned Kelly was finally trapped in Glenrowan in June, 1880, where he defied the police, protecting himself with home-made armor. Realizing that they could not penetrate his plough-share mask they shot at his feet which were unprotected. Captured, he was sentenced to death and hanged

in Melbourne on November 11, 1880. His last words were: "Such is life." Ned Kelly's last stand quickly entered the realms of folklore, and after his death the legend spread by way of ballads, poems, books, paintings and films.

AN AUSTRALIAN IDENTITY

The prosperity that gold brought to Australia accelerated the country's development. Roads and railway lines were laid down, linking the colonies and creating a new-found confidence around the nation. People began talking about an Australian identity

Dust rises as cattle are gathered on the dry expanse of a Northern Territory ranch.

that incorporated the ideas — born in the goldfields — of mateship and egalitarianism. A sense was developing that Australia, rather than Britain, was now home.

After the gold rushes Australia went through several cycles of boom and bust, and the Depression of the 1890s saw the growth of new unions and their political arm, the Australian Labor Party, which protected worker's rights within Parliament and was the most successful social democratic party in the world, forming a government in 1908.

Many men without permanent employment during the Depression took to the road to survive. Known as "swagmen," their swag being the small sack in which they kept all their worldly goods, they had a healthy disregard for authority and their exploits were celebrated in folk songs, the most famous being *Waltzing Matilda*.

Australians at the turn of the century were called "Cornstalks," just as John Bull represented Great Britain and Uncle Sam the United States of America. The Cornstalk was typically two meters (6 ft) tall, wearing corded pants, red shirt, wide blue sash and a cabbage tree hat, high boots and a stock whip wrapped around his arm. His character was described by a contemporary source as "slow, easy, indolent in the ordinary way, proud of his country and himself and capable of holding his own in anything in which he is interested." This popularly accepted view of Australians as outdoors types was at odds with the trend towards urbanization — and by the turn of the century nearly half the population lived in the six capital cities.

FEDERATION

In the colonial parliaments, visionaries promoted federation of the six independent colonies, to create one country.

In 1901 the colonies came together to form the Commonwealth of Australia and on the first day of the New Year, to celebrate the event a procession snaked its way through the streets of Sydney to the wild cheering of 150,000 onlookers. After the Queen's proclamation was read in Centennial Park a 21-gun salute was fired and a new nation was born.

Despite its new independant status, Australia remained loyal to the British Empire, and imperial foreign policy was slavishly followed.

COMING OF AGE

In 1901 the birth of the new nation was marked with parades and fireworks. But, the fireworks that saw Australia's true coming of age happened fourteen years later on the bloody battlefields of the First World War.

The first major encounter involving Australian troops was when they were thrown against a strong Turkish force at Gallipoli. Australia suffered 8,000 dead but, in spite of their impossible position, there were displays of great heroism. Australian soldiers, who were known as "diggers," went on to acquit themselves with honor on the battlefields of France.

By the end of the war Australia had lost 59,000 men, a high proportion of casualties.

Gallipoli is remembered on Anzac day, when veterans march proudly through the streets of every capital city and major town.

Along with many other countries, Australia's fortunes slumped after the First World War under the burden of debt and low export prices for its farm produce. In 1930 the Depression set in and scarred a generation of Australians. Many men took to the countryside in search of work, with their swag on their backs, and urban Australians renewed their links with the bush.

The Second World War helped end the Depression. When Japan entered the war,

Australia was thrown into a panic because its territory was threatened. Japan conducted bombing raids against Australia's northern coastline between March, 1942, and November, 1943, and with Britain fighting for its very survival and unable to help, the entry of the United States into the Pacific theater of war in 1941, was welcomed by Australia. Within weeks of the Japanese attack on Pearl Harbor, 4,600 American troops arrived in Australia. On March 17, 1942, General Douglas MacArthur arrived to establish his headquarters in Brisbane, and over the next few years hundreds of thousands of American troops passed through. The American GIs had a reputation for being free-spenders; and the Australians, especially the troops, resented the success the Americans had with the local women. GIs were criticized as being "over sexed, over paid and over here," but despite some tension, a lasting bond and mutual respect developed between the fighting men of Australia and the United States.

In the aftermath of the war, debate on Australia's future turned to its pitifully small population. To overcome this weakness the catch-cry was coined "populate or perish." And so the great postwar period of immigration began.

Britons who had seen their homes demolished during the Blitz, and the displaced people and refugees of Europe who desperately wanted an opportunity to build a new future for themselves and their children formed the first wave of migrants, and migration continues to this day. Almost 21 percent of the current population was born overseas. Australians were unused to non-English speakers, but the initial cultural shock gave way to a liberalization and an acceptance that Australia was a multicultural society.

Australians were also urged to do their bit for populating the country, and there was a sharp rise in the postwar birth rate, giving rise to a generation dubbed the "baby boomers."

At first these new settlers found their way into laboring and construction jobs. Australia's greatest engineering project, the Snowy Mountain Scheme, is evidence of immigrants' hard work. Other newcomers became retailers, and the local fruit shop, owned by an Italian, or the fish and chip shop run by a Greek family, became commonplace. Change came, albeit in very small ways. Eggplants were now on sale next to tomatoes and potatoes, and instead of fish and chips we kids would occasionally try *souvlaki*.

Immigrants established restaurants that allowed them to enjoy foods from their homelands. For a few years they had these to themselves, but in the late 1960s students would hunt out Balkan or Greek restaurants, which were not only exotic but amazingly cheap.

As ethnic communities gathered around different suburbs, the character of neighborhoods began to change. For example, walking through Cabramatta in Sydney is like visiting an Asian city, while Johnston Street

THE INFLUENCE OF IMMIGRANTS

Every aspect of contemporary Australian life has been influenced by the immigrant influx.

OPPOSITE: State Parliament building, New South Wales. ABOVE: Australia is comprised of two territories — Northern Territory and Australian Capital Territory — and five states which are each represented by a star on the flag.

in Melbourne with its tapas bars is like a little piece of Spain. In a number of capitals China-town is a major tourist attraction, with its restaurants employing the best chefs from Hong Kong, Shanghai and Singapore. Whereas once Australians might venture to the local Chinese restaurant for some chow mien, today you are more likely to find din-ers arguing the relative merits of Cantonese regional cooking and the more spicy Sichuan cuisine.

Welcome as it may be, the stamp of im-migrants goes deeper than the pleasures of the table. Newcomers have widened Aus-tralian perspectives of the world. Just as the continent itself lies over a tectonic plate sluggishly moving a few millimeters each year towards Asia, so also are Australia's attitudes and policies looking towards the Orient.

The Vietnam War brought home to Aus-tralia that it was geographically part of Asia, and Australia's involvement there provided the first local in-depth reporting of that part of the world. It was the Whitlam govern-ment of the early 1970s, not surprisingly, which turned the country's foreign policy towards its neighbors. The slow continental drift is now being overtaken by a profound cultural shift, as Australia embraces more immigrants from Southeast Asia. Although they compose just five percent of the popu-lation, East Asians are the fastest growing immigrant group.

While the cultural traditions of the mi-grants gradually permeated Australia's lifestyle, immigrants took enthusiastically to the Australian outdoors and sports. Today the game of Australian Rules Foot-ball includes the sons of these immigrants, with names such as Daicos, Silvangni and Jakovich.

Australia remains a monarchy, and Queen Elizabeth II of Great Britain is also the Queen of Australia, but over the last few years the notion that Australia should be-come a republic has been voiced in the news-papers, and fanned by politicians. A referen-dum on the subject is expected before the end of the millennium.

A quite cove near Sydney provides a haven for pleasure craft.

The traditional view is that, as the country was founded by Britain it would be denying its roots to turn itself into a republic. Needless to say the Aboriginal minority has not been impressed by this argument. Another view is that as Australia is forging new ties with Asia it needs to break its links with Europe, a *non sequitur* if ever there was one.

A few changes have occurred: in 1974 British honors were replaced by Australian ones, causing a great outcry among traditionalists. In 1984, "Advance Australia Fair" replaced "God Save the Queen" as the national anthem; but, the Union Jack still occupies a corner of the national flag.

The debate on whether Australia becomes a republic continues with passion, and occasionally, with a grain of sense.

A NATION OF HEDONISTS

For Australians, there is not much in their nation's short history to generate the sort of patriotism taken for granted in most other countries. Solitary flags fly outside some public buildings but in general Australians are seldom moved by nationalist symbols. On Australia Day, celebrating the founding of European settlement, or Anzac Day in remembrance of those soldiers who lost their lives in the wars, a few more flags are hoisted.

Rather than dwelling on patriotic platitudes, Australians prefer to enjoy themselves, and the great country that they live in. They take every advantage of their temperate climate to spend as much time as possible outdoors. Friday evening is a time for joining friends in an after-work drink on the verandah, or heading off to the beach in summer or the snowfields in winter. Saturday afternoon is usually dedicated to sports, and every town and suburb has an oval where ball games are under way. A dinner party with friends, either at home or at a restaurant is a favorite way to pass Saturday evening where etiquette demands, if invited for dinner at someone's home, you bring a bottle of wine or a bouquet of flowers for the host.

Sunday is a day for relaxing, drives in the country or just watching television.

Festivals are now run throughout the year in all capital cities and in many towns. They include parades, concerts, food stalls and sporting events. Art and film festivals, annual events in all capital cities, are a good time to sample the best of the country's culture. There are also some bizarre events, like the Henley-on-Todd in Alice Springs where teams race bottomless boats down a dry river bed. A list of festivals is included in FESTIVAL FLINGS in YOUR CHOICE.

Australia has produced more than its fair share of athletic heroes: in tennis there are

Wimbledon champions Lew Hoad, Margaret Court, Evonne Goolagong and Pat Cash; in golf there is Greg Norman; and Dawn Fraser won the 100-m freestyle in three successive Olympic Games between 1956 and 1964.

Australia's climate is quite well suited for year-round outdoor activities. Every weekend Australians are hitting or kicking all sizes and sorts of balls around an oval, splashing about in the pool, galloping around the court after a judiciously lobbed tennis ball or driving on to the next of their 18 holes of golf.

OPPOSITE: Hang gliding TOP and hire boats BOTTOM near Sydney. ABOVE: Aborigine station hand in the outback.

As well as taking to the field or swimming at the beach or poolside Australians are great sports spectators, devoting their weekends to watching football in winter, cricket and tennis in summer and horse racing in spring.

While the climate and way of life conspire to make Australia a country of hedonists, it also has a vibrant and exciting arts culture. Films such as *Shine* and *The Piano* have been honored with Academy Awards. Its novelists are producing interesting books, and some have received international acclaim like Peter Carey who won the Booker Prize and Patrick White who won the Nobel Prize. There are also many less well-known, but very talented writers such as Elizabeth Jolly, Thea Astley and David Malouf.

you want to borrow a couple of dollars and the committee room when a local political problem needs to be addressed.

Walk into a country pub the locals will cautiously look you over, and then go about their business. A remark about the weather or crops is all that is usually necessary to strike up a conversation: Country folk like nothing better than a chat with a stranger and soon the ice will be broken. By the end of the evening it will be difficult to get away. Don't forget that when you join a group, they will "shout" you drinks and it is polite to

keep up the same rate of consumption as the locals. When it comes to your turn, don't forget to buy a round of drinks. There can be no greater social blunder than missing your "shout."

Farmers from outlying regions enjoy coming to town for an outing, and local dances provide such an opportunity. These are not as popular as they once were but if a country dance is on, don't skip it. Usually held in the local hall, the festivities start with a progressive dance — a little like a slow square dance where men and women stand opposite one another in a large circle changing partners as the dance unfolds. There is no better way than one of these progressive dances of being introduced to everyone in town.

BATTLERS FROM THE BUSH

If you leave the city and enter the Outback, there is more than a change of scenery; there is a shift in perspective and lifestyle. The wit can be as dry as the red dust in the street outside the pub.

Social life in the bush revolves around the pub. It's the information office you go to if you want to locate someone is, the bank if

The social highlight of the year is the local agricultural show; farmers travel hundreds of kilometers for the big event where they have a chance to meet neighbors, buy new stock and chew the fat.

The show ring is a nonstop procession of cattle and sheep judging. An event I always enjoy watching is sheep dogs in competition. The owners send instructions to them with coded whistles, and in no time at all these highly intelligent beasts have even the most uncooperative sheep cornered and penned.

smaller than the United States excluding Alaska and Hawaii, or rather smaller than Europe. Over the last 100 to 200 million years the continent has slowly eroded, leaving most of the landscape flat and the soil relatively poor.

One of the features of the continent is the Great Dividing Range. By world standards the range is not high, but it does serve as a catchment for most of the rain. Very little falls on the rest of the continent, other than the Top End which is watered by the monsoons. Most of the center of the country is

There are cooking competitions for the best jams, cakes and pickles. After some shows all these delicious entries are offered for sale.

For all the talk of the remote Outback, life there does have its basic creature comforts: air-conditioning is generally available and television is beamed from satellites.

A number of families in the Outback offer farm holidays which allow city folk to see first-hand how country people live.

GEOGRAPHY AND CLIMATE

Australia is the largest island in the world, covering an expanse of 7,682,300 sq km (2,975,000 sq miles), which makes it slightly

desert: one and a half million square kilometers (570,000 sq miles) of sand, scrub and boulders. Lakes Torrens, Eyre and Frome, marked on maps of northern South Australia, can be salt pans for years on end.

Despite being in a dry continent the Murray–Darling River system is enormous, with a drainage area covering Queensland, New South Wales and Victoria. The past agricultural practice of indiscriminate clearing of the land has elevated the water tables and caused severe salt contamination of this important river system. Increasing salinity

Tasmania's Cradle Mountain and Dove Lake OPPOSITE, and Uluru National Park ABOVE, Australia's "Red Center," dramatize the country's climatic contrasts.

An Ancient Continent

has reduced the potential of the river for irrigation, and in South Australia drinking water taken from the Murray river is of poor quality.

The furthest point north is latitude 10°41' south of the Equator, which puts Australia well within tropical climes, while the southern tip of Tasmania has a latitude of 43°39' south, equivalent to the northern hemisphere latitude of Rome in Italy or Toronto in Canada.

In the southern hemisphere, seasons are the opposite of the seasons in the northern

hemisphere so January and February are high summer. The climate is generally temperate in most state capital cities, and in winter it never gets cold enough to snow at sea level except occasionally in Hobart and Canberra.

The mean maximum temperature in Sydney ranges between 15.9° and 25.8°C (55° to 78°F), and the best time to visit Sydney is between September and November when the temperature is mild and the rainfall is lightest. Summer can be extremely humid.

Average temperatures in Melbourne range between 13° and 26°C (60° to 78°F). Spring is the wettest season while the most stable weather arrives in autumn, which is also quite dry. During a summertime heat wave the temperature can plummet in just a half hour more than 10°C (18°F) as a cool southerly wind prevails, and local folklore says that Melbourne can pass through four seasons in one day. North of the Great Dividing Range the weather tends to be more stable.

Tasmania is the coldest state but remains mild because of its island climate. The average temperatures range between 13° and 22°C (54° to 71°F). Nights can be chilly throughout the year. In winter the prevailing winds come from the northwest. When the wind occasionally turns southerly, an icy blast straight from Antarctica cuts straight to the bone. In the Highlands care should be taken as the weather can collapse suddenly.

Adelaide has the lowest total rainfall of all state capitals. The average temperatures vary between 15° and 22°C (59° to 71°F) and winter is the wettest season.

Summer in Perth can consist of days on end of temperatures between 30° and 40°C (85° to 105°F), and the only relief is an afternoon breeze from the west, called the "Fremantle Doctor". Fortunately, the heat is dry and therefore easier to bear. The rest of the year is mild and winter in Perth can be wet.

Brisbane has a subtropical climate and temperatures throughout the year are quite toasty. In winter the average temperature is 20°C (68°F), and in summer 29°C (84°F). Summers can be particularly moist and humid.

The furthest inland of all Australian capital cities, Canberra is not moderated by the ocean. Maximum temperatures range between 11° and 28°C (51° to 81°F), while in winter the average minimum temperature is 0°C (32°F). Early mornings in Canberra can be very frosty.

Darwin has two seasons: a monsoon season from November to April and a dry season for the remainder of the year. It is generally hot all year round and even in the coolest months, June and July, the daily temperatures are between 19° and 30°C (65° to 85°F)

Towards the center of the continent it can be extremely hot, the highest temperature ever recorded being 53.1°C (127°F) at Cloncurry in 1889.

RELIGION

In the last census, 73 percent of Australians said they were Christian. Observance, however, is low as most Australians prefer to be outdoors on Sunday than in church.

This has not always been the case. Irish Catholics, who constituted a high proportion of convicts and early immigrants, were kept apart from the better-heeled Protestant middle class by religion. In towns across the countryside Catholics and Anglicans competed for the highest hill on which to erect their churches. Religion also had an influence on political allegiances: for many years the Australian Labor Party received the support and votes of Irish Catholics because it claimed to stand for the (white European) underdog. These divisions are no longer

During Orthodox Easter the streets of Melbourne and Sydney are lit up by the candles of thousands of people in procession, participating in the most important celebration of their calendar.

Non-Christian denominations have established themselves as well: the oldest of these is Judaism. Several Jews were on the First Fleet and in 1844 the first synagogue was built in Sydney; their numbers were significantly bolstered by postwar immigrants and strong communities thrive in all states.

strong, and Australians in generally are apathetic about religion; still, the Catholic population is quite excited because it appears that the Vatican might soon canonize Mary McKillop, which would make her the first saint from Australia.

At the last census the Catholics were slightly more numerous than the Anglicans, with the nonconformist denominations and Eastern Orthodox church making up the remainder.

While most religions have declined in numbers, the reverse is true for the Orthodox Church. Its emphasis on family and community life and pride in ethnic traditions are strong influences in the Greek and Orthodox Slavic communities.

The Moslem population consists largely of Turkish, Lebanese and Indonesian immigrants who built mosques in the metropolitan areas, their number bolstered by more recently-arrived adherents.

Small faith communities of Hindus, Sikhs and Buddhists flourish throughout Australia as well.

OPPOSITE: A drought scene in New South Wales.
ABOVE: St. Andrew's Church in Launceston, Tasmania's "garden city".

An Ancient Continent

New South Wales

The Premier State

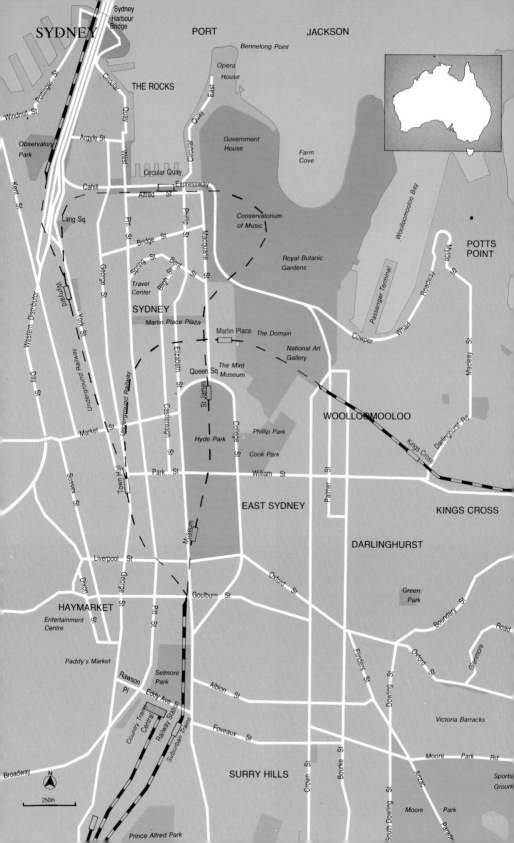

SYDNEY: A NATURAL WONDER

Sydney's reputation is based on its natural beauty. Built on one of the most magnificent harbors in the world, framed by the Harbour Bridge (known irreverently by the locals as the coat-hanger) and the sails of the Opera House, Sydney is one of the world's truly great cities.

Sydney also has history and atmosphere, whether it be "The Rocks" early colonial streetscape, with its sandstone and bluestone buildings, or cosmopolitan Bondi Beach.

Rather than take their breathtaking setting for granted, Sydneysiders would almost kill for a glimpse of water from where they live, even if it's a sliver of blue only visible from the top floor bathroom by standing tiptoe on a chair. The real estate market feeds off this mania and apartments or houses with a view of the water fetch astronomical prices.

Fortunately Sydney Harbour contains numerous inlets and estuaries, maximizing the opportunities to acquire real estate with a view of the water. There are 300 km (188 miles) of foreshore and 56 km (35 miles) of city beaches for locals to fight over.

The harbor is always packed with pleasure cruisers, yachts, commuter ferries and motor boats, as Sydneysiders take advantage of the temperate climate that allows outdoor activities to be pursued in all seasons by the intrepid.

At night the streets of suburban Manly, Paddington and Bondi are packed with people taking the air. Sydney is made for promenading.

The *nouveaux riches* feel comfortable in Sydney, reveling in brash and unashamed admiration of financial success.

BACKGROUND

When Captain Phillip ignored his original orders to establish a penal colony in Botany Bay, he landed instead at Port Jackson, a few kilometers to the north, which he judged a better site. Here he raised the Union Jack where the ferry terminal now stands and the 759 convicts, few hundred seamen and guards, and a handful of officials set about erecting tents and crude shelters.

The first settlers were ill-prepared and the colony almost foundered. Food was scarce, they did not know how to farm the new land and the indigenous population was hostile.

As this sad rabble overcame its early privations and the population grew, it sought to venture across the natural barrier of the Blue Mountains west of Sydney. Once this hurdle was surmounted, the local Aborigines subdued and the rich pastoral land beyond the mountains made available for exploitation their future was assured.

The Victorian era brought prosperity to Sydney and endowed it with scores of handsome buildings. Many survive to this day, nestling amongst modern office blocks.

The twentieth century and two World Wars established its industrial base and today it is the premier city in the country.

GENERAL INFORMATION

General information for tourists can be obtained from booths at Wynyard Station and Circular Quay. To make travel arrangements in New South Wales contact the **New South Wales Travel Centre** ((02) 9224-4744 or 132-077, at 31 York Street.

Maps showing major attractions can be obtained free from **The Rocks Visitor Centre** ((02) 9255-1788, at 106 George Street.

There are information booths at Manly ((02) 9977-1088, and at Darling Harbour (1902-260-568.

Commuter ferries are the perfect way to see Sydney Harbour.

For all information on buses, trains and ferries phone (131-500 from 6 AM to 10 PM. For information on the Sydney monorail phone ((02) 9552-2288.

WHAT TO SEE AND DO

Sydney Harbour

Sydney's biggest lure is its magnificent harbor. Governor Phillip described it as "the finest harbour in the world, in which a thousand sails of the line may ride in the most perfect security." While Phillip was probably

thinking of the English fleet, today his prediction has come true as thousands of pleasure craft, yachts and commuter ferries enjoy the safe waters and stunning beauty of Sydney Harbour .

Sydneysiders are energetic water-lovers and appreciate their waterways to the full. Each summer the numerous beaches and shoreline of the harbor are dotted with people enjoying their attractive environment.

The best way to see the harbor is from the water, and there are a number of organized cruises available. **Captain Cook's Harbour Explorer** ((02) 9206-1111, operates a variety of tours. The Explorer Cruise makes a circuit of the harbor, stopping at major attractions,

such as The Rocks, Sydney Opera House and Tooronga Zoo. Ferries leave every two hours, from 9:30 AM to 3:30 PM from Jetty Number 6 at **Circular Quay**. It is possible to hop off at any stop and then catch the next ferry to continue the tour. The Coffee Cruise circles the harbor, passing from the middle harbor to the heads and back past the gracious mansions on the north shore. It departs at 10 AM and 2:15 PM, and takes about two hours.

Another other way to see Sydney Harbour is how locals see it — from a commuter ferry. Timetables and information on routes can be obtained from the **Sydney Ferry Information Centre** (131-500, opposite Wharf 4 at Circular Quay. The best time to take a ferry is at sunset when the colors of the sky tinge the harbor with yellows and pinks. Regular services across the harbor take 30 to 90 minutes.

The Old Quarter

The historic precinct called **The Rocks** is close to the Harbour Bridge on the south shore. The Rocks is Sydney's oldest section, where Governor Phillip established the first settlement, built around winding streets connected by flights of narrow stone steps, giving it a distinctive character.

The history of The Rocks is an unhappy one. In the nineteenth century it became an iniquitous den of vice; as Sydney grew, so the nasty streets of The Rocks became nastier, terrorized by gangs, thugs and bandits. With colorful names such as "The Forty Thieves," "Cabbage-tree Boys" and the "Golden Dragons," various gangs engaged in pitched battles around **Argyle Place**, which at that time was the village green.

The neighborhood became increasingly run-down and it surprised nobody when in 1900 there was an outbreak of bubonic plague, which prompted the city fathers to react by demolishing parts of the area.

After degenerating into a slum the original face of The Rocks was whittled away by successive developments. When the Sydney Harbour Bridge was built, further destruction of historic houses occurred, but the last assault which was almost the fatal and final one in the 1960s was when speculators in league with the government tried to redevelop the entire quarter and tear down its historic buildings. Thankfully local residents resisted, and restoration of the buildings in the 1970s and 1980s has revitalized The Rocks, making it a worthy destination for tourists.

At 110 George Street is Sydney's oldest surviving dwelling, **Cadman's Cottage** ((02) 9247-8861, built in 1816. When John Cadman was alive his house was on the shoreline and boats would moor at his front door. The cottage is now open to the public. Call for hours.

4,500 paintings, sculptures and works on paper, and from visiting international collections. The museum is open daily and an admission fee is charged. On the terrace outside is **MCA Café**, which has a good view of the bustle of Circular Quay and the harbor beyond.

On Saturday and Sunday, George Street, just under the Bridge, becomes the crowded **Rocks Market** with crafts, antiques and jewelry sold from its many stalls.

Step out with **Classic Walks of Sydney** ((02) 9555-2700, which offers organized

Convict houses have been transformed into arcades housing taverns, boutiques and craft shops, such as the **Argyle Arts Centre** at 16–20 Argyle Street.

There is even an authentic village green, surrounded by nineteenth-century cottages and the pseudo-Gothic **Garrison Church**, built between 1840 and 1843. The inside of the church is adorned with the dusty flags of the British regiments of the line who once worshipped here.

Adjacent to The Rocks is **Circular Quay**, the main commuter terminal for harbor ferries. On Circular Quay's west side is the **Museum of Contemporary Art** ((02) 9252-4033, an imposing six-story art deco building. It exhibits modern art from a collection of

tours explaining the fascinating history of The Rocks and other parts of old Sydney.

The Opera House
At Bennelong Point on the opposite side of Sydney Cove from The Rocks, fly the white sails of the Opera House ((02) 9250-7111 FAX (02) 9221-8072, Box 4274, G.P.O. Sydney, NSW, Australia 2001.

The design was selected from submissions to a competition in 1956, won by a 37-year-old Danish architect, Joern Utzon. Originally budgeted at AU$7.5 million, the

OPPOSITE: The convict-built Argyle Centre, once a warehouse, now houses shops and taverns. ABOVE: Sydney's most famous landmarks, the billowing sails of the Opera House and the Harbour Bridge.

cost began escalating and politicians, public servants and the architectural Establishment began to express reservations as to whether Utzon could realize his bold design. Ten years after he started the project Utzon fled the country under an assumed name to escape the hostility of officialdom and press harassment. When finally the Opera House opened in 1973 the cost had ballooned to over AU$100 million. While costs were escalating, one wit suggested that it would have been cheaper to build it overseas and sail it to Australia! Ballet companies have complained that the stages are too small and opera singers grumble about the acoustics. Although functionally flawed, the Opera House is truly a spectacular sight. In 1978, Mr. Utzon won the Queen's Gold Medal for Architecture, which cited him as "the greatest architect of the twentieth century."

It is worth taking a tour of the building to gain an appreciation for its architecture. Guided tours leave from the Lower Concourse Arcade daily from 9 AM to 4 PM. There are numerous performances on at the Opera House, and attending one provides another chance for you to make up your own mind about the merits of this world-famous building.

Darling Harbour

Darling Harbour, just southwest of Circular Quay, can be reached by foot from The Rocks or by Monorail from the city center.

Once a derelict area of rotting wharves and decrepit warehouses, Darling Harbour has undergone a major transformation. Today it has been redeveloped as a leisure area with restaurants, museums, shops and an exhibition center. Over weekends the place is crowded, and its management seems determined to find any excuse for a fireworks display over the harbor.

Sydney Aquarium ((02) 9262-2300, provides an opportunity to see fish, sharks and stingrays swimming around you as you walk inside a plexiglass tube running through the Aquarium. This experience greatly appeals to children.

The **Powerhouse Museum** ((02) 9217-0111, at the corner of Macarthur and Harris streets in Ultimo, is a sympathetically converted power station which once supplied the electricity for Sydney's trams. Exhibitions are changed regularly, the themes being everyday life, social history, science and technology. Its high roof allows the curator to develop imaginative displays utilizing the space to its best advantage. The museum is open daily 10 AM to 5 PM.

City Walks

The haphazard layout of roads in Sydney and its inner suburbs owes its pattern to random paths created by the meanderings of the bullock carts which moved goods between the business district and Sydney Cove.

Today most streets are flanked by high rise buildings, making them appear even

narrower. Streets to the south of the city are more orderly, with **Pitt**, **George** and **Castle-reagh streets** forming the heart of the shopping district.

Macquarie Street leads from the Opera House, skirting the eastern boundary of the city, and ending at Hyde Park. This road passes several neoclassical buildings associated with the early history of the colony. The **State Library**, fronted by an imposing Doric colonnade, contains the Mitchell Wing housing the finest collection of early Australian books and manuscripts. Almost next door is **Parliament House**, the oldest section of which was built between 1811 and 1816 as a hospital and then donated to the state in return for a concession for importing rum. Just before reaching the

park, on your left you will see **Hyde Park Barracks** and on your right **St. James' Church**. Both structures were built by Francis Greenway, the colony's best known architect.

To the east of the city, a pleasant stroll through the Domain, is the **Art Gallery of New South Wales** which has an extensive collection of late nineteenth- and twentieth-century Australian art, and has recently opened up a gallery devoted to Aboriginal artists. Continuing past the gallery, heading north, you will come to the **Royal Botanic Gardens**, a favorite locale for Sydneysiders to picnic. From **Mrs. Macquarie's Chair**

Darling Harbour, a once derelict part of town imaginatively rejuvenated to house museums, restaurants and shops, is especially lively on weekends.

New South Wales   *107*

there is a fine view of the Opera House and **Farm Cove**.

Catch the monorail at the corner of Market and Pitt streets and weave your way between buildings through a loop of 3.6 km (2.2 miles), linking Darling Harbour to the city center. While it may be an eyesore, the monorail provides an admirably convenient form of transport around the center of Sydney.

For a bird's eye view of the city take a ride on the elevator in **Sydney Tower** at the corner of Castlereagh and Market streets up to

Oxford Street

The liveliest street in Sydney is **Oxford Street**, snaking through the inner suburbs, lined by working men's cottages and pubs (with one on almost every corner). Oxford Street is always bustling with people walking to work, to the local pub for a drink, or simply on the prowl; most are promenaders just out for a stroll and hankering for a cappuccino, shopping or casting an eye over the passing parade. The street is a popular haunt for Sydney's gay community, reputedly second only to San Francisco in popu-

the Observation Level. Both night and day this vantage point, 305 m (1,000 ft) above street level provides panoramic views of Sydney and the harbor. There is an admission fee to the Observation Level; open Sunday to Friday from 9:30 AM to 9:30 PM and Saturday from 9 AM to 11:30 PM.

Sydney also has the liveliest **Chinatown** in Australia. Located just beyond the southern end of the main city shopping area in **Haymarket** with its fragrant aromas which would not be out of place in Singapore or Hong Kong, it contains some of the finest Chinese restaurants in the country, centered around Dixon Street where there are also Chinese cinemas, grocers and curio and gift shops.

lation, and each late February, provides the venue for the flamboyant Gay and Lesbian Mardi Gras.

Oxford Street starts at Hyde Park in the city and runs southeast to form the border between **Darlinghurst** and **Surry Hills**.

There are various inexpensive restaurants, bookshops and interesting emporia selling a plethora of goods, as well as a number of good galleries in the area. At the **Brett Whitely Studio Museum**, Two Raper Street, Surry Hills, the artist's former home and studio is open to the public on weekends from 10 AM to 4 PM. Situated just north of Oxford Street off William Street is the infamous **Kings Cross**, a red light district peppered with strip joints and porn shops where aggressive hawkers importune likely customers.

O innocent Travelers, lock up your wives and daughters! And at night, avoid dark streets.

Back on Oxford Street, the next suburb is **Paddington** (or "Paddo" to the locals) where the shops are upmarket and call themselves "boutiques." It is worth taking a detour off the main drag — so to speak — at Elizabeth Street to see restored two-story Victorian terraced houses, as well as the **Carr-Olson Gallery** ((02) 9360-9854, on the corner of Paddington Street. If you are tired of walk-

Museum located in the former jailhouse, reputed to be haunted.

It is then only a short distance to **Centennial Park** at the junction of Oxford Street and Lang, Darley and York Roads, which was built in 1888 to commemorate Sydney's first hundred years. The 220-hectare (550-acre) complex of sporting fields, rose gardens and ornamental lakes is a soothing oasis of peace after the bustle of Oxford Street. The best way to see the park is on wheels, and conveniently, **Centennial Park Cycles** ((02) 9398-5027, hire out bicycles and roller blades.

ing then this may be a good moment to drop into the **Berkelouw's Bookshop** at 19 Oxford Street. You can take your purchase into the upstairs café, part of the bookshop, and have coffee or a light meal. Afterwards, visit the **Co-ee Aboriginal Art Gallery** at 98 Oxford Street.

To garrison British troops **Victoria Barracks** was built in 1848, replacing the original quarters on George Street. It housed British army regiments until 1870. Hidden behind high sandstone walls, the architecture of the Barracks is symmetrical and orderly, reflecting the military profession of its designer, Colonel George Barney. On Wednesday at 10:30 AM witness the changing of the guard and afterwards visit the Army

Beyond Centennial Park, Oxford Street is residential until it meets **Bondi Junction**.

Bondi Beach

With good surf beaches so close to Sydney, it is no surprise that a warm summer's day will see teenagers heading down to catch a wave. Just seven kilometers (five miles) from the city, Bondi Beach has become synonymous with sun-bronzed Australians. The country's first lifesaving club was established there in 1906.

During any summer weekend a carnival celebrating sea and surf is bound to be held

OPPOSITE: Sydney's harbor and beaches are its summer playground. ABOVE: The best known beach of them all: Bondi.

on at least one of Sydney's surf beaches. The most exciting are the boat races in which teams of five men work hard to maneuver their boats through waves and breakers.

Bondi has been through several transformations, from fashionable seaside suburb to home for successive generations of immigrants. When I first visited it in 1969 the foreshore was a seedy, depressing place. In the intervening years the area has transformed itself and today Bondi is a lively mixture of good cafés, excellent ethnic restaurants and a foreshore crowded with

people. And, of course, there is the surf. Swimming has become rather more agreeable since the government stopped the discharge of raw sewage into the sea, but regrettably the local council has authorized several large, ugly construction developments, spoiling parts of the foreshore.

The North Shore
People who live on the **North Shore** are quick to identify themselves as a race apart from the unfortunates on the other side of the Sydney Harbour Bridge. The general image conveyed by the North Shore is of affluence; there mansions line the streets and the chatter of yuppies brings life to the cafés of Neutral Bay and Mosman.

Manly can be reached by the Harbour Bridge or Harbour Tunnel but the best way across is by the Manly Ferry, a leisurely 45-minute journey. Alternatively, take the Hydrofoil and whiz across in 20 minutes.

ABOVE: Secluded moorings on Sydney's North Shore. OPPOSITE: Elegant Victorian era ironwork drapes a Sydney terrace like lace curtains.

A hundred years ago Manly was a fashionable seaside resort; today it remains a popular place for Sydneysiders to go for a meal or a stroll along its bustling streets. The main pedestrian mall, the **Corso**, runs between the harbor shore and the surf beach and overflows with cafés, shops and people enjoying the sea air. Free walking-maps of Manly and its environs are available at the information booth, open from 10 AM to 4 PM daily. If you have three or four hours to spare, pick up a map of the **Manly Scenic Walkway**, which follows the edge of the harbor from Manly through quiet inlets and bushland reserves to **Spit Bridge**; it crosses over to **Balmoral Beach** at **Mosman**, which being in the harbor has no waves and is preferred by windsurfers and families with small children.

SYDNEY AFTER DARK

Sydney at night can be loud and wild or quiet and cultured, but never dull.

Lovers of music and traditional performing arts can enjoy the **Opera House** where there are fine performances of opera and ballet, and where good plays and concerts are always on the program at one of its various halls. While the interior of the Opera House has its detractors, its location is unsurpassed and the views at night are bewitchingly lovely.

Numerous playhouses are found in the suburbs. The **Stables Theatre** ((02) 9361-3817, at 10 Nimrod Street, Kings Cross, and the **Belvoir Street Theatre** ((02) 9699-3444, situated in a converted tomato sauce factory, at 24 Belvoir Street in Surry Hills, shows good plays in season. **Sydney's Original Comedy Store** ((02) 9565-3900, at 450 Parramatta Road in Petersham, showcases Australia's best humorists, and Tuesday night is when new talent is let loose on the audience.

Half price tickets for some plays are available on the day of performance from the **Halftix** booth in Martin Place which is open on weekdays from noon to 5:30 PM and Saturday from 10:30 AM to 4 PM.

On warm evenings the streets come to life as Sydneysiders promenade along the mall at Manly, Bondi foreshore or Oxford

Street's busy pavements, settling themselves into an outdoor restaurant for a convivial meal.

Sydney after dark can be a naughty place, as the profusion of strip joints and prostitutes in Kings Cross attest. Its streets are alive with neon and noise as passersby are accosted by hustlers touting for trade. Prostitutes (clad in alarmingly little attire) stand on street corners ready to negotiate with anyone interested. Lively shows and restaurants in the Cross abound but there are better places to eat around town.

As you would expect in a city this size there is no shortage of choice; one can dine and dance in a sedate ambiance or gyrate to ear-bruising disco music. For cabaret try the **Sydney Show Club** ((02) 9552-2592, at the corner of Pyrmont and Allen streets in Darling Harbour. Sydney has long been a stronghold of jazz and many well-established clubs are situated near The Rocks. **Soup Plus** ((02) 9299-7728, at 383 George Street, and **The Basement** ((02) 9251-2797, at 29 Reiby Place, are venues which dish out supper with hot music. A number of pubs have live music at night: try **Mercantile Hotel** ((02) 9247-3570, at 25 George Street, The Rocks, and the **Cock 'n' Bull** ((02) 9389-3004, in the Grand Hotel at 89 Ebley Street, Bondi Junction. Depending on the band some pubs may charge admission. **The Bridge** ((02) 9810-1260, at 135 Victoria Road, Rozelle, known for its rock music, appeals to younger people. At the **Rhino Club** ((02) 9251-1255, in The Orient Hotel, 89 George Street, The Rocks, you can disco to live music until 3 AM.

Unique to Sydney, there is a wide range of entertainment at 1,500 licensed clubs which offer relatively inexpensive shows and meals to entice patrons to gamble on their poker machines. Run by sporting bodies and returned servicemen's associations, the larger ones stage shows at which international stars perform.

George Street, near the Town Hall, is movieland and Sydney's other main entertainment center. Two theater complexes screen more than a dozen movies at once, at least one of which is usually the premiere of an Australian film.

Information on what's on in Sydney can be found in the Metro section of Friday's *Sydney Morning Herald,* which can also be found on the web at http://www.smh .com.au. On the streets of inner Sydney you can pick up a free copy of *Beat* newspaper, or check out its gig guide on the Internet, http://www.ozonline.com.au:80/beat/ s_giggui.htm.

WHERE TO SHOP

In the city, Pitt, George and Castlereagh streets are the heart of the shopping district. Multi-story centers and arcades offer a plethora of shops while major department stores, such as Myer, David Jones and Grace Brothers straddle several blocks joined by elevated walkways. Four floors at the base of **Centrepoint Tower**, at the corner of Pitt and Market streets, contain 170 retail businesses. In nearby King Street is the **Glasshouse Centre,** that has several levels of shopping floors. Each one, with its own theme, is built around a glass-domed hall. Gift shops are on the lower level and above them, elegant fashion boutiques. The complex also houses the **Theatre Royal** ((02) 9224-8444, one of the city's most respected performance venues, as well as several open-air cafés.

A world away from the ambiance of modern shopping centers is the nineteenth-century **Strand Arcade** in George Street. Its galleries gleam with wrought iron and polished wooden balconies, while shop signs are restricted to discreet shingles. In **Strand Hatters** on the ground floor of the Strand Arcade, famous Australian akubra hats can be purchased. Also on George Street is the magnificently restored **Queen Victoria Building**, built in 1898, endowed with a choice of over 200 shops, cafés and restaurants. The center modestly advertises itself as "the world's most beautiful shopping center." Nine awards for excellence, including the Australian Heritage Award, uphold this characteristically self-effacing claim.

Access to the central city shopping district is easy from all stations on the subway loop, other than Circular Quay.

The Strand Arcade houses some of Sydney's most elegant shops.

For the upmarket shopper, **Double Bay**, approximately 15 minutes from the city, provides an opportunity to browse through designer clothes, jewelry and shoes in the company of the well-heeled of Sydney's North Shore.

Ken Done's bold paintings and designs with their views of Sydney Harbour, the Opera House and bridge are popular with visitors, recalling as they do the warmth and vivid colors of the city and its setting. His work can be bought from the more fashionable shops or from his three galleries at 123–125 George Street, The Rocks, Shop 141 Festival Market Place, Darling Harbour and Shop G42 in the Queen Victoria Building.

Amongst the excellent galleries in Paddington where good local art can be purchased are **Sherman Galleries** ((02) 9331-1112, at 16 Goodhope Street and **Hogarth Galleries** ((02) 9360-6839, at 7 Walker Lane, opposite Liverpool Street, which exhibit contemporary Aboriginal art. **Australian Galleries** at 15 Roylston Street, largely confine themselves to mainstream artists such as Brett Whiteley and Arthur Boyd,

On weekends a number of flea markets offer all manner of wares. An example is **Paddy's Market** at the corner of Hay and Thomas streets, Haymarket, just a short walk from the city. Saturday, on the grounds of the Eastside Parish Church on Oxford Street, is the **Paddington Village Bazaar** where 250 stalls sell antiques, jewelry, crafts and bric-a-brac.

games to see are international sides against Australia, guaranteed to attract a monstrous crowd.

There are 69 golf courses in Sydney open to the public. Get in touch with the New South Wales Golf Association ((02) 9439-8444, for details.

Top-class tennis can be seen at **White City** ((02) 9331-4144, at 30 Alma Street, Paddington, and at the **Sydney Entertainment Centre** ((02) 9211-2222, at Darling Harbour. It is wise to purchase tickets well ahead for major tournaments.

SPORTS

Sydney offers the choice of three football codes during winter — Rugby League, Rugby Union and Australian Rules. Football is played between March and September and information on venues for games can be obtained from Friday's newspaper. Rugby League is by far the most popular sport in New South Wales. Its Grand Final takes place at the Sydney Football Stadium at Moore Park and tickets can be obtained through BASS Booking Agency (11566.

When the football season is over, cricket commences. Details of where games are can be obtained from the New South Wales Cricket Association ((02) 9261-5155. The best

WHERE TO STAY

Luxury

Within The Rocks there are small, but top-class, hotels with intimate surroundings not found in larger establishments. **The Observatory Hotel** ((02) 9256-2222 TOLL-FREE 1800-806-245 FAX (02) 9256-2233, at 89–113 Kent Street, is comfortably furnished and recreates the atmosphere of an English country house. For views of Campbell's Cove stay at the **Park Hyatt** ((02) 9241-1234 or 131-234 FAX (02) 9252-2419, at 7 Hickson Road, which has an unassuming lobby and friendly staff. Not all the rooms have such good views so when making reservations it is advisable to express your preference.

The **Russell Hotel** ((02) 9241-3543 FAX (02) 9252-1652, at 143A George Street, The Rocks, has combined its nineteenth-century charm with twentieth-century conveniences.

Several good "boutique" hotels — those smaller hotels which combine luxury with intimacy — provide more personal service than do the larger luxury hotels. In North Sydney, **The McLaren Hotel** ((02) 9954-4622 FAX (02) 9922-1868, at 25 McLaren Street, North Sydney, is located in a beautiful turn-of-the-century house; with just

In the style of a guesthouse of the nineteenth century, **Periwinkle** ((02) 9977-4668 FAX (02) 9977-6308, at 19 East Esplanade, Manly, offers bed and breakfast. In a similar style, **Cremorne Point Manor** ((02) 9953 7899 FAX (02) 9904 1265, 6 Cremorne Road, is a Federation mansion on the edge of the harbor with million dollar views, and is located a short distance from the Cremorne ferry terminal.

In Paddington, stay at **Paddington Terrace** ((02) 9363-0903 FAX (02) 9327-1476, 76 Elizabeth Street. Hosts Dianne and Ron

25 rooms, guests are assured of personal service. Located in a row of charming nineteenth-century terrace houses, the **Kendall Hotel** ((02) 9357-3200 FAX (02) 357-7606, at 122 Victoria Street, Potts Point, is another boutique hotel with lots of character and attention to detail.

Moderate
Staying close to the city center is generally expensive—moderately-priced hotels are thin on the ground. For authentic Aussie pub atmosphere try **O'Malley's Hotel** ((02) 9357-2211, at 228 William Street, Kings Cross. This turn-of-the-century pub has been carefully restored, and provides bed-and-breakfast accommodation in a great location.

are quite friendly and helpful; and their delightfully restored Victorian terrace house provides a comfortable and homey atmosphere.

The **Garden Studios** ((02) 9356-2355 FAX (02) 9356-4943, at the corner of Bourke and Plunkett streets, Woolloomooloo, are self-contained units, a 10-minutes walk from the city and can be reached through the Domain.

Opposite the University of New South Wales is **Barker Lodge Motor Inn** ((02) 9662-8444 FAX (02) 9662-2363, at 32 Barker Street in Kingsford, midway between the city and

OPPOSITE: A well preserved terrace in The Rocks. ABOVE: An old façade for a modern business.

airport. Near the University of Sydney and close to good inexpensive restaurants is the **Rooftop Motel** ((02) 9660-7777 FAX (02) 9660-7155, at 146-148 Glebe Point Road, Glebe. The **Metro Inn** ((02) 9319-4133 FAX (02) 9698-7665, at One Meagher Street, Chippendale, is close to Chinatown and handy to Central Station.

Inexpensive

The **Astoria Hotel** ((02) 9356-3666 FAX (02) 9357-1734, at 9 Darlinghurst Road, and **Barclay Hotel** ((02) 9358-6133 FAX (02) 9358-

4363, at 17 Bayswater Road, are very close to everything in lively Kings Cross.

Established in 1873, the **Wynyard Hotel** ((02) 9299-1330, at the corner of Clarence and Erskine streets, is well placed for access to most of Sydney's major attractions.

There are also quite a few places in Kings Cross, Bondi and Coogee that cater solely to backpackers. Youth Hostels of Australia (YHA) ((02) 9281-9111 FAX (02) 9281-9199, has two hostels in Sydney. The Sydney Central YHA is opposite Central Station, on the corner of Pitt Street and Rawson Place. The Glebe Point YHA ((02) 9692-8418 FAX (02) 9660-0431, at 262 Glebe Point Road, Glebe, is smaller and more relaxed.

WHERE TO EAT

When you have a city with such a beautiful harbor, is it little wonder that some of the most exclusive restaurants are on the waterfront, or that many of them specialize in seafood? They have the added advantage of splendid views — considered justification for a bill which may seem unreasonably high. Beware!

Ask any Sydneysider to name the city's best seafood restaurant and **Doyles on the Beach** ((02) 9337-2007, at 11 Marine Parade, Watsons Bay (expensive), is sure to be his response. Situated near the Heads, it looks back along the length of the harbor, and while Doyles may no longer be truly the best seafood restaurant it remains a local institution. Another restaurant gaining in reputation is **The Bather's Pavilion** ((02) 9968-1133, at 4 The Esplanade on Balmoral Beach (expensive), with great views over the beach. The emphasis is on fresh food, especially seafood, simply prepared but with a touch of exotic influence from Asia, Africa and Europe. The nearby **Freshwater** ((02) 9938-5575, on Moore Road, Harbord (expensive), resembles a rambling old guesthouse and looks out over a surf beach. At Manly, **Le Kiosk** ((02) 9977-4122, on Shelley Beach (moderate), is popular, and on hot days the outdoor tables are crowded.

A number of good restaurants serve dishes other than seafood, and are close to the city to boot; most are located in The Rocks and around Darling Harbour and have good water views. Kept full by a constant flow of tourists some have become blasé. Not so at **Nº7 at the Park** ((02) 9256-1630, in the Park Hyatt Sydney at 7 Hickson Road, The Rocks (expensive). This establishment takes particular care in the presentation of its food with unusual combinations of Japanese ingredients. You need connections to get a window seat where below you can take in a bird's eye view of the Harbour Bridge and Opera House, but the views are good from anywhere in the restaurant. The outlook from of **The Wharf** ((02) 9250-1761, at Pier 4 Hickson Road, Walsh Bay (moderate), is uninspiring, a factor which appears not to have discouraged its patrons, actors by and large; its atmosphere is Bohemian.

What better way of enjoying the harbor than aboard a catamaran fitted out as a restaurant? **Sail Venture Cruises (** (02) 9262-3595 (expensive), leaves Aquarium Wharf at Darling Harbour at lunchtime and evenings for a dinner cruise of the harbor.

The best view of the city is from the **Centre Point Tower revolving restaurant (** (02) 9233-3722 (expensive), which provides an à la carte menu upstairs and has a **bistro** (moderate) below. On a clear day you can

lar Quay (expensive), overlooks the harbor and the bridge.

To find restaurants which are both good and moderately priced you will have to get away from the water.

Chinatown in the city has some of the best Chinese restaurants around, although Melbournians would challenge this claim. For Cantonese cuisine try **Marigold's (** (02) 9264-6744, at 299–305 Sussex Street (moderate). You'd better believe that the seafood is fresh at this restaurant, as you can choose your dish (alive) from large tanks; a few

see as far as the Blue Mountains west of the city and also have a panoramic view of Sydney Harbour.

Three restaurants situated in or near the Opera House provide the chance to dine before attending a concert or the convenience of a late supper afterwards. **Bennelong (** (02) 9250-7578 (expensive), is located under the smaller sails at the back of the Opera House and offers special pre-theater meals and supper, if available, upstairs. The **Concourse Restaurant (** (02) 9250-7300 (moderate), is less formal, serves better food than the Bennelong (some say), and provides a wide selection of meals, from snacks to a full dinner. The view from the **Harbour Front Restaurant (** (02) 9247-6661, at Circu-

minutes later the lobster or crab will appear (cooked) in front of you. It brings tears to your eyes.

Cantonese *yum cha*, consisting largely of steamed and fried dumplings, has become very popular in Sydney and is traditionally served as a brunch. **East Ocean (** (02) 9212-4198, at 421 Sussex Street (moderate), offers a wide selection of dishes which come around on trolleys for you to select. Just point to what you fancy. For food typically sold from stalls in Southeast Asia try **Dixon House Food Hall in Dixon Street** (inexpensive), where dishes from a dozen Asian

OPPOSITE: One of Sydney's many fountains, this one in Hyde Park. ABOVE: Doyles on the Beach—a long-time favorite for seafood.

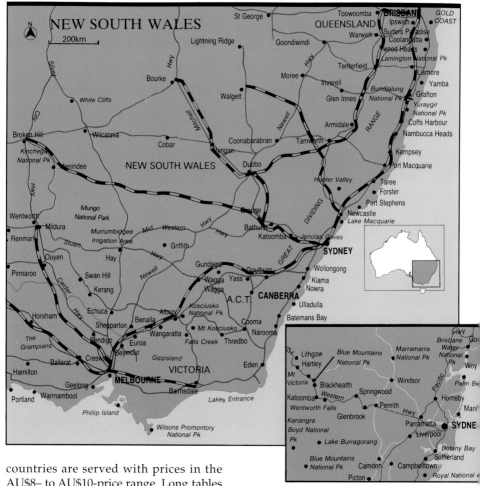

countries are served with prices in the AU$8– to AU$10-price range. Long tables populated with hungry dinners are surrounded by food stalls to tempt every taste. There is no cheaper, nor more interesting place to dine in Chinatown.

On the lower North Shore are a number of sensibly-priced establishments, with more expensive ones around Crows Nest. **Armstrong's Brasserie (** (02) 9955-2066, at One Napier Street, North Sydney (expensive), has a reputation for serving the best steaks on the North Shore. **Pino's (** (02) 9439-2081, at 49 Willoughby Road, Crow's Nest (moderate), a humble pizzeria, has some of the best pasta in town. The place is usually full, which is its own recommendation. **The Red Centre (** (02) 9906-4408, at 70 Alexander Street (moderate), serves pizza with a difference: they use deliciously unusual toppings. Moving away from

Crows Nest to Mosman, the restaurants along Military Road generally become more pricey. The **Rattlesnake Grill (** (02) 9953-4789, at 130 Military Road, Neutral Bay (moderate), is famous for its volcanic chili dishes; while in Mosman, **Spitler's Restaurant (** (02) 9968-3811, on the waterfront at Spit Bridge (moderate), serves contemporary Australian seafood.

The choice of restaurants widens around Oxford Street between the city and Paddington, where the best places to eat have good views of Oxford Street and watching the passing parade of trendsetters adds interest to the meal. **Café Flicks (** (02) 9331-7412, at 3 Oxford Street, Paddington, next to the Academy Twin Cinema (inexpensive), is a good spot to pause for a light meal or a *café au lait* while you watch the world go by.

The Golden Dog ((02) 9360-7700, at 388 Oxford Street (moderate), is an Italian bistro serving both traditional pasta and some inventive specialties of its own. Another good Italian place is Il Trattoraro ((02) 9331-2962, at 10 Elizabeth Street (moderate), and next door at 8 Elizabeth Street you'll find the wickedly indulgent Chocolate Factory Coffee Shop ((02) 9331-3785 (inexpensive), serving delicious cakes and snacks.

They must run the chefs on a roster at Morgan's ((02) 9360-7930, at 304 Victoria Street, Darlinghurst (moderate), as the day starts at 6 AM for breakfast and continues late into the night. The prices are very reasonable and the menu always interesting.

For excellent Thai food, go to the Siam Restaurant ((02) 9331-2669, at 383 Oxford Street (moderate). At 149 Oxford Street, Jo Jo's ((02) 9331-3293 (moderate) serves traditional North Indian cuisine.

On either side of the University of Sydney are good cheap restaurants frequented by students. In Newtown are various Thai restaurants which have sprung up in recent years, offering good value for money such as Ban Thai ((02) 9519-5330, 115 King Street (moderate). Glebe Point Road is a bit of a mixed bag, offering a number of inexpensive ethnic restaurants. Borobudur ((02) 9660-5611, at 125 Glebe Point Road (inexpensive), has deliciously spicy Indonesian food, and very good Indian cuisine will be found at Flavour of India ((02) 9692-0662, 142 Glebe Point Road (inexpensive).

HOW TO GET THERE

As well as being the major international gateway to Australia, Sydney is also the hub of the transport network along the eastern seaboard.

By air Sydney is an hour from both Melbourne and Brisbane, and two hours from Adelaide. As for Sydney's airports, the less said about them, the better. They are a disgrace, as are the roadways leading to them. Transferring from an international to domestic flight requires a short bus trip between terminals. When connecting to a domestic flights give yourself more than 30 minutes as undermanned transfer desks, particularly with Ansett, can lead to missed flights.

The bus takes 17 hours from Brisbane, 13 hours from Melbourne, 23 hours from Adelaide and two and half days from Perth on the other side of the continent. Sydney is the eastern terminus for the transcontinental *Indian–Pacific*. If you fancy train-travel this 62-hour trip is one of the world's last great train journeys.

DAY TRIPS FROM SYDNEY

KU-RING-GAI CHASE NATIONAL PARK

Sydney is fortunate to have at the edge of its suburban sprawl and 24 km (15 miles) from the city center a national park of great beauty. Visitors can take a scenic drive through it or stroll along its many tracks.

Bordered by Pittwater to the east, Broken Bay to the north and Sydney's suburbs towards the south, the Ku-ring-gai Chase National Park covers over 15,000 hectares (37,000 acres) and contains rivers, gorges and more than 100 km (62 miles) of navigable water.

Caves and sheltered overhangs in sandstone provided protection for the Aborigines who once lived there. Rock engravings of kangaroos, dolphins, emus and sharks are their memorial. Maps on where to see Aboriginal paintings can be obtained from the Bobbin Head Information and Retail Centre ((02) 9457-9322, or Kalkai Visitor Centre ((02) 9457-9853, both open 9 AM to 5 PM daily.

How to Get There

A ferry to the park leaves from Palm Beach, or follow the signs from either the Berowra, Ku-ring-gai or Cowan railway stations.

THE BLUE MOUNTAINS

The Blue Mountains, an leisurely hour-and-a-half drive from Sydney, were *the* vacation place for locals before the advent of inexpensive overseas air fares. Fifty years ago the Blue Mountains were lauded for their healthy "mountain air." These days their vistas have been rediscovered by day trippers from Sydney who continue to be attracted to this especially beautiful region. Make the trip in a day or stick around and enjoy the hills as a base from which to explore the surrounding countryside.

From a distance the mountains really appear blue, caused by the haze of eucalyptus vapor, from the gum trees, which absorbs the red component of sunlight.

General Information

Information on touring around the Blue Mountains can be obtained from the **Blue Mountains Tourist Authority** ((02) 4739-6266, on the Great Western Highway, Glenbrook, or drop by their booth at Echo Point two kilometers (one mile) from Katoomba, which has a good collection of books about the area and walking guides for sale.

What to See and Do

Man's encroachment on the sandstone ramparts is confined to the procession of small towns and villages straddling the Great Western Highway linking the mountains and Sydney. The mountains, despite their name, are really a 1,000-m (3,280-ft) sandstone plateau. Millions of years of erosion have created a scenic wilderness of valleys, ravines and cliffs.

Most of the area is a conservation region; numerous walking tracks run parallel to the edge of the escarpment and lookouts are clearly signposted. They provide breathtaking panoramas of the harsh but spectacular land; walking tracks within the national park lead to more than 40 waterfalls.

There are several pretty villages along the Great Western Highway approach to the Blue Mountains: **Leura**, **Blackheath** and the village of **Springwood** are worth visiting.

Author and artist Norman Lindsay lived at Faulconbridge via Springwood for over 50 years, etching and painting satyrs and nude women in compositions of Bacchanalian revelry. Although his works scandalized generations of prudes, his prints and paintings can now be appreciated without the tut-tutting of that sanctimonious age. Lindsay also wrote the children's story, *The Magic Pudding* with his tongue in his cheek to prove that any stories about animals and food appeal to children. His homestead has been converted into the **Norman Lindsay Gallery and Museum** ((02) 4751-1067, on Norman Lindsay Crescent, Faulconbridge, via Springwood, where his paintings hang and memorabilia from his life are on display. His studio has been preserved as it was when he died.

The main town in the Blue Mountains is **Katoomba**, perched near cliffs which rise from the Jamieson Valley. What is claimed to be the world's steepest railway plunges 250 m (820 ft) down the cliff wall on a 400-m (1,300-ft) track and a cable car sways out over the valley to give a truly heart-stopping ride. Both the **Scenic Railway and Skyway** ((02) 4782-2699, start at the corner of Cliff Drive and Violet Street.

At Katoomba is the **Three Sisters** rock formation with the best views from Echo Point or Queen Elizabeth Lookout. Rising out of the Jamieson Valley, these three sheer rock columns are steeped in Aboriginal folklore. Three maidens, Meenhi, Wimlah and Gunedu were menaced by a witch doctor. Their father saw their plight from the valley below and — to protect his daughters — turned them to stone using a magic stick; however, in his excitement the father dropped his stick and the witch doctor turned him into a lyrebird. The sound of the lyrebird is believed by Aborigines to be the girls' father looking for his magic stick so that he can bring his daughters back to flesh and blood.

While in Katoomba drop into the **Paragon Café** at 65 Katoomba Street, for some tea or a light meal. This art deco café was built in 1916 and appears not to have changed much in the intervening years, nor has the menu. Try the homemade chocolates displayed in leadlight cabinets dating back to 1925.

Katoomba and surrounding villages are also the place for a mid-year Christmas. Being in the Southern Hemisphere Australians are used to celebrating Christmas at the height of summer, and the Christmas lunch is often a barbecue outdoors; the northern hemisphere traditions are missed, so the tourist industry has come up with a solution. Between June and August the area celebrates Yuletide. There are Christmas decorations in the streets, including a Christmas tree in Katoomba, and a snowman in Leura. More than 30 guesthouses, restaurants, hotels and resorts in the Blue Mountains serve the full traditional Christmas dinner to the accompaniment of carol singing, open fires and mulled wine. How agreeable, a mid-year Christmas devoid of squabbling relatives.

If all this indulgence niggles the conscience then go play 18 holes of golf on the picturesque greens of **Leura Golf Club** ((02) 4782-5011, on Sublime Point Road, or go horseback riding through the Kanimbla Valley on day trips organized by the **Centennial Glen Horse and Sulky Hire** ((02) 4787-7179, Blackheath.

than style; and, for a sample of history, the **Balmoral House** ((02) 4788-2264, at 196 Bathurst Street, built in 1876. Several motels in town provide moderately-priced accommodation.

Leura is one of the prettiest towns in the area, without the hustle and bustle of Katoomba. It has a number of nice bed-and-breakfast places. At **The Greens** ((02) 4784-3241, 24 Grose Street, hosts Jean and Peter provide a friendly welcome and facilities include a spa, library and full-size billiard table. **Where Waters Meet** ((02) 4784-3022

About an hour and half west of Katoomba are the limestone caverns of the **Jenolan Caves** which are open daily; the best way to see these natural cathedrals in lime is to join a guided tour, which leaves every 30 minutes from the **Jenolan Caves Reserve Trust** ((02) 6332-5888.

Where to Stay

There are some wonderful guesthouses and hotels in the Blue Mountains with prices ranging from moderate to luxury. The rates usually go up over weekends.

In Katoomba, in the luxury category, there are **The Cecil** ((02) 4782-1411 FAX (02) 4782-5364, at 25 Lurline Street, a traditional guesthouse built more for comfort rather

FAX (02) 4784-3343, at 15 Mt. Hay Road, is an elegant and secluded guesthouse, about three kilometers (two miles) out of town.

At Medlow Bath there is the famously luxurious **Hydro Majestic** ((02) 4788-1002 FAX (02) 4788-1063, a hotel in the grand style (see LIVING IT UP in YOUR CHOICE).

The **Sky Rider Motor Inn** ((02) 4782-1600, is at the intersection of Scenic Cliff Road and the Great Western Highway, Katoomba, while in nearby Blackheath you can try out the **Gardners Inn** ((02) 4787-8347 and **Jemby-Rinjah Lodge** ((02) 4787-7622 FAX (02) 4787-6230, at 336 Evans Look-

LEFT: Sandstone walls of the Blue Mountains National Park. These cliffs are perfect for abseiling RIGHT.

out Road, set into the bush adjacent to the Grose Valley.

The **Jenolan Caves House** ((02) 6359-3322 FAX (02) 6359-3227, has the relaxed atmosphere of a country homestead, and provides a chance to get away from it all.

Mid-year **Yuletide** accomodation packages are available at the Cecil guesthouse, Balmoral House, Hydro Majestic and Jenolan Caves House.

Where to Eat

For light meals, snacks and coffee, try the **Parakeet Café** ((02) 4782-1815, in Katoomba. In Leura, **Gracie's on the Mall** ((02) 4784-1973, serves homemade pies, soups and flower-pot dampers, as well as breakfast every day. For a superb meal in a charming setting and relaxed atmosphere, have dinner at **The Ferns** ((02) 4784-3256, at 130 Megalong Street, where the seafood sausage is a favorite of mine. If you are traveling with kids, or to revive your own memories of childhood, go to the **Candy Store Old Time Lolly Shop** ((02) 4782-5190, inside Leura's Strand Arcade, where you can select from over 1,000 jars of your favorite old-fashioned sweets, including hard candies, nougats, toffees and chocolates.

How to Get There

Katoomba is about two hours by train from Sydney. The drive along the M4 Highway takes one and a half hours, and on the Great Western Highway slightly longer.

Trains to the Blue Mountains leave from Central Station in Sydney, stopping at Springwood, Leura, Katoomba, Mt. Victoria and Lithgow.

The local bus lines connect with some of the train services, running frequent services on weekdays and Saturday morning.

Daily tours are offered by **Australian Pacific Tours** (131-304, and **AAT King's Tours** ((02) 9252-2788, with stops at popular lookouts in the Blue Mountains and the Jenolan Caves.

THE SOUTH COAST

The coastal road south of Sydney passes through the industrial cities of Wollongong and Port Kembla and then onto rich pastoral country dotted with dairy herds. The road occasionally turns towards the coast to pretty fishing villages and small holiday resort towns.

GENERAL INFORMATION

Kiama's Visitor Centre ((02) 4232-3322, at Blowhole Point, is open every day from 9 AM to 5 PM.

The **Shoalhaven Tourist Centre** ((02) 4421 0778, at 254 Princes Highway, Bomaderry, is open daily 9 AM to 5 PM.

For information about the area around Bowral and Berrima contact the **Southern Highlands Information Centre** ((02) 4871 2888, on the Hume Highway at Mittagong, which is open daily 9 AM to 4:30 PM.

The **Bateman's Bay Visitor Centre** ((02) 4472-6900, is at the corner of Princes Highway and Beach Road, and is open daily from 9 AM to 5 PM.

WHAT TO SEE AND DO

Kiama, a charming seaside town 17 km (73 miles) south of Sydney, is famous for its blowhole that can spurt water as high as 60 m (200 ft) into the air when the sea is rough and the wind is blowing from the southeast. **The Terrace**, a row of historic timber cottages built in 1886, has been restored as a home for art galleries, craft shops and restaurants.

The walks along the cliffs to Cathedral Rocks and Kaleula Head are recommended. Maps of walking trails are available from the visitor center.

Inland from Kiama are the small towns of **Berrima** and **Bowral**, both of which merit a detour from the coastal route.

Berrima has changed very little since it was settled, in fact virtually no buildings have been erected there since 1890. One establishment that still functions as it did when started in 1834 is the sandstone **Surveyor General Inn**, although the food is more upmarket and these days Guinness is on tap. There are numerous restaurants, tea rooms, antique shops and galleries in town; to appreciate it best, go for a stroll.

Bibliophiles should not miss **Berkelouws' Antiquarian Books** ((02) 4877-1370

FAX (02) 4877-1102, located on the Old Hume Highway towards Mittagong where there are shelves filled with second-hand and rare books.

Bowral has retained its buildings from the late nineteenth century, many of which can be seen on Wingecarribee and Bendooley streets. The town and surrounding area have traditionally been used as a resort by affluent Sydneysiders, as a consequence of which many fine restaurants and places to stay can be found in and around town.

in which a profusion of blossoms paint the town red... yellow, blue, white....

Back on the coast, **Nowra** is the agricultural and business center of the Shoalhaven River district. The high escarpment and plateau immediately inland are bounded by high sandstone cliffs which can be seen to the west of the road into the village, from which there is access to the high tableland 28 km (17 miles) away, preserved as the **Morton National Park**. This features the spectacular **Fitzroy Falls** and is a haven for a large number of indigenous animals and wild birds.

Bowral is frothing with tributes to its favorite son, Donald Bradman — the greatest batsman Australian cricket has ever produced. A **museum** in St. Jude Street dedicated to this cricketing immortal has an impressive collection of memorabilia which includes an oak bat from the mid-eighteenth century, and mementos from the current test team. An admission fee is charged and the museum is open daily 10 AM to 3 PM. After visiting the museum, have afternoon tea at the **Marmalade Café** ℂ (02) 4861-3553, at 362 Bong Bong Street. Sharon and Keith serve delicious homemade food, including the tastiest hot scones in the district. In September–October, Bowral hosts a spectacular **Tulip Festival**,

Batemans Bay is spread along the Clyde River estuary and is a popular seaside resort where rumor has it that you can simply pick up oysters on the shore, but it's probably easier to buy a couple of dozen — or a crayfish — for which the area is famous, and picnic with a bottle of Chablis on the foreshore. On the coast north of Batemans Bay is **Murramarang National Park**, renowned for its broad beaches and towering headlands.

Central Tilba, 79 km (50 miles) south of Batemans Bay, is surrounded by rugged coastal mountains. Frozen in time, this

A Dutch touch among the spring blossoms at Bowral's Tulip Festival in New South Wales.

village of 25 wooden buildings was built between 1889 and 1906 during a short-lived gold rush and has remained unaltered to this day.

WHERE TO STAY

In Kiama moderately-priced accommodation is offered by the **Grand Hotel** ((02) 4232-1037, at the corner of Manning and Bong Bong streets, and the **Kiama Inn Hotel** ((02) 4232-1166 FAX (02) 4232-3401, at 50 Terralong Street, within easy walking distance of all the sights of note. Also in this category, the **Berrima Bakehouse Motel** ((02) 4877-1381 FAX (02) 4877-1047, is at the corner of the Hume Highway and Wingecarribee Street.

Staying in Bowral can be expensive but the accommodation available is quite special. Particular noteworthy are: **Milton Park** ((02) 4861-1522 FAX (02) 4861-4716, on Hordern's Road, on a 300-hectare (740-acre) estate which serves excellent meals to its guests, with wine from its cellar. The **Craigburn Resort** ((02) 4861-1277 FAX (02) 4862-1690 has been providing accommodation since 1910 and has its own nine-hole golf course.

Excellent value weekend packages in Nowra can be obtained at the **Riverhaven Motel** ((02) 4421-2044 FAX (02) 4421-2121, at One Scenic Drive, located on the banks of the Shoalhaven River. A little out of Nowra but well worth the trip, is the **Coolangatta Historic Village Resort** ((02) 4448-7131 FAX (02) 4448-7997, which is the site of the first settlement on the South Coast in 1822. Suites are moderately priced. Located in the Murramarang National Park, 10 km (six miles) from Batemans Bay are inexpensive self-contained bungalows on the beach at the **Murramarang Caravan and Camping Resort** ((02) 4478-6355 FAX (02) 4478-6230. In Batemans Bay itself a range of accommodation is offered by the **Coachhouse Marina Resort** ((02) 4472-4392 FAX (02) 4472-4852, from inexpensive cabins to moderately-priced villas. For a little luxury try the **Old Nelligen Post Office Guest House** ((02) 4478-1179, at 7 Braidwood Street, Nelligan, which provides a weekend getaway package which includes meals in its admirable restaurant.

HOW TO GET THERE

Pioneer Motor Services of Nowra operates a bus service connecting with trains from Sydney and following the route along the 325-km (200-mile) coastline to the Victorian border.

Most of the sights on the south coast are on or near the Princes Highway, a good route by car and easy to connect from town to town using local buses. The train from Sydney stops at Kiama and Nowra.

SNOWY MOUNTAINS

While most parts of Australia are hot and dry, the alpine regions are much visited by skiers and other winter sport enthusiasts who flock to the higher peaks along the Great Dividing Range, from Victoria to southern New South Wales. The best skiing areas are the Snowy Mountains, 200 km (125 miles) south of Canberra along the Monaro Highway.

Snow gums OPPOSITE bent by the alpine winds at Mount Kosciusko National Park. Australia's snowfields are more extensive than those of Switzerland. The bleached landscape of Mungo National Park ABOVE where the earliest evidence of Aboriginal man in Australia has been uncovered.

In snowy months of winter the high peak of Mt. Kosciusko glitters in brilliance or disappears in a shroud of mist. There are beautiful passes through the mountains and many top ski resorts. In summer the high country is a favorite haunt of trout fishermen. In spring it is flower hunting time.

GENERAL INFORMATION

The **Tourist Information Centre** ((02) 6947-1849, is on the Snowy Mountains Highway at Tumut, provides useful advice on current road and skiing conditions. The center is open daily from 9 AM to 5 PM.

The New South Wales National Parks and Wildlife Service runs the **Snowy Region Visitor Centre** ((02) 6450-5600, on the Kosciusko Road at Jindabyne, open every day from 8 AM to 6 PM. It has a good range of information on the Kosciusko National Park and the Snowy Mountains.

The **Cooma Visitor Centre** ((02) 6450-1740, is at 119 Sharp Street, Cooma, and is open 9 AM to 5 PM.

WHAT TO SEE AND DO

The slopes of **Thredbo, Perisher, Blue Valley, Selwyn, Smiggins Holes, Charlotte Pass** and a few other resorts on the mountains are packed from June to September with skiers. There is also cross-country skiing throughout the whole area, the major ski fields being in the **Kosciusko National Park**, covering 690,000 hectares (1,700,000 acres), making it the largest national park in New South Wales.

Glacial lakes, limestone caves, windswept moors and the headwaters of the Murrumbidgee River all contribute to the park's scenic beauty.

In summer the mountain's slopes are a tapestry of yellow, white and purple wildflowers, delighting nature lovers and photographers, making this alpine region as popular in summer as it is during the winter skiing season. The moment the snow recedes hikers take to its tracks, climbers head for its sheer rock walls and anglers cast their lines into clear alpine streams and lakes for trout.

Dominating the Snowy Mountains is **Mt. Kosciusko**, 2,228 m (7,307 ft) above sea level. Although modest by world standards, this is Australia's highest peak. Take a chair lift, which operates year-round, from Thredbo or walk up to the peak, an leisurely eight-kilometer (five-mile) hike through alpine meadows. A more challenging 20-km (12-mile) walk begins at the information office at Sawpit Creek making its way up Perisher Valley. It's great fun to explore the mountains on horseback. **Reynella Kosciusko Rides** TOLL-FREE 1800-029-909 FAX (02) 6454-2530, offer three- to five-day rides from November to May into the high country where wild horses roam and wildflowers cover the meadows.

Australia's most ambitious engineering undertaking, the Snowy Mountain Scheme, involved the construction of 16 large dams and 160 km (100 miles) of tunnels rerouting water formerly running to waste into the Pacific Ocean, to irrigate land west of the Great Dividing Range. On its way west the drop of some 1,000 m (3,000 ft) is utilized to drive the hydroelectric turbines feeding southeastern Australia's power grid. At **Tarbingo** on the New Dam Road, take a narrated tour of the **Tumut Nº3 Power Station** to gain an idea of the magnitude of the engineering involved.

WHERE TO STAY

During the winter it is essential to book well ahead. Rooms above the snow line can be expensive and some places will only accept reservations in blocks of a week or more. The tariffs during summer can be 50 percent cheaper than during winter.

There are several reservation services both on and off the mountains which can save you the bother of hunting around for lodging. Contact the **Snowy Mountains Reservation Centre** ((02) 6456-2633 TOLL-FREE 1800-020-622 FAX (064) 561-207, at Shop 16, Town Centre, Jindabyne, **Kosciusko Accommodation Centre** ((02) 6456-2022 TOLL-FREE 1800-026-354 FAX (02) 6456-3945, at Shop Two Nugget's Crossing, Jindabyne, or the

A bushwoman near Broken Hill, New South Wales prepares a meal in the open over a coal fire.

Thredbo Accommodation Services ((02) 6457-6387 TOLL-FREE 1800-801-982 FAX (02) 6457-6057, at Shop 9 Mowamba Place, Thredbo Village.

In the center of Thredbo Village, luxury accommodation is available at the **Thredbo Alpine** ((02) 6459-4200 TOLL-FREE 1800-026-333 FAX (02) 6459-4201. **Bernti's Mountain Inn** TOLL-FREE 1800-500-105 FAX (02) 6456-1669, at 4 Mowamba Place, is moderately priced.

At Jindabyne there are the **Alpine Resort** ((02) 6456-2522 FAX (02) 6456-2854, at 22 Nettin Circuit, and the less expensive **Lakeview Plaza Motel** ((02) 6456-2134 FAX (02) 6456-1372, located at Two Snowy River Avenue.

The **Kosciusko Chalet** TOLL-FREE 1800-026-369 FAX 1800-802-687, is a rambling luxury guesthouse in Charlotte Pass, above the snowline in winter. The Chalet is also popular in summer.

If you have a car then you can save on accommodation by staying in one of the lowland towns. In **Cooma**, there is inexpensive accommodation at the **Bunkhouse** ((02) 6452-2983, at 28 Soho Street, and **Hawaii** ((02) 6452-1211, at 192 Sharp Street.

HOW TO GET THERE

Car access is by way of the Snowy Mountains Highway, the Alpine Way and Kosciusko Road. During winter it is advisable to carry tire chains.

There are Skitube trains to Perisher, Smiggins Holes and Blue Cow Mountain which leave Bullock's Flat in Jindabyne every twenty minutes in winter and on the hour in summer. Savings can be made by purchasing a return Skitube pass and chair-lift ticket package.

There are daily flights to Cooma from Sydney by Eastern Australian Airlines and from Melbourne by Kendall Airlines.

Coach companies include a stop-over in the mountains on their itineraries, and day trips from Canberra can be arranged.

THE FAR WEST

The north and west of New South Wales are flat, arid and sparsely populated; this is part of the **Outback**. In 1883 Charles Rasp discovered rich lead, silver and zinc deposits near **Broken Hill**, which became the center for mineral exploration in this part of the state. The company formed to exploit the mine was The Broken Hill Proprietary Company which used its wealth to invest in steel manufacture and petroleum exploration. Today BHP is Australia's largest multinational company.

GENERAL INFORMATION

Tourist information is available from the **Broken Hill Visitor Information Centre** ((08) 8087-6077, at the corner of Bromide and Blende streets. Its staff will handle reservations for local tours and provide information on Outback attractions, and the information booth is open daily from 8:30 AM to 5 PM.

WHAT TO SEE AND DO

Broken Hill could justifiably be known as "Silver City"; its mines once produced a third of the world's silver. The town itself is dreary beyond words, but explore **Delprats Underground Tourist Mine** ((08) 8088-1604, in Crystal Road. A 120-m (400-ft) drop in a cage takes you to the start, where visitors are herded through a labyrinth of tunnels. Tours begin at 10:30 AM weekdays and at 2 PM on Saturday.

The abysmal landscape around Broken Hill has inspired a generation of bush painters who have created styles unique to the area. Best known are Pro Hart who has a gallery at 108 Wymam Street, and Jack Absalom whose gallery is at 638 Chapple Street. Works by other painters calling themselves "brushmen from the bush" can be seen at the **Ant Hill Gallery** at 24 Bromide Street.

To gain some understanding of the wealth generated in the area visit the **Broken Hill City Art Gallery** ((08) 8088-9252, at the Entertainment Centre in Chloride Street. Silver craftwork is on display, and the pride of the collection is *The Silver Tree*, commissioned by Charles Rasp. An admission fee is charged, and the gallery is open Monday to Saturday.

If you really want to get off the beaten track, book a seat on the **Bush Mail Run**, the light aircraft which delivers post and supplies to 25 remote sheep stations in Outback New South Wales. The plane can hold up to five passengers and reservations are made with **Crittenden Airlines** ((08) 8088-5702. Traveling only a few thousand meters above the endless plain you gain an appalling insight into the hinterland — forbidding, harsh and bereft of beauty. Morning tea and lunch at a homestead are included for passengers. The plane leaves the Broken Hill Airport every Tuesday and Saturday morning and the round-trip voyage of approximately 1,100 km (680 miles) takes about 10 and half hours. (Read Patrick White's epic novel, *Voss*.)

Another way to explore the Outback is to take a safari tour. **Broken Hill's Outback Tours** ((08) 8087-7800, in Crystal Street, takes small groups out in their four-wheel drive vehicle to explore the surroundings areas, including **Mootwingee and Kinchega National Parks**, **White Cliffs** and its opal fields. Alternatively, hire a four-wheel drive vehicle from **Silver City Vehicle Hire** ((08) 8087-3266 FAX (08) 8088-5775, at 320 Beryl Street, and explore the Outback at your own pace.

About 25 km (16 miles) from Broken Hill is the "ghost town" of **Silverton** which was deserted when silver mines in the area were exhausted. The population now stands at around 100 and it is not unusual to see a camel walking down the main street. Check out the **Silverton Hotel**, which features contemporary art from the West Darling Ranges.

A three-hour drive from Broken Hills is **White Cliffs**, a town built underground to avoid the searing heat of the Outback. This area is Australia's oldest opal field where visitors have been known to pick up valuable opals by fossicking around the old diggings. **Ross Jones** ((08) 8091-6607, is a local guide who will show you the best places to fossick for blue-green opals, tell tall tales and true about local history and arrange visits to underground homes in White Cliffs. While in White Cliffs improve your golf game on the local course which has no green fees because it has no greens, having the

distinction of containing not one blade of grass. The sandtraps, however, are something else! Indeed, the whole place is... something else.

WHERE TO STAY

There is a good choice of moderately-priced motels in Broken Hill. The **Charles Rasp** ((08) 8088-1988, at 158 Oxide Street, and the **Old Willyama Motor Inn** ((08) 8088-3355 FAX (08) 8088-3856, at 30 Iodide Street, are near the center of town. Inexpensive accommodation is offered by **The Tourist Lodge** ((08) 8088-2086, at 100 Argent Street.

In White Cliffs, the **Underground Motel** ((08) 8091-6647 TOLL-FREE 1800-021-154 FAX (08) 8091-6654, may not have any views (as there are no windows) but will provide a memorable stay. The proprietor, Leon Hornby, excavated its 32 rooms himself, and vertical shafts provide natural light to rooms.

HOW TO GET THERE

A number of airlines fly into Broken Hill. Monarch Air Services runs from Sydney and Melbourne via Mildura; Kendall flies in daily from Adelaide.

THE NORTH COAST

Traveling north along the New South Wales coast the countryside becomes increasingly lush and subtropical as it runs the 900 km (560 miles) from Sydney to the Queensland border.

Broad cultivated valleys — with names such as Big River Country and Summerland — mark a succession of wide sluggish rivers which flow to the east.

Farming and timber bring prosperity to the towns in the valleys while small fishing villages cluster around the river mouths. During the summer months these villages see an influx of thousands of vacationers from the south who come to the excellent beaches or to try their hands at angling along the coast or in the rivers. Finding accommodation during the summer and school holidays may not be easy but during the rest of the year hotel and motel rooms are plentiful and prices are competitive.

There are also pristine sections of coast preserved as national parks. **Yuraygir** and **Bundjalung National Parks** stretch 80 km (50 miles) along the shore north of Coffs Harbour and feature secluded beaches, untouched coastline and wetlands full of water birds; there is good surfing at Angourie Beach. The area can be explored from one of the many tracks that meander along the coast.

GENERAL INFORMATION

Port Macquarie-Hastings Tourism TOLL-FREE 1800-025-935, has an office in Horton Street, which is open daily from 9 AM to 4:30 PM.

Coffs Harbour Tourist Information Centre ((02) 6652-1522, on the corner of Pacific Highway and Marcia Street, is open weekdays from 8 AM to 5 PM, and from 8 AM to 6 PM on weekends.

The **Byron Bay Tourist Association** ((02) 6685-8050, has an office at 80 Jonson Street, which provides visitors with maps and brochures about the local sites of note.

WHAT TO SEE AND DO

To the north of Sydney is **Port Macquarie**, a major holiday town which can be a little on the pricey side but has all kinds of attractions and activities sure to appeal to the whole family.

The town started as a penal settlement in 1821 and several examples of colonial architecture have survived: at the corner of William and Hay streets stands **St. Thomas Church**, built by convicts between 1824 and 1828 and open to the public weekdays from 9 AM to noon and 2 PM to 4 PM.

Sea Acres Rainforest Centre ((02) 6582-3355, in Pacific Drive, provides excellent educational displays on rain forest ecology. A boardwalk gives visitors an opportunity to wander through Australia's last remaining pocket of coastal rain forest. The reserve is open daily from 9 AM to 4:30 PM and an admission fee is charged. **Fantasy Glades** ((02) 6582-2506, in Parkland Close, is a theme park introducing children to the wonders of this vanishing phenomenon, open from 9 AM to 5 PM daily.

Another 150 km (95 miles) to the north is the self-proclaimed **Banana Coast**. To prove it is the monstrous Big Banana north of **Coffs Harbour**, the capital of the Banana Coast.

Coffs Harbour itself is surrounded with banana groves with bunches of fruit covered with plastic bags to shorten the ripening process from two years to 18 months.

Just 10 km (six miles) north of Coffs Harbour is **Woolgoolga**, where a little piece of India has been transplanted. Sikhs have established themselves here and turbaned men and women in saris are part of local color now, with their white-domed temple at the top of the hill. (You may visit it by arrangement.)

An area only recently discovered by tourists is **Byron Bay** which has the advantage of the climate and facilities of many of the larger resorts to the north and south, but without the crowds. Its coastline has been called the Rainbow Country because hippies flocked into the area in the 1970s; a decade later they were followed by disciples of the New Age. From their farms and communes in the hinterland they come into Byron Bay to shop, do business and meet friends. The result is a relaxed and laid-back place which also caters to visitors who have no inclination to chant or meditate, but seek an attractive beach to lie on and a cocktail to lead the way into Nirvana. Byron Bay's atmosphere and charm attract celebrities: Paul Hogan and Linda Kozlowski of *Crocodile Dundee* fame and Olivia Newton-John live nearby.

WHERE TO STAY

Staying at Port Macquarie can be expensive, particularly in the holiday season. Located on the river is **Sails Resort** ((02) 6583-3999 TOLL-FREE 1800-025-271 FAX (02) 6584-0397, on Park Street, a complex of luxury accommodation, restaurant and bars with sporting facilities for guests. Various motels offer a more basic and moderately-priced alternative, such as the **Arrowyn** ((02) 6583-1633, at 170 Gordon Street, and almost next door **Bel Air** ((02) 6583-2177 FAX (02) 6583-2177, at 179 Gordon Street. For longer stays, you can rent a self-contained unit at **Beach House Holiday Apartments** TOLL-FREE 1800-025-096, at 50 Owen Street.

A large choice of accommodation in Coffs Harbour can be arranged through **Variety Holidays Information and Booking Service** ((02) 6651-2322, at 23 Vincent Street. During summer demand is high so it is necessary to make reservations early. If you want to make your own arrangements there is good moderately-priced accommodation around Coffs Harbour. **Bo'suns Inn Motel** (/FAX (02) 6651-2251, at 37 Ocean Parade, and **Midway Motor Inn** ((02) 6652-1444, on the Pacific Highway, are convenient to the city center.

There are daily air flights going from Sydney to Coffs Harbour and Port Macquarie; Oxley Airlines provides service between Coffs Harbour and Brisbane. Coast to Coast provides service to Port Macquarie from Brisbane, Lismore and Newcastle.

Lindsay Coach Service provides daily bus shuttle service between Sydney and Brisbane with stops at most of the major towns. The Pioneer bus service runs between Melbourne and Brisbane and stops at Byron Bay.

Tucked away in 2.6 hectares (6.5 acres) of rain forest near Byron Bay is the luxury-priced **Wheel Resort** ((02) 6685-6139 FAX (02) 6685-8754, at 39–51 Broken Head Road, which has one- and two-bedroom self-contained cabins in a bush setting. If Byron Bay isn't relaxed enough for you try **Cooper's Shoot Guesthouse** ((02) 6685-3313 FAX (02) 6685-3315, at Cooper's Creek, a moderately-priced converted schoolhouse located on a quiet hilltop overlooking Tallow Beach.

HOW TO GET THERE

The Pacific Highway runs along the north coast, and is a very good road for long distance driving.

NATIONAL PARKS

General information and entry conditions for the national parks in New South Wales can be obtained from the **National Parks and Wildlife Service** ((02) 9585-6333, at 43 Bridge Street Hurstville, open daily 9 AM to 5 PM. Information can also be obtained from the **National Parks Association of New South Wales** ((02) 9233-4660.

Within the boundaries of the **Barrington Tops National Park** ((02) 4987-3108, 96 km (60 miles) northwest of Newcastle, are widely differing ecologies, including a high

Houseboating on Myall Lake, near Newcastle, New South Wales.

plateau where snow gums and Antarctic beech proliferate, and a plain at 1,550 m (5,000 ft) above sea level with subtropical vegetation.

The **Great Lakes of New South Wales** ((02) 4987-3108, consist of Myall, Wallis and Smiths lakes with an area four and a half times the size of Sydney Harbour, totaling more than 1,300 sq km (495 sq miles) of cruising waters. One third of the Great Lakes has been set aside in national parks or state forests, and the region has 27 beaches along its 145 km (88 miles) of Pacific coastline. The park is the largest coastal freshwater and saline lake system in New South Wales and numerous tracks allow walkers to get a close look at the waterfowl drawn to the area. Alternatively, take a boat out onto its waterways, about half of which are navigable.

Mount Kaputar National Park is located 53 km (32 miles) east of Narrabri and features the remnants of an 18-million-year-old volcano, the slopes of which are covered with open forest and savannah woodland. The park is a popular place for rock climbers and has some great short wilderness walks. Camping is permitted at Dawsons Spring or the Bar Hut ((02) 6792-4724 or (02) 6792-4731.

The **Wollemi National Park** is situated 100 km (62 miles) northwest of Sydney. Wollemi is New South Wales' second largest park and contains the state's largest wilderness area. This park is a maze of narrow canyons and gorges channeling through a region of precipitous basalt mountains covered with thick undisturbed rain forest. Although the extremely rugged terrain makes access difficult, for the properly equipped and experienced bushwalker the park offers plentiful rewards. The wilderness areas have abundant fauna living in their native habitat. The Bob Turners Track descends toward the beaches along the Colo River, through one of the state's longest and most scenic gorges. Other attractions include white-water canoeing down the Colo, Wolgan, and Capertee rivers and a glow worm-filled railway tunnel near Newnes. There are camping areas at Newnes, Wheeney Creek or Dunns Swamp. **Brisbane Water National Park** ((02) 4324-4911, nine

kilometers (six miles) southwest of Gosford and 60 km (37 miles) north of Sydney, is off the Pacific Highway, where a number of Aboriginal art galleries may be seen on the sandstone landscape with engravings at Bulgandry on Woy Woy Road. Panoramic views spread out from 100-m (300-ft)-high cliffs overlooking the Hawkesbury River at Warrah Trig and Staples lookouts. Displays of Christmas Bells and Waratah are stunning in November and December. In the northwest corner of the state is the **Sturt National Park** ((08) 8091-3308, 330 km (205 miles) north of Broken Hill, with examples of desert ecosystems from red dunes to stony plains over which red and grey kangaroos and emus range. There are about 300 km (185 miles) of dirt roads to explore and a four-wheel drive vehicle is essential here. The Sturt National Park can be unpleasantly hot in summer, so plan to visit in winter or spring.

CANBERRA: THE NATION'S CAPITAL

Running down their politicians is a popular pastime among Australians. In fact, in public opinion poles, politicians rank less honorable than real estate agents and only marginally more trustworthy than used-car salesmen (a malicious slur on used-car salesmen).

Canberra — 286 km (177 miles) from Sydney and 653 km (404 miles) from Melbourne — with its broad thoroughfares and manicured suburbs, is a planned city where the placment of every public edifice has been carefully predetermined. Buildings are set well back from the roads, numerous parklands break up the neat rows of houses and no building is taller than six stories. Even outdoor television antennae are forbidden lest they disturb the clean outlines of houses.

To the extent that it is a pre-planned capital, Canberra has something in common with Brasilia, Islamabad and Washington, DC. As a planned city, it showcases some of the most impressive public architecture in Australia, which complements its natural beauty with Lake Burley Griffin at its center.

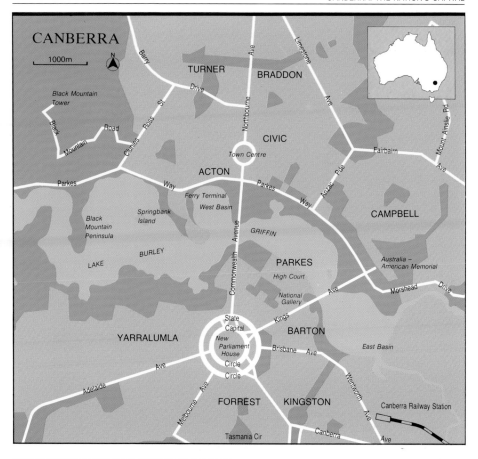

BACKGROUND

When the first federal legislature convened in 1901 in Parliament House in Melbourne the understanding was that in future a new and permanent location would be found between that city and Sydney.

The selection of a site by a committee of politicians established standards of behavior which successive generations of federal politicians have striven to perpetuate: in 1902, these people toured the countryside being lavishly wined and dined by locals who hoped to benefit from having the national capital on their doorstep. Their pattern of behavior has stood the test of time; a contemporary newspaper ridiculed the junketing politicians in verse. It wrote:

Each hill and dale, each stream and lake,
Seems all the more alluring,
When sandwiches and bottled ale,
Alleviate the touring.

It appears that the Federal Capital Committee had ample opportunity to indulge this predilection for bottled ale and sandwiches because a site was not chosen until 1908 when a spot in the Molongo Valley was selected. This they named Canberra, after the Aboriginal word for "meeting place."

A competition to design the national capital was won by 35-year-old American architect Walter Burley Griffin. Griffin was a student of the Chicago School of Architecture, and forerunner in the Australian tradition of not trusting local architects to do anything of value. In designing Canberra, Griffin was aware of the natural amphitheater formed by the surrounding mountains, and the street plan and placement of buildings were designed to integrate these features. Griffin began work turning his vision into reality when he was appointed Federal Capital Director of Design. His task was made difficult by the spite and venom of envious architects, public servants and politicians to whom courage, taste and vision were alien. Often his plans and drawings were "lost" by the Works Department, causing deliberate, endless delays. Not surprisingly, Griffin eventually gave up in frustration. The momentum he had created, however, was sufficient to ensure that the enduring local tradition of mediocrity did not modify his original layout too much. He left much that is good there, evidence of a vision not altogether dimmed by a succession of myopic "bottled ale" guzzlers.

On May 9, 1927 the Duke of York opened Parliament House and the national capital was all set for the business of government. At the time, the population of Canberra was less that 6,000, most of whom were construction workers. As the city grew construction workers were replaced by public servants, today the largest occupational group in Canberra's population of 220,000. Who knows? Perhaps one of these days government will begin.

GENERAL INFORMATION

The **Canberra Visitor Information Centre** TOLL-FREE 1800-026-192, located on Northbourne Avenue near Morphett Street, and the **Queanbeyan Tourist and Information Centre** ((02) 6298-0241, at One Farrer Place, offer information about accommodation, events and attractions around Canberra. The main bus terminal is at the **Jolimont Travel Centre** in Northborne Avenue near Alinga Street and it also provides tourist information.

For information and timetables on bus services contact **Action Bus Service** ((02) 6207-7611.

WHAT TO SEE AND DO

Dominating Canberra is **Lake Burley Griffin**, which was created artificially in 1964 by damming the Molongo River. The best way to get a feel for the city is to hire a bike from **Mr. Spoke's Bike Hire** ((02) 6257-1188, located in Barrine Drive, Acton. The circumference of the lake is 35 km (22 miles), an easy ride.

Roads in Canberra form a series of circles, linked by radiating boulevards. The lake is bisected by Commonwealth Avenue, running through the two foci of the city — Civic, the main business and shopping center, and Capitol Hill, which is dominated by the new **Parliament House** ((02) 6277-5399. The centerpiece of the new Parliament House, opened in time for the bicentennial in 1988, is an 81-m (265-ft) flag pole which towers over the landscape. The building itself is understated, with part of it underground to main-

tain the original topography of Capitol Hill. In the forecourt a mosaic by Northern Territory artist Michael Tjakamarra Nelson represents an Aboriginal meeting place. The mosaic, containing 100,000 tiles, is surrounded by water, symbolizing Australia as an island-continent. In the Great Hall hangs a magnificent tapestry designed by Arthur Boyd, while in the Foyer and scattered around the building are paintings by leading Australian artists—Sidney Nolan, Albert Tucker and Tom Roberts among them. In a display cabinet in the Members' Hall is a detailed copy of the *Magna Carta*. There are tours of the building, leaving every 30 minutes. Alternatively, visitors can take time out and watch Australian democracy at work from the public gallery, if Parliament is sitting. "Debate" consists of heapings of abuse, where words such as "scumbag" are standard Australian political jargon, alternating with mind-numbing drone from back-bench hacks. The best time to gaze is during Question Time at 2 PM, when the Opposition is given the opportunity to interrogate the incumbents who are judged by how well they defend themselves before attacking the Opposition. The contents of the responses are beside the point, it seems. Parliament is open daily 9 AM to 5 PM, or later

works including bark paintings and the works of foreign masters, such as Jackson Pollock's controversial *Blue Poles* and paintings by Picasso, Warhol and Matisse. The gallery has eleven halls over three levels, and the top one is invariably devoted to indigenous art. Opening hours are from 10 AM to 5 PM daily, and an admission fee is charged. Major visiting exhibits are frequently hosted, and an additional entrance fee is charged for these shows.

Next door to the gallery is the **High Court** ((02) 6270-6811, in King Edward Terrace,

when the legislature is sitting, and entry is free.

The **Old Parliament House** ((02) 6270-8222, in King George Terrace, housed the legislature before 1988, and is now a museum. Its back rooms and halls echo with spirits of great Prime Ministers of the past and are haunted by party leaders who ended their career at the knife end of an opponent. Exhibits provide an insight to the colorful politicians of the past and history of Australian democracy. It's open daily 9 AM to 4 PM and a small admission fee is charged.

The **National Gallery of Australia** ((02) 6240-6502, in Parkes Place, overlooking the lake, holds an outstanding collection of over 70,000 Australian paintings, Aboriginal

Parkes, where judges deliberate constitutional disputes; their decisions have shaped the changing relationship between the state and federal governments. Organized tours of the High Court are possible.

Further around the lake shore is the **National Library of Australia** ((02) 6262-1111, in Parkes Place, which is required by law to receive a copy of every book, newspaper and magazine published in Australia. In its keeping are one and a half million books and thousands of audio recordings. A changing exhibition of rare and historic documents in the library's collection is on

Australia's Old Parliament House, now a museum, on the shores of Lake Burley Griffin.

display in the Exhibition Gallery. Entry is free, but call ahead for opening hours.

Every day the chimes of the imposing **National Carillon** ((02) 6271-2888, waft across the placid waters of Lake Burley Griffin. Built on three pillars, this 50-m (150-ft) structure houses 53 bronze bells, and depending on the season several recitals are held every day. Call for recital times.

The nearby **Royal Australian Mint** ((02) 6202-6999, in Dennison Street, Deakin, provides a glimpse of the past with its rare

coin collection dating back to the days of Spanish galleons. On a more up-to-date note visitors can also watch the mint make the country's money. Unfortunately no free souvenirs are offered.

To gain an appreciation of the early contributions made by Australia to cinema from its genesis at the turn of the century, visit the **National Film and Sound Archive** ((02) 6209-3035 TOLL-FREE 1800-067-274, in McCoy Circuit, Acton. The exhibition hall has continuous screenings of newsreels and films from its collection; the archive is housed in an art deco building designed by Walter Haywood Morris in 1929, constructed of Hawkesbury River sandstone and featuring a foyer with a stained-glass skylight depicting a stylized platypus as its centerpiece. Opening hours are 9 AM to 5 PM daily. Entry is free but their may be a charge for certain special events and displays.

The Snowy Mountains, near Canberra, are popular in spring and autumn for outdoor recreation.

The **Australian National Botanic Gardens** are on the lower slopes of Black Mountain, three kilometers (two miles) west of the business district. The largest collection of native flora in Australia can be seen in the gardens. More than 170,000 plant species from every corner of the country are on display. Visitors can walk through a rain forest that thrives in a former gully thanks to hundreds of fine mist sprays controlled by automated time-switches. One of several trails leads past trees with signs explaining how they were used by local Aboriginal clans. The garden is open 9 AM to 5 PM and entry is free.

Above the gardens is **Telstra Tower**, a 195-m (640-ft) telecommunication tower and major Canberra landmark. It's open to the public and provides a panoramic view of Canberra and the surrounding landscape. The best place to go is the revolving **Tower Restaurant** ((02) 6248-6162.

More than 60 countries have diplomatic representation in the national capital. Lovers of kitsch will find themselves in paradise in this architectural hodgepodge: for example, the Japanese embassy is set in traditional gardens, the Thai embassy is a landmark with its elevated roof and gold-colored tiles and the Italian embassy blends modern design with inspiration from ancient Rome.

CANBERRA AFTER DARK

Canberra's nightlife has come a long way. Ten years ago the choice was between watching a Bernard Shaw play at the Canberra Theatre or dropping into the club for a quiet drink.

These days the **Graphix Brasserie** in Jardine Street, Kingston, has hot jazz, Thursday to Saturday night, while you can rock away to the coolest live bands in town at the **Gypsy Bar and Brasserie** at 9 East Row, or **Tradesmen's Union Club** at Two Badham Street, Dickson.

The *Canberra Times* publishes a liftout Good Times guide on Thursday with a comprehensive list of gigs and entertainment in the capital, and the *Muse* is a free monthly arts newspaper which reviews the cultural events on offer.

WHERE TO STAY

Luxury

Canberra has few distinguished hotels, but an exception is the **Hyatt Hotel Canberra** ((02) 6270-1234 FAX (02) 6281-5998, in Commonwealth Avenue, Yarralumla. The hotel has an exterior in the so-called garden pavilion style, its interior containing many art deco features. Another hotel with character is the **Olims Canberra Hotel** ((02) 6248-5511 TOLL-FREE 1800-020-016 FAX (02) 6247-0864, at the corner of Ainslie and Limestone Avenues, Braddon, set around a pleasantly landscaped courtyard.

Moderate

The **Telopea Park Motel** ((02) 6295-3722 FAX (02) 6239-6373, at 16 New South Wales Crescent, Forrest, and the **Diplomat Boutique Hotel Canberra** ((02) 6295-2277 TOLL-FREE 1800-026-367 FAX (02) 6239-6432, in Canberra Avenue, are modern hotels on the Parliament side of Lake Burley Griffin. On the city side of the lake and a five minutes walk to the center of town is the **Acacia Motor Lodge** ((02) 6249-6955 FAX (02) 6247-7058, at 65 Ainslie Avenue, in a very quiet neighborhood.

Inexpensive

Not far out of the city is the **Kambah Inn** ((02) 6231-8444 FAX (02) 6231-2450, at Marconi Crescent, off the main highway in a quiet suburban setting. A little further out, in Queanbeyan, is the **Burley Griffin Motel** ((02) 6297-1211 FAX (02) 6297-3083, at 147 Uriarra Road.

WHERE TO EAT

A popular pastime in Canberra is going to restaurants frequented by political figures and watching them engage in the character assassination of a party leader or plot the destruction of a minister. Some guides to the capital even include a list of politicians who frequent certain restaurants. In any case, you can usually identify the politicians; they're the ones whispering across the table and accompanied by an entourage of flunkies.

Fringe Benefits ((02) 6247-4042, located at 54 Marcus Clarke Street, is one of the best restaurants in Canberra with an imaginative menu of Mediterranean dishes.

Jehangir Indian Restaurant ((02) 6290-1159, at 15 Swinger Hill Shops in Mawson, specializes in dishes from northern India and the service is friendly. Joseph Cotter is a Canberra fixture and widely respected as one of the best Indian chefs. Unfortunately, the location of his latest venture, **Geetanjali** ((02) 6285-2505, in Duff Place, Deakin, is out of the way, though the good news here is that reservations are only required at weekends. It is rumored that at one gathering here, members of the governing party concluded a deal to overthrow the incumbent prime minister over *gulub jamun* and coffee.

The **Hyatt Hotel Promenade Café** ((02) 6270- 8930, in Commonwealth Avenue, has an excellent menu and their desserts are heavenly.

HOW TO GET THERE

Both major domestic airlines run frequent flights into Canberra from Melbourne and Sydney; there are less-frequent flights from Brisbane, Launceston, Perth, Townsville, Gold Coast, Rockhampton and Adelaide.

Pioneer Greyhound stops at Canberra on their Melbourne-to-Sydney route and connects with Adelaide. Trip durations are three and a half hours from Sydney, eight hours from Melbourne and sixteen and half hours from Adelaide. **Murray Australia** (132-251, is a regional bus line that runs routes into Canberra from the Snowy Mountains, Sydney and the coast between Naroom and Nowra.

By car, Canberra is 286 km (177 miles) from Sydney along the Hume Highway; turn off just after Goulburn.

Canberra is 653 km (404 miles) from Melbourne, and the turn-off from the Hume Highway is near Yass. If you can afford a leisurely pace, it is possible to take the scenic route to Canberra from Melbourne on the Princes Highway east through Gippsland to Cann River, and north onto the Cann Valley Highway which passes the **Coopracambra National Park**.

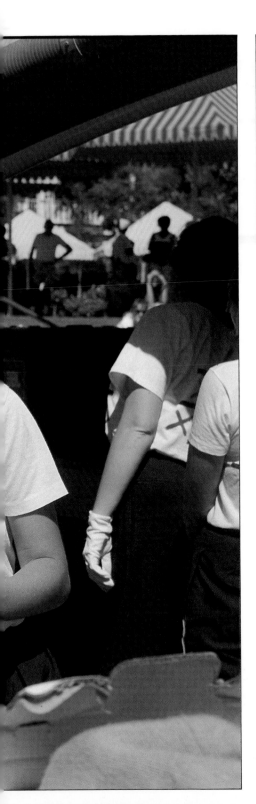

Queensland

Paradise and
Beyond

TO MOST southerners, Queensland is another country. Its inhabitants are stereotyped as slow-talking and extremely conservative. There is a hint of truth in this: the contrary northeast shares similarities with the Deep South in the United States. Queensland's government until quite recently was run by an incorrigibly independent and ruthlessly canny politician called Joh Bjelke-Petersen. Before him there was the reactionary Labor premier, Vince Gair.

Despite Queensland's reputation for archaic political proceedings its people are as warm and friendly as the climate. Southerners come north and are quickly seduced by the informality and kindness of the Queenslanders.

BRISBANE

Brisbane is a subtropical city where mango trees and banana palms adorn many front gardens. The older houses are built on stilts to allow cooling breezes to circulate on sweltering days.

In the afternoon children scamper home from school barefoot, their shoes in their school bags, while in the evening men return home from the office wearing shorts and long socks, most likely without their ties. As the final rays of sunlight penetrate the jacaranda foliage heavy with lavender flowers, the first fruit bats arrive to feast on ripe mangoes.

BACKGROUND

Brisbane began its days as a penal settlement for convicts who had committed new offences after their exile to Australia. Soldiers and recalcitrant convicts first established a settlement on Moreton Bay in 1824, but it proved to be an unsuitable site. The following year they moved up the Brisbane River to the spot where the city center stands today. The convict population never exceeded 1,000 and by 1839 their number had reduced to 29; on February 11, 1842, it became a free settlement.

In 1859, the Moreton Bay District, as Queensland was then known, separated from New South Wales to become a colony in its own right.

In the early days there was constant friction between the local Aborigines and the white settlers. In 1845 several tribes forged an alliance under the leadership of Dundalli, who led a guerrilla campaign against the colony for the next nine years.

Once the hinterland had been opened, despite determined opposition from the Aborigines, the wealth of natural resources there helped Brisbane grow. Cattlemen from New South Wales drove their herds north to the wide plains and tableland, occupying large tracts of grazing land. The discovery

of gold and the establishment of a successful sugar industry added to the colony's wealth, but the expansion of coal exports after the Second World War, and the more recent tourist boom have make Queensland a powerhouse in Australia's economy.

GENERAL INFORMATION

Queensland Government Travel Centre (131-801, at the corner of Adelaide and Edward streets, provides information and takes booking on attractions and package holidays, and will arrange accommodation anywhere in Queensland. The center is open weekdays 8:30 AM to 5 PM and Saturday 8:30 AM to midday. The **Brisbane Visitor and Convention Centre** ((07) 3229-5918, is located on the ground floor of City Hall opposite King George Square, and provides information on attractions, events and accommodation in Brisbane only.

ABOVE and OPPOSITE: Australia's favorites entertain the kids at Brisbane's Lone Pine Sanctuary.

Public transport information is available for suburban buses, ferries and trains at (131-230; and for long distance train reservations (132-232, and inquiries at (132-235 (phone lines open daily from 6 AM to 9 PM).

WHAT TO SEE AND DO

Central City Precinct

The shopping and business districts are bounded by a bend in the Brisbane River, with cultural and recreational attractions concentrated on the opposite south bank.

Overlooking the city in Wickham Terrace is **The Old Windmill**, a reminder of the city's convict past. Built in 1828 to crush corn, it failed to function because of a design fault; whereupon, the sails were removed and convicts put to work on a treadmill to get the job done. Offenses as trivial as using "disgusting language" and "insolence" earned convicts 14 hours of backbreaking shifts on the treadmill.

Walk down the hill to Edward Street which leads into the city. Past the railway bridge running between Ann and Queen streets is **Anzac Square**, the focal point of which is a rotunda of Doric columns. Built

One of four bridges which links central Brisbane with its south bank.

in 1930, the **Shrine of Remembrance** is dedicated to Australian soldiers who died during the First World War.

Queen's Street Mall, a major shopping precinct, runs between Edward and George streets, and off it run several arcades brimming with boutiques and restaurants.

Behind Parliament House are the **Old Botanic Gardens**, first used by convicts for growing vegetables. The southern tip jutting into the river is still known as **Garden Point**. The first Director of the Botanic Gardens laid them out much as they appear today, and you can still walk down the avenue of bunya pines he planted. On the Point is the French Renaissance-style **Parliament House** ((07) 3406-7562, built in 1868. Free public tours are available when Parliament is not in session. Call to check tour times.

Queenslanders have a passion for the beach; for many years Brisbanites envied the southern capitals of Perth, Adelaide, Melbourne and Sydney for their beach suburbs. Then the solution to this shortcoming arose in the form of **Southbank**: spread across the opposite bank of Brisbane River from the city is **Kodak Beach**, a part of the 16-hectare (40-acre) recreational development. Within the parkland displays of different ecosystems can be explored, where it is possible to walk through the **Gondwana Rainforest Sanctuary** or swim around a giant lagoon. Visitors to the **Butterfly House** can discover the literal meaning of "butterfly kisses," and the **Formal Gardens** with beautiful floral displays have ornamental fountains. On weekends, concerts and street theater entertain visitors and in the **Suncorp Piazza** you can choose any one of the 16 restaurants or cafés for a splendid meal or just a coffee. Admission to Southbank is free, although there may be a entrance fees for some special events and exhibitions. For information on entertainments, visit or call the **Southbank Information Centre** ((07) 3867-2051, on the Piazza, which is open seven days a week from 8 AM to 8 PM.

Northwest of Southbank is the **Queensland Cultural Centre**, including the **Queensland Art Gallery** with a good collection of colonial era paintings. Next door is the

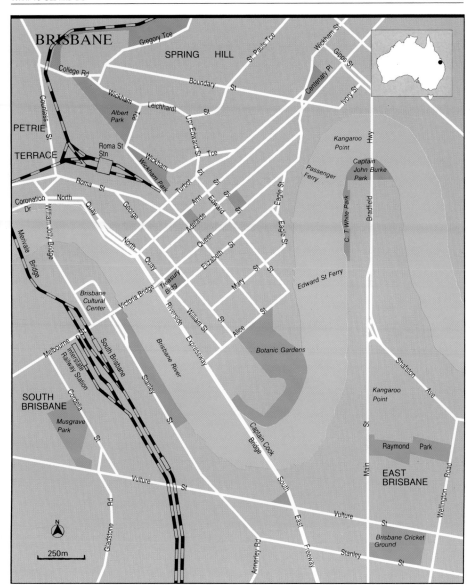

Queensland Museum, Performing Arts Complex and the State Library of Queensland. Tours leave on the hour from 10 AM to 4 PM, Monday to Saturday.

Historic Houses

Unfortunately not much of early Brisbane has survived within the city. For examples of colonial architecture you will have to travel four kilometers (two miles) away from the center to the **Early Street Historical Village** ((07) 3398-6866, in Norman Park at 75 McIlwraith Avenue, which has exhibits ranging from a slab hut to **Auchenflower House**, described as a Victorian gentleman's residence. The village is open daily and an admission fee is charged. The Discalced Carmelite Nuns once inhabited Auchenflower House but in the 1960s moved to **Ormiston House**, built in 1854. After the interior was restored Ormiston House on Wellington Street was opened to the public; you can visit the house and grounds on Sundays from 1:30 PM to 4:30 PM, from March through November. An admission fee is charged.

Newstead House ((07) 3216-1846, is situated in parkland overlooking the Brisbane River at Breakfast Creek. Built in 1846, this magnificent mansion has been restored and was once the unofficial Government House, being the Government Resident's home. Sit out on the verandah and enjoy a Devonshire tea of scones, jam and cream. An admission fee is charged.

Parks and Sanctuaries

Can anyone resist cuddling a koala bear? Eleven kilometers (seven miles) upriver of

A few kilometers past the sanctuary is the **Mt. Coot-tha Reserve and Botanic Gardens** ((07) 3403-2533, on Mt. Coot-tha Road. A mixture of parklands and forest, the 57-hectare (140-acre) reserve is Australia's largest subtropical gardens in which the collection includes plants from native rain forests spread around lagoons, ponds connected by streams, and displays of vegetation found in the arid zones of Queensland. Opening hours are from 8 AM to 5 PM, and narrated tours can be reserved by calling ahead.

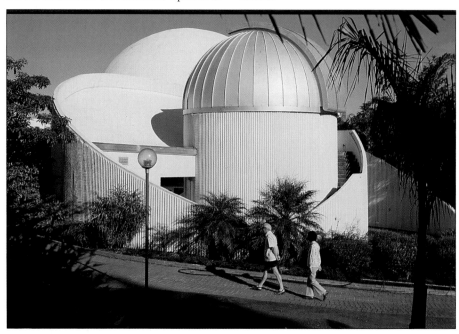

Brisbane at Fig Tree Pocket live more than a hundred of them in the **Lone Pine Koala Sanctuary** ((07) 3378-1366, on Jesmond Road. You can have your photograph taken holding one — but watch those claws which can make the cuddling rather less cuddly. Elsewhere in the park are over 80 types of native wild animals, all in a natural bushland setting. You can hand-feed the kangaroos and flightless emus, ostrich-like birds, or get a close look at hedgehog-like echidnas or wombats. A launch leaves Hayles Wharf at North Quay on the Brisbane River daily at 1:15 PM, with additional departures on Sunday. Alternatively, take a bus from "Koala Platform" leaving the Myer Center hourly.

BRISBANE AFTER DARK

A few years ago a copy of *Playboy* magazine was banned, as a result of which Queenslanders were thought by southerners to be prissy and straightlaced, but once the sun sinks below the horizon, Brisbane kicks up its heels and starts to party.

City Rowers nightclub at One Eagle Street jives until 3 AM with dance floors on two levels, and in Petrie Terrace the **Brisbane Underground** features live music on Friday, Saturday and Sunday. **Nightworx** at the intersection of Albert and Queen streets, and **Margaux's** inside the Brisbane Hilton at 190 Elizabeth Street, are just two of Brisbane's classier nightspots.

Several pubs and clubs have excellent jazz. The Jazz-n-Blues Bar in Annie Street, Kangaroo Point, has live music on weekends; for rock music try the **Mary Street Nightclub** at 138 Mary Street, or **St. Paul's Tavern** on Wharf Street.

The best way to find who's playing where is to consult Thursday's *Brisbane Courier-Mail's* What's on in Town section. Consult Brisbane's gig guide *Timeoff*, which is also published on the Internet, http://www .peg.apc .org/~timeoff, and is updated every Wednesday.

WHERE TO SHOP

Brisbane's main shops are on **Queen Street** which is closed to traffic between George and Edward streets. Converted into an imaginative pedestrian mall it has an information kiosk for visitors, and off Queen Street is the **Myer Centre**, whose atriums, balconied walkways and large choice of 200 shops make it a delight.

A rash of redevelopment has resulted in several new shopping complexes such as

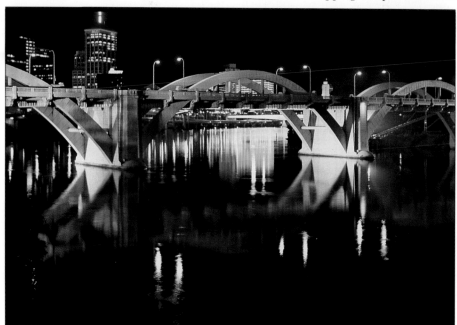

For something a bit more racy, **The Red Garter** ((07) 3252-2608, at 693 Ann Street in Fortitude Valley, has what are politely called "exotic dancers."

The Brisbane Theatre Company ((07) 3840-7000, maintains a full season of plays including *Australia*, productions which are performed at Suncorp Theatre at 170 Turbot Street and the Cremorne Theatre inside the **Queensland Performing Arts Complex** on Southbank. You can enjoy cutting-edge plays at **La Boite** ((07) 3369-1622, at 57 Hale Street.

Several tours of the city are on offer; **Sunstate Day Tours** ((07) 3868-2400, arranges visits to a woolshed bush dance or nightclub.

the Wintergarden and Broadway on the Mall, which are complexes containing cafés, boutiques, and shops selling the latest in fashions and jewelry. **Rowes Arcade**, off of Post Office Square, has an Edwardian charm with dark cedar paneling and stained-glass windows. A good place to buy an Australian bush outfit is **Greg Grant Saddlery and Western Stores** in the Myer Centre. Just outside Brisbane, go shopping in the bustling **Fortitude Valley**, which has an excellent Chinatown.

Every Sunday from 7 AM a **market** sets up outside the Riverside Complex, where

OPPOSITE: The domes of Australia's largest planetarium in Brisbane's Mt. Coot-tha Botanic Gardens. ABOVE: View south from the city center.

stallholders sell a variety of arts and crafts and food-stall vendors provide sustenance to shoppers at the end of their tether. Friday night and Saturday from 11 AM to 5 PM, a part of Southbank becomes a craft market.

Queensland has opal fields and a number of shops in Brisbane specialize in these; black and white opals are on sale at **Opal Strike (** (07) 3221-0470, at 226 Queen Street.

SPORTS

Basketball is popular in Queensland, where the Brisbane Bullets attract a good crowd when they play National Basketball League games inside the **Boondall Entertainment Centre.**

Queenslanders are torn between the three codes of football. None predominates here. Rugby League is played at **Lang Park** at Milton and at the **ANZ Stadium** at Nathan, and the **"Gabba"** is the home of the local Australian Football League team, the *Brisbane Lions*. Rugby Union is played at Ballymore Park at Herston.

During the winter, Brisbane's climate is perfect for horse racing. Race meetings are held at **Eagle Farm** and **Doomben**, with several major race meetings occurring between June and August.

WHERE TO STAY

Luxury

For a treat stay at **The Heritage Beaufort Hotel (** (07) 3221-1999 TOLL-FREE 1800-773-700 FAX (07) 3221-6895, in Edward Street, which couldn't be in a nicer spot: it overlooks the Brisbane River and Botanic Gardens. The hotel has three restaurants and two bars to choose from at night.

Boomajarril ((07) 3268-5764 FAX (07) 3268-2064, at 58 Derby Street, Hendra, is a quintessential colonial Brisbane house with its white wooden verandah, in the middle of a tropical garden. The guesthouse provides accommodation and meals.

Indulge yourself at the **Carlton Crest (** (07) 3229-9111 TOLL-FREE 1800-777-123 FAX (07) 3229-9618, on King Street Square, which features a rooftop swimming pool, sauna, and gym. If this sounds all-too-

healthy, then trot down to one of its three fine restaurants before partying the night away in the hotel's four popular bars.

The **Brisbane Hilton (** (07) 3234-2000 TOLL-FREE 1800-222-255 FAX (07) 3231-3199, at 190 Elizabeth Street, is notable for its covered atrium towering 25 floors above the lobby.

Moderate

The **Metro Inn Tower Mill (** (07) 3832-1421 TOLL-FREE 1800 806-553 FAX (07) 3835-1013, at 193 Wickham Terrace, is a multistory motel with agreeable balcony views. A bit closer to the center of town is the **Wickham Terrace Motel (** (07) 3839-9611 TOLL-FREE 1800-773-069 FAX (07) 3832-5348, located at 491 Wickham Terrace, in a quiet parkland location.

Six kilometers (four miles) from the city and a convenient walk to the Eagle Farm Racecourse is the **Raceways Motel (** (07) 3268-4355 TOLL-FREE 1800-077-474 FAX (07) 3868-1640, at 66 Kent Street, Hamilton.

Inexpensive

There are several economical hotels and backpacker hostels in New Farm. Catering to the older backpacker is the **Atoa House Travellers Hostel (** (07) 268-2823 TOLL-FREE 1800-062-693, located at 95 Annie Street. The **Budget Brisbane Motel (** (07) 3358-5832, located at 3 Moreton Street, provides basic accommodation.

WHERE TO EAT

The **Bays Seafood Restaurant (** (07) 3262-5250, at 147 Alexandra Road, Clayfield (expensive), is located in a fine old building with the wide verandahs typical of Queensland. Local mud crabs are a specialty of **Gambaro's (** (07) 3369-9500, at 33 Caxton Street, Perrie Terrace (moderate). For spectacular views of Brisbane take Sir Samuel Griffith Drive to Mt. Coot-tha and enjoy a top meal at the **Summit Restaurant (** (07) 3369-9922 (expensive).

Opposite the Botanic Gardens in the Heritage Hotel, is **Kabuki (** (07) 3232-0232

Exuberant Gold Coast garden shop TOP, and a king-size chess game BOTTOM at Surfers' Paradise in Queensland.

(moderate), a *teppan-yaki* restaurant where the food is cooked before your eyes.

Across the river on Southbank's boardwalk is **Ned Kelly's Tucker Restaurant (** (07) 3846-1880 (moderate). It serves such local dainties as emu, crocodile and witchetty grubs (if you dare), which enthusiasts describe as tasting "a little like chicken". There are many more good restaurants from which to choose at Southbank; most are moderately priced.

Several inexpensive restaurants are found in South Brisbane. Vegetarian meals can be obtained from **Squirrels of Newmarket (** (07) 3856-0966, at 184 Enoggera Road, and honest pub food at the **Sly Fox Hotel (** (07) 3844-2514, at 73 Melbourne Street, a favorite hangout for backpackers.

HOW TO GET THERE

There are flights into Brisbane's domestic airport from all capitals and regional cities. Brisbane is serviced by more than twenty international airlines providing regular services from ports throughout the world. The airports are situated approximately 15 km (just over nine miles) from the city center and taxis are plentiful at the international and domestic terminals. Regular bus services operate to the Brisbane Transit Centre and to major hotels.

Queensland Rail operates several modern long distance passenger services to Brisbane from stations at Queensland's coastal and inland cities. Long distance services are also available from the southern states. Inter- and intra-state coach services operate daily into Brisbane's Transit Centre **(** (07) 3236-4444, in Roma Street, close to the city center.

THE GOLD COAST

About an hour's drive south of Brisbane along the Pacific Highway is Australia's answer to Miami, Florida. Located just 42 km (26 miles) from Brisbane, the Gold Coast is Australia's most famous playground, providing visitors with an abundance of sun, surf and sand. This glitzy, brash and unashamedly hedonistic resort region caters to the desires of both the wealthiest and the most pedestrian vacationer... and everyone in between.

GENERAL INFORMATION

There are several sources of information on attractions along the Gold Coast. The **Gold Coast Visitor and Convention Bureau (** (07) 5593-1199, at 105 Upton Street, Bundall, and information kiosks in Cavill Mall, Surfers' Paradise, as well as in Marine Parade, Tweed Heads, have a wide range of information about the region.

WHAT TO SEE AND DO

The Gold Coast runs southwards from Brisbane to the New South Wales state border through a string of resort towns.

For decades it has been colonized by southerners seeking escape from the rigors of winter. More recently, retirees are moving north in search of a permanent place in the sun. During the 1970s and 1980s this brought an explosion of development along the magnificent beaches of the Gold Coast — some would say too much. The number of summer visitors attracted annually to this popular holiday destination now exceeds the year-round population of Queensland.

Centered on **Surfers' Paradise** (known as just "Surfers'"), high-rise buildings have sprouted along the sea-fronted highway, as though a slice of a major metropolis had been transplanted on the beach. With this ugly development have come streets jammed with traffic, unable to handle ill-conceived, uncontrolled development. In consequence, a system of canals was constructed to allow additional access to the water through private jetties.

Despite its frenetic pace and indiscriminate development the influx of so many

16 km (10 miles) northwest of Surfers' Paradise at Oxenford. There are tours of special effects studios and rides, admission is AU$37 for adults and AU$22 for children under 13.

Dreamworld ((07) 5588-1111, is another theme park, located 17 km (10 miles) north of Surfers' Paradise at Coomera. The price of admission is AU$35 for adults and AU$21 for children.

A wildlife reserve well worth visiting is the **Currumbin Sanctuary** ((07) 5534-1266, at Currumbin Beach, 19 km (12 miles) south

visitors to the Gold Coast has its benefits: the area has more major man-made attractions than any other tourist region in Australia.

The whole family can be kept constantly entertained here (see FAMILY FUN in YOUR CHOICE). The main attractions are **Seaworld** ((07) 5588-2222, at The Spit Main Beach, three kilometers (two miles) north of Surfers' Paradise. A monorail takes visitors around the 150-hectare (370-acre) park. It's open 9:30 AM to 5 PM daily, except Christmas Day and Anzac morning. Admission is AU$37 for adults and AU$22 for children. The revival of the Australian motion picture industry inspired the creation of **Warner Bros. Movie World** ((07) 5573-3999, located

of Surfers' Paradise, where you can feed the flock of brightly colored wild lorikeets. Breakfast and dinner times are from 8 to 9 AM and 4 to 5 PM. Kangaroos, wallabies and other Australian wildlife wander freely around the reserve and there are many educational displays for children. On your way back into Surfers' Paradise is the **Burleigh Heads National Park,** a prominent headland on the southern end of the Gold Coast. The area is ideal for picnics, and a walk along easy tracks through the park's rain forest, eucalypt forest, pandanus groves, tussock grassland, coastal heath, rocky foreshore,

Despite miles of high-rise development, the vast expanse of soft surf and sand dominate the shoreline at Surfer's Paradise.

mangroves, creeks, and ocean beaches. In the wintertime humpback whales can be seen off this stretch of the coast. For further information contact the **Burleigh Heads Information Centre (** (07) 5535-3855, on the Gold Coast Highway.

At night Surfers' goes into high gear with its restaurants dotting the sidewalks and offering everything from gourmet cuisine to junk foods. There are many choices of what to do after dinner: take in a show, go nightclubbing or have a fling at **Jupiter's Casino**.

WHERE TO STAY

Packages to the Gold Coast fly tourists from any state capital to Surfers' and provide a week's accommodation, all at discounted prices.

There are a large number of luxury hotels and apartments along the Gold Coast. Most are high-rise and although they may lack character, the ocean views from the upper floors are quite magnificent. In Surfers' Paradise **ANA Hotel Gold Coast (** (07) 5579-1000 TOLL-FREE 1800-074-440 FAX (07) 5570-1260, at 22 View Avenue, and **Ramada Hotel (** (07)

5579-3499 TOLL-FREE 1800-074-317 FAX (07) 5539-8370, at the intersection of the Gold Coast Highway and Hanlan Street, have spectacular ocean or hinterland views. **Coomera Motor Inn (** (07) 5573-2311, is situated next to Dreamworld just 20 minutes from Surfers' Paradise and 40 minutes from Brisbane, and the **Broadbeach Motor Inn Holiday Apartments (** (07) 5570-1899, at 2651 Gold Coast Highway, is centrally located in the heart of the Gold Coast's many activities.

Outside the school holiday period there is keen competition between motels in the lower price bracket, and driving down the Gold Coast Highway you should be able to pick up significant out-of-season discounts.

For inexpensive accommodation good deals can be obtained by shopping locally. If you decide to stay on the Gold Coast for a week or more, renting a self-contained apartment is an inexpensive option. Prices start at AU$200 a week for a two-bedroom unit. Reservations for apartments can be arranged through **Broadbeach Real Estate (** (07) 5539-0000 FAX (07) 5538-3280, located at 2703 Main Place, and **Coolangatta Realty (** (07) 5536-2000 FAX (07) 5536-1084, at 72–74 Griffith Street. It is best to book well in advance.

HOW TO GET THERE

For domestic plane arrivals there are two ports of entry: Coolangatta Airport and Brisbane Domestic Airport. Ansett and Qantas have daily services. Limousine , taxi, coach and hire car services are available from Coolangatta and Brisbane airports to Gold Coast accommodation. For visitors flying into Brisbane, a 24-hour door-to-door coach service is available with either Sunbus or Airporter. It is approximately a one-hour drive from Brisbane city to Surfers' Paradise. It is advisable to pre-book transfer services.

There is a new electric train service operating between Brisbane and Helensvale at the northern end of the Gold Coast. Regular interstate coach services with Greyhound Pioneer and McCafferty's depart and arrive at the Surfers' Paradise Bus Station. Long distance coach services are also available

Flocks of rainbow lorikeets fly in to be fed by visitors to Currumbin Sanctuary on the Gold Coast.

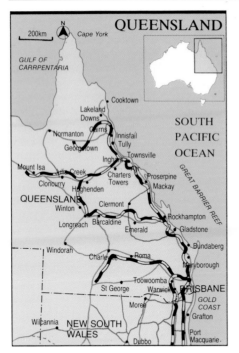

exotic flowering trees, is where the well-heeled promenade or just sit outside in a sidewalk café. Noosa also attracts young people and those in search of good surf; some less expensive accommodation and eating houses are available to meet their needs.

The main beach runs parallel to Hastings Street, with the best restaurants and hotels on the east side of the road overlooking the ocean. After lunch or a hard day shopping take a short walk up Noosa Hill, above Hastings Street, and enjoy its extensive views of Laguna Bay and the river estuary. Occupying the headland is the **Noosa National Park** which encompasses a dramatic rocky coastline dotted with sheltered beaches and coves. Enter the park at the northeast end of Hastings Street and walk along the path which takes you along the cliffs to Granite Bay with its pebble beach and the popular nudist beach at Alexandria Bay. A series of tracks through the national park offer visitors a chance to explore tranquil rain forest, open forest, wallum headlands, scrubland and grasslands.

Inland from the Sunshine Coast are the **Glasshouse Mountains**. These curiously-shaped rocky peaks rise some 500 m (1,640 ft) out of the surrounding scrub. Dedicated rock climbers will find challenges among the sheer faces and there are walks to the lower reaches of the mountains along rough paths. Viewed from a distance, the Glasshouse Mountains shrouded in mist, have an eerie mystery about them.

into the Brisbane City Transit Centre. Via automobile, the Gold Coast Highway branches off the Pacific Highway at Gaven, and Surfers' Paradise is an hour's drive from Brisbane.

THE SUNSHINE COAST

The Sunshine Coast lies to the north of Brisbane and is more sedate than its brash counterpart to the south. Several resort towns, a string of beaches and rocky headlands make up the 56 km (35 miles) of Sunshine Coast. There has been some development modeled on Surfers' Paradise, but mercifully restricted. The Sunshine Coast, therefore, has many of the benefits of the Gold Coast with a more relaxed pace.

This resort area extends from Peregian Beach in the south to Noosaville on the banks of the Noosa River and includes the localities of Marcus Beach, Sunrise Beach, Sunshine Beach, and Noosa Heads; within Noosa Heads are the communities of Little Cove, Noosa Sound and Noosa Junction which is the main shopping center.

The Mecca in the Sunshine Coast is **Noosa**, with its chic restaurants and exclusive boutiques. Hastings Street, lined with

WHERE TO STAY

Noosa attracts upmarket visitors and most of the accommodation is priced accordingly. The best hotels are along Hastings Street facing Laguna Bay. The **Sheraton Noosa** ((07) 5449-4888 TOLL-FREE 1800-073-535 FAX (07) 5449-4753, and **Netanya Noosa** ((07) 5447-4722, at 75 Hastings Street, offer luxury accommodation and direct access to the beach.

Moderately-priced accommodation is available in Noosaville at **Sandy Beach Resort** ((07) 5474-0044 FAX (07) 5474-0788, at 173–175 Gympie Terrace. If you are willing to travel five kilometers (two miles), Noosaville has inexpensive motel accommodation at **Palm Tree Lodge ⟨** (07) 5449-7311, and at 233 Gympie Terrace, **Noosa Gardens Riverside Resort ⟨** (07) 5449-9800, at 261 Weyba Road. At the end of Hastings Street is the inexpensive **Noosa Tewantin Caravan Park ⟨** (07) 5449-8060 FAX (07) 5474-1171, which offers camping spots with electrical facilities and vans.

HOW TO GET THERE

Noosa can be reached by plane from Bris-

THE SUGAR COAST

North of the Sunshine Coast plantations of sugar cane grow on the flat coastal plain. Each year at harvest time the sky is alight with cane burning, clearing the fields for mechanized harvesting. Most of the work on the plantations is now done by machines but this was once a labor-intensive industry. Before Federation in 1901 and the implementation of the White Australia Policy, many cane-cutters were Melanesian or Asian. This

bane or Maroochy Airports, with daily flights from Sydney and Melbourne which are met by a local Sunshine Coast bus operator that will bring you to Noosa with just a short half-hour drive from the airport.

By bus, **Suncoast Pacific** runs five daily services from Brisbane's **Roma Street Transit Centre**. This is approximately a three hour trip by coach. They also pick up travelers from both the domestic and international airports in Brisbane.

By car, the Sunshine Coast is, approximately, a 60-minute drive along an excellent divided highway. Noosa is another 30 minutes along at the northern end of the coastline — around a hour and a half trip from Brisbane.

made for interesting days on the Sugar Coast, as town names such as Melekula and Tanna remind us.

GENERAL INFORMATION

The **Maryborough Tourist Information Centre ⟨** (07) 4121-4111, at 30 Ferry Street, is open daily.

Open weekdays only, the **Bundaberg District Tourism Centre ⟨** (07) 4152-2333, at the corner of Mulgrave and Bourbong streets, can give you general information on the region.

The **Hervey Bay Whale Information Centre ⟨** (07) 4128-9387, will advise on the best times to view whales.

WHAT TO SEE AND DO

To get a feel for what it must have been like in those boom times when sugar built fortunes, visit **Maryborough**, founded in 1865. A fine example of its early architecture is **Baddow House** at 364 Queen Street, which is open to the public. Built in 1883, this two-story mansion lost some of its features during the war but there is enough left to justify a visit. Walk around the streets and see other examples of Maryborough's early architecture, featuring ornate wooden verandahs.

Bundaberg on the Burnett River is one of the few sugar towns that all Australians have heard of because of one of its other products — Bundaberg Rum, a hearty dark spirit from a distillery attached to one of the town's five sugar mills. A visit to Bundaberg would not be complete without a stop at the **Rum Distillery (** (07) 4152-4077, in Avenue Street. Here you will see how the renowned rum is processed. This tour is informative but hazardous as it ends with a sampling of the distillery's product. There are guided tours on the hour from 10 AM to 3 PM weekdays and 10 AM to 1 PM on weekends. An admission fee is charged.

Not far from Bundaberg is **Mon Repos Beach** Australia's largest, most accessible turtle rookery where many species of turtles come ashore from November to February to lay their eggs. At the **Mon Repos Turtle Rookery** these fascinating reptiles can be sighted making their way up the beach one hour before high tide or up to two hours afterwards. They lay their eggs at the top of the beach on a grass-covered bank. From January to March you can observe the miracle of birth when the baby turtles hatch from their eggs.

The Sugar Coast has two other attractions unrelated to cane which draw thousands of visitors to the region every year:

Fraser Island takes its name from Eliza Fraser, who, with her husband Captain Fraser and his crew were shipwrecked there in 1836. Captured by Aborigines, the survivors were used as slaves. Only Eliza got away, escaping after three weeks in captivity. Her ordeal unhinged her so gravely that she was eventually committed to a lunatic asylum.

Fraser Island has excellent beaches. There are colored dunes, some towering 240 m (790 ft) above the island, while inland are scrub and over 40 small freshwater lakes which attract all manner of bird life. Many people explore in four-wheel drive vehicles or just take to the walking tracks. The **Great Sandy National Park** preserves 184,000 hectares (454,500 acres) of the northern part of the island.

Opposite Fraser Island is **Hervey Bay**. Between June and October humpback whales migrate along the coast towards

warmer waters in the north to mate and give birth. They can be seen off Hervey Bay, one of the best places anywhere in the country to see these great mammals.

A third of Australia's sugar crop is grown in the canefields surrounding **Mackay**, 334 km (210 miles) from Rockhampton. This is the "sugar capital of Australia" and you would be amiss not to take a look at a working sugar plantation while in the region. At **Poistone Cane Farm (** (07) 4959-7359, on Homebush Walkerstone Road, 20 km (12 miles) inland from Mackay,

Lifeguards: Demonstrating rescue skills OPPOSITE, and keeping watch on the beach ABOVE, as part of the Surf Carnival.

visitors can see every stage of sugar production on this farm and finish the day with a cool drink of sugar cane juice. Back in town, see the exquisite blooms of orchids in the conservatory at **Queens Park**, which is also a showcase of ferns and colorful tropical flowers.

Mackay, together with **Proserpine**, 130 km (80 miles) to the north, are the departure points for the popular Whitsunday Passage Islands. Tourist information on the islands can be obtained at nearby **Airlie Beach** from **Whitsunday Visitor and Convention Bureau (** (07) 4946-6673, at the intersection of Shute Harbour and Mandalay Roads, open weekdays only. Airlie Beach, 24 km (15 miles) from Proserpine, is an ideal mainland base from which to explore the magical Whitsundays. It is also a good place to take SCUBA diving lessons and there are a number of schools from which to choose.

Crocodiles were sunning themselves on the banks of Ross Creek when the first settlers arrived to establish **Townsville**. Today, only 120 years later, the city is the third largest in Queensland and the crocodiles have had to find a more secluded river bank on which to bask. Visitors can get the best view of Townsville from **Castle Hill**, a 300-m (980-ft) red granite outcropping which rises steeply immediately behind the business district. The vantage point looks down on the growing city which has nonetheless succeeded in retaining much of its colonial elegance.

The **Great Barrier Reef Aquarium (** (07) 4750-0891, at 68 Flinders Street East, contains the world's largest coral reef aquarium and a touch tank where some of the hardier marine specimens can be handled.

For great food, the restaurants along **Fisherman's Wharf (** (07) 4721-1838, in Townsville allow diners to enjoy a meal under the stars, or watch street theater and live entertainment. On Sunday morning, wander along Flinders Malls' **Cotters Market (** (07) 4722-0380, North Queensland's largest arts and craft market.

From Townsville travel to **Paluma**, a clear mountain stream which is fed from a waterfall half way up Mount Spec, and walk through its peaceful rain forest.

WHERE TO STAY

Moderately-priced accommodation on Fraser Island can be found at **Happy Valley (** (07) 4127-9144, and **Eliza Sands (** (07) 4127-9132.

At Mackay the **Dolphin Heads Resort (** (07) 4954-9666 TOLL-FREE 1800-075-088 FAX (07) 4954-9341, on Beach Road, is surrounded by palms and has its own pool.

Staying on Magnetic Island is an alternative to Townsville, **Magnetic International Resort (** (07) 4778-5200 TOLL-FREE 1800-079-902 FAX (07) 4778-5806, on Mandalay Avenue, is set on the side of a hill in a pretty bush setting. In Townsville the **Arcadia Hotel Resort (** (07) 4778-5177 FAX (07) 4778-5939, at 7 Marine Parade, is moderately priced, while **Midtown Hotel-Motel (** (07) 4771-5121, at 718 Sturt Street, is also a good value.

HOW TO GET THERE

Townsville has an international airport which receives twice weekly services from Europe and the United Kingdom; and Garuda Airlines flies in from Indonesia. There are frequent daily domestic flights from the southern states.

Buses run along the Queensland Coast, stopping at the major towns. At the other end of the Sugar Coast, Bundaberg can be reached by air; **Sunstate Airlines** and **West Airlines** have daily flights. McCafferty's and Pioneer Greyhound run daily services from both the north and south. The rail line runs up the northern coast and many towns from Brisbane to Cairns can be reached by train.

The Bruce Highway, starting at Brisbane, links all the towns along the north coast.

THE GREAT BARRIER REEF

Off the coast near Bundaberg is Lady Elliott Island which marks the southern edge of the Great Barrier Reef — stretching a staggering 2,000 km (more than 1,200 miles) up the coast, covering an area of approximately 350,000 sq km (130,000 sq miles) and consisting of nearly 3,000 individual coral reefs.

The reef is indisputably one of the natural wonders of the world.

The reef is built on the calcium skeletons of billions of minute coral polyps laid down over thousands of years. Above the calcareous remains of its predecessors new coral grows, nurtured by the unique conditions on the eastern coastal strip — warm, clear, shallow waters rich in nutrients which promote the diverse aquatic life in the coral: there are an estimated 2,000 types of fish and 500 species of coral polyps within its boundary. The colors of this underwater wonderland are astounding. Fish, brilliant as jewels, glide between waving sponges and delicate

facilities for visitors. A good base is the **Green Island Reef Resort** ((07) 4031-3300 TOLL-FREE 1800-673-366 FAX (07) 4052-1511. There are also a number of uninhabited low-lying coral cays around the reef that can be visited. Many of the islands are national parks and permits are required to camp on them.

Along the reef are ordinary islands unconnected with it and covered with thick vegetation. Resorts have been established on a number of these islands where the reef is usually only a short trip away.

coral formations. On the sea floor starfish and sea urchins forage in the underwater grottoes.

In and around the reef are about 900 islands.

Cays are sterile coral outcrops which over the centuries have acquired a fertile surface layer on which grasses and shrubs have established themselves. Sand-filled lagoons have formed on these, providing a platform for exploring the underwater swirl of color and movement.

Only a handful of islands are cays, and only three — **Lady Elliott Island** 80 km (50 miles) from Bundaberg, **Heron Island** 81 km (50 miles) off Gladstone and **Green Island** 27 km (16 miles) from Cairns, have

SCUBA diving provides freedom to explore the sea bed at will. If you ever thought about taking up this sport, what better time to start than during a visit to the Great Barrier Reef? There are schools in all the major resorts catering to learners. A simpler way to explore is with a snorkel, and glass-bottomed boats can be hired for nonswimmers to enjoy the reef.

There are major resorts on the larger islands, most of which are owned by one company. Each offers total packages that include accommodation, meals (excluding alcoholic drinks), use of aquatic sports

Some 500 species of coral thrive along the Great Barrier Reef.

equipment, SCUBA lessons and entertainment. Contact numbers are included below for each resort group.

The **Keppel Island Group** are continental islands near Rockhampton. On **Great Keppel Island** guests can linger on one of its seventeen beaches, skip over the water on skis or go parasailing. At night there is leisurely dining in the **Admiral Keppel** and afterwards disco dancing at the **Anchorage Bar** or **Neptune Nightclub**. The resort is operated by Qantas TOLL-FREE 1800-812-525 FAX (07) 7939-1775, and marketing is aimed at families and the younger crowd. **Keppel Haven (** (07) 4933-6744, provides inexpensive accommodation and also appeals to families.

At **Middle Island** one and a half kilometers (one mile) from Great Keppel Island, is an **Underwater Observatory** that gives excellent coral viewing through large panoramic windows. Access is from Rosslyn Bay via Great Keppel Island with **Keppel Tourist Services (** (07) 4933-6744, which has daily trips at 2:30 PM, except Thursdays. Get a fish-eye view of the hundreds of colorful species that swim these waters. It's open daily from 9 AM to 4:30 PM, and an admission fee is charged. Nearby **North Keppel Island** appeals to locals looking for an inexpensive camping holiday.

The **Whitsunday Passage Islands** are a collection of about 74 idyllic islands with some of the best-developed resorts on the Great Barrier Reef — definitely not off the beaten track — but nevertheless, wildlife abounds; Whitsunday Island is home to the unadorned rock wallaby and is an important rookery for brahminy kites, ospreys, white-bellied sea eagles and peregrine falcons.

The surrounding waters of the Whitsundays are marine park, and the best way to see this area is underwater. A popular SCUBA diving location is at the northern end of Hook Island which is sheltered from the southerly weather. Bookings can be made with **Club Whitsunday** TOLL-FREE 1800-678-755 FAX (07) 4946-6890, who also arrange day trips and extended cruises departing from Shute Harbour at Airlie Beach. The best time to visit is spring and autumn when the weather is milder.

A seven-kilometer (four-mile) trip from Shute Harbour, brings travelers to the main jumping-off point for the Whitsunday Passage, **South Molle Island Resort (** (07) 4946-9433 FAX (07) 4946-9580, where a good range of activities are provided and children are well looked after. Day visitors and guests are welcome.

At adjacent **Hook Island** there is an **Underwater Observatory (** (07) 4951-4644, providing some of the best views of coral on the reef. It is open 11 AM to 2 PM, and an admission fee of AU$5 is charged.

Across Cleveland Bay lies **Magnetic Island,** a suburb of Townsville just 30 minutes to reach by boat. Most of the island is a national park with 22 km (14 miles) of walking tracks. The cane toad is an introduced species which has reached plague proportions in Queensland. These ugly amphibians are raced at **Arcadia Hotel Resort (** (07) 4778-5177, every Wednesday at 8 PM. Before the race, toads competing are auctioned off, so anyone can participate. There is a prize for the winner, but first he or she has to kiss the winning toad, none of whom to date has turned into a prince or princess. You can cap off the evening at **Trix** nightclub, which rocks on into the early hours.

Imagine walking out of a pristine tropical rain forest onto a magnificent white sand, blue water, ocean swimming beach... and finding it totally deserted. You can do that on **Hinchinbrook Island** one of the most beautiful islands along the coast, and one that hasn't suffered from inappropriate development. To protect its delicate ecology, management restricts numbers of visitors to the island. It covers an area of 39,350 hectares (97,200 acres) and is the world's largest island national park. Exploring by foot has its rewards, as the terrain changes from coastal mangroves and sandy beaches to mountains in the interior, **Mt. Bowen** at 1,142 m (3,745 ft) being the highest point. At **Missionary Bay** watch for dugongs. These rare mammals look like overfed seals, but in the water they glide gracefully among the extensive sea grass beds in the area, where

OPPOSITE: Flying low TOP over a tiny island resort and the turquoise waters of the Great Barrier Reef is an exciting preview of a visit to this natural wonder. BOTTOM: Sunning at Surfers' Paradise.

they graze. They grow up to three meters (18 ft) in length and weigh up to 420 kg (1,000 lbs).

The **Hinchinbrook Island Resort** TOLL-FREE 1800-777-021 FAX (07) 4066-8742, is small and exclusive and definitely for the well-heeled. Camping is also possible. **Hinchinbrook Island Adventures (** (07) 4066-8270 TOLL-FREE 1800-682-702, conducts daily cruises to Hinchinbrook Island, starting at 6 AM out of Cairns and guides take you through some of the prettiest parts of the island's national park, imparting their deep knowledge of the flora and fauna of the area and narrating its colorful Aboriginal and early European history.

Lizard Island ((07) 4060-3990 TOLL-FREE 1800-812-525 FAX (07) 4060-3991, is the most northerly resort on the Great Barrier Reef, 90 km (56 miles) north of Cooktown. Captain Cook visited the island in 1770, seeking a way through the reef. From the highest point on the island Cook saw the outer reef, only 15 km (nine miles) away where waves pound the edge of the continental shelf. Lizard serves as a base for marlin fishermen from September to November.

HOW TO GET THERE

The best time to go to the Great Barrier Reef is between April and October. Contact the Government Tourist Office for the most convenient hopping-off points to the various islands, some of which can be reached by air. There are daily flights into Proserpine from Brisbane, and flights six days a week from Adelaide, Rockhampton, Cairns and Mackay.

It takes about 22 hours by train to get from Brisbane to Proserpine, nearest rail town to the Whitsundays.

To tour the reef, you can take a launch or catamaran, leaving daily from Mackay. Airlie Beach is the main embarkation point. A visit to the reef is also on the itinerary of many long-distance coach tour operators.

FAR NORTH QUEENSLAND

Cairns is easily accessible by road and water, has its own airport and is therefore a popular base from which to explore Far North Queensland, Cape York and the Gulf Country. It offers the Great Barrier Reef on one side, while inland are many attractions to cater to all tastes.

GENERAL INFORMATION

In Cairns, the **Far North Queensland Promotion Bureau (** (07) 4051-3588, is located at the corner of Grafton and Hartley streets, and is open daily. The **Gulf Savannah Tourist Organisation (** (07) 4051-4658, located at 55 Macleod Street, provides information on attractions in the Gulf of Carpenteria. The **Cape York and Gulf Savannah Hotline** TOLL-FREE 1800-629-413, operates 8:30 AM to 5 PM daily.

WHAT TO SEE AND DO

Going north, Cairns is the last stop of any consequence, 1,807 km (1,130 miles) from Brisbane. The main rail line ends at Cairns, as does the Bruce Highway. This is a tourist town, with an amazing 600 tour options available each and every day out of Cairns.

Life in Cairns is casual and its inhabitants take it at a leisurely pace, advisable in a climate so often hot and humid. The city itself is where much of the accommodation is situated with international standard restaurants, boutique shopping, modern art galleries and classy nightclubs to keep visitors entertained.

Want to play the didgeridoo? Throw a boomerang? Do this and a lot more at the **Tjapukai Aboriginal Cultural Park (** (07) 4042-9999, on the Kamerunga Road in Smithfield, which is a theme park that introduces visitors to aspects of life, traditional culture, music and customs of the local Aboriginal people. It takes about two and a half hours to explore the exhibits and take part in activities that include cultural and dance theaters. At the traditional Aboriginal camp, visitors can talk with Tjapukai people, learn about bush foods and medicines, play a didgeridoo and throw boomerangs and spears. Spend your lunchtime at the **Boomerang Restaurant** and try dishes made from local food sources. The park is open daily 9 AM to 5 PM; the price of admission is AU$21.

From Trinity Harbour, cruise boats depart for the Great Barrier Reef which is, at this point, at its closest to the coast. The **Great Adventures Outer Reef Island Cruises** ((07) 4051-5644, on Wharf Street, provides two trips a day to Green Island, Lizard Island and other attractions along the reef.

Big game fishermen from around the world congregate in Cairns for the **Marlin Meet**, which coincides with the migration of these fighting fish along the outer side of the Great Barrier Reef. Celebrities of the ilk of Greg Norman are known to keep an

day. It is important to have a good skipper on fishing expeditions and Ross McCubbin of **Lucky Strike Charters** TOLL-FREE 1800-735-570 FAX (07) 5591-8624, comes highly recommended.

A leisurely way of seeing the attractions inland of the coast is on the **Kuranda Scenic Railway** ((07) 4052-6249. From Cairns Railway Station, the 100-year-old train sluggishly winds its way up through 15 tunnels to the **Atherton Tableland**, a trip of 34 km (21 miles). The track clings to the face of the escarpment, passing through lush forest and

annual appointment with the giant black marlin ready for battle off the Cairns Coast.

These marvelous creatures can reach four meters (14 ft) in length and weigh over 420 kg (1,000 lbs), in which case they are known as "granders." The fishing season is from mid-September to mid-December, and at around AU$1,600 per day this is not a cheap pastime; for packages that include luxury accommodation aboard the mother ship add another AU$1,000. At night, over cocktails, you can wind your companions up with yarns about the "one that got away." If you do happen to catch a black marlin, you can get a fiberglass mold made, but if this idea is unappealing then I suggest you release it so it can fight another

over 40 bridges. The old beast wheezes past the edge of **Barron Falls** which, after heavy rain, becomes a thundering torrent plunging hundreds of meters into a gorge colored with rainbow-flecked mist. When in full flow, the **Stoney Creek Falls** is so close to you that its spray envelopes the track. There are several trips each day; you can take organized tours to the surrounding national park from **Kuranda**, described as the "village in the rain forest."

There are two roads to the isolated town of **Cooktown**. Going via Cape Tribulation requires a four-wheel drive because parts of the inland road are rough tracks.

Towering palms in a rain forest north of Cairns.

Cooktown is where Captain Cook first landed on the mainland — he put in there to make repairs on the *Endeavour* after running aground on a coral reef. Cookstown boomed after gold was discovered there in 1883, and the town went from a one horse town to one that supported 68 bordellos, 64 pubs and numerous gambling dens, an indication of the miners' priorities. At the time it was the second largest town in Queensland after Brisbane. Once the goldmines were exhausted, Cooktown became a backwater, today its population is just 1,500. The main attraction in town is the **James Cook Historical Museum (** (07) 4069-5386, at the intersection of Helen and Fureaux streets. The building is typical of early Queensland architecture with emphasis on wide verandahs and airy rooms — a practical arrangement designed to capture every cool breeze that might happen by. The museum has several exhibits containing artifacts to acquaint visitors with the early history of the town.

Eons ago, when the sea level was lower and Torres Strait shallower, **Cape York Peninsula**, the northernmost part of Australia, formed a land bridge to New Guinea. As a result, its flora and fauna are closely related to those found in New Guinea.

The area starts at Cooktown on the east coast and takes in some of the wildest, most isolated country in Australia, the best way of seeing it is on an organized safari.

In the heart of the Gulf Country is one of the most curious train tracks in the world. It leads nowhere and serves no practical purpose. Starting at **Normanton**, the *Gulflander* winds 152 km (94 miles) inland to **Croydon**, once a gold mining town. It is a leisurely journey, and unscheduled stops are not because of mechanical breakdowns but rather the driver's desire to show his passengers something of interest near the track. The train leaves Normanton on Wednesday and returns from Croydon on Thursday. Reservations can be made at Normanton Station **(** (07) 4745-1391, or at the **QR Travel Centre (** (07) 4052-6249, in Cairns. In 1993 the Queensland government tried to close down the *Gulflander* but decided otherwise in the face of the ensuing public outcry.

North of the cape are the **Torres Strait Islands** with 5,000 inhabitants occupying 17 islands. Pearling was a major industry in the nineteenth century and pearls are still profitable for the islanders. Permission to visit pearling areas should be obtained from the traditional land owners.

WHERE TO STAY

As you would expect in a large tourist center such as Cairns, there is a wide range of accommodation from which to choose.

Most of the luxury hotels are along the Esplanade overlooking the harbor. The **Pacific International (** (07) 4051-7888, is found at the corner of Spence Street and the Esplanade, and **Sunshine Tower Hotel (** (07) 4051-5288, is at 140 Esplanade. The **Flying Horseshoe Motel (** (07) 4051-3022 FAX (07) 4031-2761, at 281–289 Sheridon Street, is moderately-priced and close to town.

Inexpensive accommodation is available at **Compass (** (07) 4051-5466, at 232 Mulgrave Road. About 75 km (47 miles) from Cairns is **Port Douglas**, a popular holiday spot. For total luxury stay at the **Sheraton Mirage Port Douglas (** (07) 4099-5888 TOLL-FREE 1800-073-535 FAX (07) 4098-5885, on Port Douglas Road.

There are several choices of moderately-priced accommodation in Kuranda. The **Cedar Park Rainforest Resort (** (07) 4093-7077 FAX (07) 4093-7841, at One Cedar Park Road, is about 15 km (nine miles) out of town. Being off the main road this resort is filled only with the noises of the rain forest — gurgling of the Clohesy River, wind in the trees or the occasional screech of a sulfur-crested cockatoo flying overhead. In town there is a mixture of good quality cabins and inexpensive bunkhouse accommodation at the **Kuranda Rainforest Resort (** (07) 4093-7555, at Two Greenhills Road.

Most of the accommodation in the Torres Strait Islands is on **Thursday Island**, the largest in the Torres Strait group. The **Jardine (** (07) 4069-2555, at the corner of Normanby Street and Victoria Parade, provides luxury accommodation, while the (also luxury-priced) **Grand Hotel (** (07) 4069-1557, at One Victoria Parade, claims that Somerset Maugham stayed there.

HOW TO GET THERE

There are direct flights to Cairns from Alice Springs, Townsville, Mackay, Gladstone, Brisbane, Perth, Melbourne and Sydney, and a number of international flights enter Australia via Cairns.

There are four Qantas Australian flights a week out of Cairns to Thursday Island.

The train runs between Melbourne, Sydney, Brisbane and Cairns, the final leg of the journey taking 32 hours and leaving Brisbane on Saturday, Sunday, Tuesday and Thursday.

The Trinity Wharf Coach Terminal is the hub for all the main and some regional bus services while the trains come in at McLeod Street Station.

NATIONAL PARKS

GENERAL INFORMATION

For information on national parks phone the **Queensland Department of Conservation and Heritage** ((07) 4227-7111 and the **National Parks Association of Queensland** ((07) 4367-0878 FAX (07) 4367-0890.

WHAT TO SEE AND DO

Lamington ((07) 4533-3584, 110 km (68 miles) west of Brisbane and 54 km (33 miles) from Surfers' Paradise is the state's first national park. It features subtropical rain forests and wet eucalypt forest. See the park on foot by way of its 160 km (100 miles) of walking paths, taking time to visit some of its 500 waterfalls, picnic beside crystal clear streams, and explore cliffs, and fern-filled gullies and wonder at mountain lookouts with spectacular views.

Mountainous, often mist-shrouded, **Eungella National Park** is a 45-minute drive west from Mackay and takes its name from the local Aboriginal word for "land of cloud." The sound of water is ever-present as sparkling creeks splash over rocks and plunge down inaccessible mountain slopes into deep ravines. The luxuriant rain forest is carpeted with ferns, which thrive in this damp atmosphere. There are 25 km

(16 miles) of walking tracks in the park for those who want to take a closer look at its beauty or the profusion of delicately colored birds that come to feed on berries and fruit.

The **Daintree** ((07) 4051-9811, 111 km (69 miles) north of Cairns and five kilometers (three miles) north of Mossman, is a large rain forest park with rivers gorges and waterfalls, with limited access even for walkers. Trails start at Mossman Gorge, and pass through rain forest and excellent swimming holes. Cruises are available up the Daintree River and are a great way to spot birds and

animals, including crocodiles. Winter is the best time to visit this park.

Girraween ((07) 4684-5157, 34 km (21 miles) south of Stanthorpe, is inland from the Gold Coast. The gravity-defying **Balancing Rock** is one of the attractions.

Lakefield National Park is 200 km (125 miles) north of Cairns. The state's second largest park has rain forest, woodlands, grassy plains and coastal mudflats along Princess Charlotte Bay. On Flinders and Stanley islands are Aboriginal galleries of marine life — stingrays, crabs, flying fish, turtles and the rare dugong.

A crystal-clear stream is surrounded by dense rain forest at the remote Daintree park near Mossman.

Northern Territory
It's All Outback

"CROC THREAT" screamed the headline in *The News*, the Northern Territory's main daily newspaper. The stories below recounted the story of of a two-meter (six-foot) saltwater crocodile trapped in a pool at the foot of Twin Falls, of water buffalo bulls hunted from helicopters, and of a Greek migrant celebrating Easter by letting off sticks of dynamite. All these appeared in *The News* on a single day, revealing the wild and untamed nature of the region. There is more than a little truth in the old Australian saying that "all madmen travel north and once there can't get away."

There are few towns in the territory, but 78,000 of its 173,500 residents live in Darwin and 22,000 live in Alice Springs.

The Northern Territory has the highest proportion of Aboriginal people of any of the states, forming 22 percent of the total population. The Aboriginal Lands Rights Act of 1976 returned ownership of large tracts of land to the traditional owners, including Uluru (Ayers Rock) and Kata Tjuta (the Olgas). While these major tourist attractions are still open to the public, traditional owners are now involved in their management.

It is a place of great distances, where the doctor comes by plane, children take their classes by short wave radio and cattle are rounded up using motorbikes or helicopters. The weather is tropical and can shift violently from drought to flood.

The landscape of the territory can only be described as bizarre; over the eons nature and geological forces have played havoc with the earth's surface to create flamboyant rock masterpieces in red and ochre. Rivers have sliced deep gorges through sandstone plateaus. Spectacular waterfalls tumble down vertical rock faces. And there is quite a lot of very flat terrain too… an awful lot!

DARWIN

There have been two serious attempts to demolish Darwin. The first occurred during World War Two when the Japanese conducted 64 bombing raids bringing the loss of 243 lives. The second came on Christmas Eve of 1974 when Cyclone Tracy unleashed

four hours of destruction, flattening much of Darwin, injuring thousands and leaving 66 dead.

Darwin has recovered from both of these catastrophes, a tribute to the spirit of its inhabitants. Such persistence in the face of repeated disasters is evidence, for many southerners, that its inhabitants must truly be "madmen." But for the people of Darwin, living anywhere else would truly be out of the question. Every setback only reinforces their ties to this bizarre tropical town.

Set on a peninsula, Darwin's lush fertility, tropical nonchalance and suburbs set in a colorful sea of bougainvillea, frangipani and poinsettia provide a exotic backdrop to Australia's most northerly capital city.

The best time to visit the territory is during the dry season, between May and October when the days are warm, the weather stable and the humidity relatively low. The rest of the year is the wet season, when the monsoons bring rain and attendant lightning storms late in the afternoon and overnight, making the days humid.

GENERAL INFORMATION

The **Darwin Regional Tourism Association** ((08) 8981-4300, at 38 Mitchell Street, is open weekdays from 8:30 AM to 6 PM, on Saturdays from 9 AM to 3 PM and on Sundays from 10 AM to 2 PM. The opening hours are shorter during the wet season. Accommodation can be arranged by staff at the center.

OPPOSITE: A road train, workhorse of the north.
ABOVE: A ranch hand feeds stock during a drought.

WHAT TO SEE AND DO

Much of Darwin has been rebuilt since Cyclone Tracy. Although the city and its suburbs look relatively new this northern city, in reality a provincial town, does not lack attractions.

Darwin's central business district is at the northwest corner of the peninsula jutting into Darwin Harbour. The main shopping area is along Smith Street mall, between Bennett and Knuckey streets. A stroll

through town is the best way to get a feel for the place.

Start at the northeast end of Smith Street where the modern **Christchurch Anglican Cathedral** stands. Built after the devastation of Tracy, the design incorporated the original porch, all that survived the cyclone.

The Chinese community was also devastated when its temple was ripped apart by Tracy's 280-kph (175-mph) winds. A new **Chinese Temple** has been erected at 25 Woods Street; its lines retain the feel of the original structure of 1887 formerly situated on the same spot. It is open to the public on

Larger than life display at the Grand Parade, part of Darwin's Bougainvillea Festival.

weekdays from 8 AM to 4 PM and on weekends from 8 AM to 3 PM. Admission is free. The temple is still used by the local Chinese who have had a long and at times troubled association with Darwin. Tourists are requested to respect the sanctity of this place and the dignity of its worshipers. Next door to the temple the Chung Wah Society has built a museum which provides interesting information on the history and everyday life of Chinese migrants in Australia.

Most of the historic buildings spared by Cyclone Tracy are to be found towards the harbor end of town. **Government House** is on the Esplanade overlooking the harbor. It is not open to the public, except for an Open Day sometime in July or August, but at other times by peering through the gate you will see a reminder of more gracious times. The century-old building has lived through Japanese bombing raids, a succession of cyclones and even an attack of white ants. Nevertheless, with its grand verandahs and gables the whole edifice has a colonial elegance now rare in Darwin.

Since gaining limited statehood, in 1994 the territory government has built itself a magnificent AU$120 million Parliament Building to house just 25 members, which makes the Taj Mahal look like a modest low-cost outhouse.

At the other end of Esplanade, near the corner of Daly Street is Doctor's Gully. At high tide hundreds of fish swim into the shallows where they know that they will get a free feed from visitors. **Aquascene (** (08) 8981-7837, at 28 Doctor's Gully provides visitors with the opportunity to participate in this unique spectacle. It is advisable to ring first to find out feeding times, which change depending on the tides. Admission is AU$4 for adults and AU$2.50 for children.

Picnic on the lawns of the **Botanical Gardens** off Gilruth Land, or wander among its collection of over 400 species of tropical and subtropical plants. It contains an amphitheater which serves as the setting for cultural events varying from concerts to Aboriginal dance performances, and is open daily from 7 AM to 7 PM; entry is free.

A superb collection of Aboriginal artifacts and Oceania art are on show at the **Museum and Art Gallery of the Northern Territory**

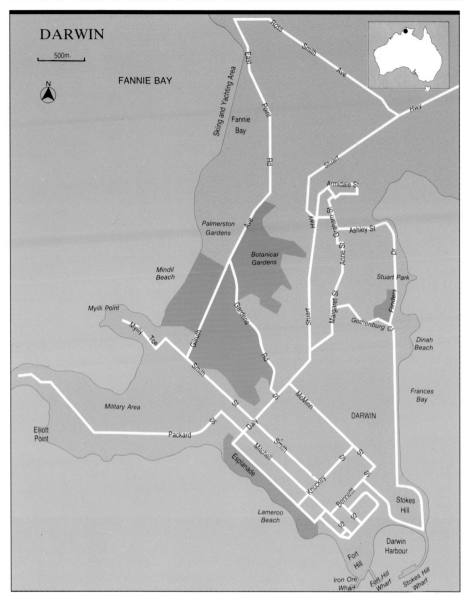

DARWIN

500m.

N

FANNIE BAY

Ross

Smith

Ave

Hwy

East

Perth

Fannie
Bay

Skiing and Yachting Area

Rd

Stuart

Armidale St

HWY

Graham St

Ashley St

Ave

Anne St

Dr

Palmerston
Gardens

Botanical
Gardens

Stuart Park

Mindil
Beach

Margaret St

Flinders

Myilli Point

Gardens

Stuart

Gothenburg Cr

Dinah
Beach

Myilly Tce

Gilruth

Rd

McMinn

Frances
Bay

Military Area

St

Smith

St

Daly

DARWIN

Elliott
Point

Packard

St

Mitchell

Smith

St

Esplanade

St

St

Knuckey

Bennett

Stokes
Hill

Lameroo
Beach

St

St

Darwin
Harbour

Fort
Hill

Iron Ore
Wharf

Fort Hill
Wharf

Stokes Hill
Wharf

((08) 8999-8201, on Conacher Street, Fanny
Bay, about four kilometers (2.5 miles) out of
town. There is also a good collection of
modern Australian works in the gallery,
open 9 AM to 5 PM weekdays and 10 AM to
5 PM weekends; entry is free.

Off the Stuart Highway on the Cox Peninsula Road, Berry Springs, is the **Territory
Wildlife Park** ((08) 8988-7201. It consists of
400 hectares (990 acres) of bushland where
the territory's animals can be seen in their
native habitat. A special treat is to watch

wedge-tailed eagles and other birds of prey
soar around park handlers at 10 AM each day.
At 1:30 PM, see greedy pelicans go into a
feeding frenzy at Wader Lagoon. Give yourself at least three hours to look around this
immense reserve; open daily from 8:30 AM to
4 PM; gates close at 6 PM. **Darwin Day Tours**
((08) 8981-8696, provides a package that
includes transport from Darwin hotels and
entry fee to the park.

Some of these tours include a visit to the
Darwin Crocodile Farm ((08) 8988-1450, at

Noonamah along the Stuart Highway, 40 km (25 miles) out of Darwin. More than 10,000 reptiles can be seen at various stages of growth, from chicks crawling out of eggs to jaw-snapping monsters. If you are frightened by the belligerence of these ancient beasts then you will probably suffer no qualms about purchasing a handbag or belt from the farm's souvenir shop, or having your revenge by dining on a Croc Burger in the kiosk. The farm is open 10 AM to 4 PM daily; admission is AU$9.50 for adults and AU$5 for children.

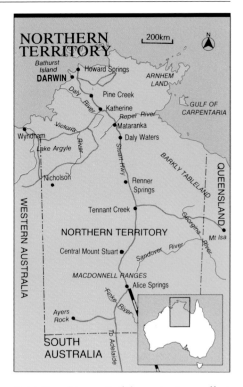

DARWIN AFTER DARK

If the thrills of Darwin by day with its spectacles revolving around the dining habits of giant reptiles have not jaded you, get ready to enjoy Darwin by moonlight, where the weather is kind to night-owls.

If it's Thursday or Sunday, start the evening on **Mindil Beach** where there is a sunset market, open throughout the dry season. Shop for local crafts or try the food from one of the 60 stalls.

Plays and performances, from the mainstream to the fringe, can be seen at **Brown's Mart Community Arts Theatre ℂ** (08) 8981-5522, at 12 Smith Street. The 1885 stone building is also of historic significance.

Overlooking Mindil Beach, the squat, pyramid-shaped **MGM Grand Darwin Casino ℂ** (08) 8943-8888, on Gulruth Avenue, is popular with tourists. If you are not interested in gambling there are live shows to watch, or music to dance to at **Sweethearts Downunder**. The casino also provides jazz concerts on its lawns at sunset during the dry season.

Friday's edition of the *Northern Territory News* has a gig guide which summarizes what's on at night in Darwin.

SPORTS

The **Gardens Park Golf Links ℂ** (08) 8981-6365, opposite the Casino has nine holes, and clubs and buggy for hire.

The best sport in town is fishing, and the Top End is famous for its barramundi (known locally as "barra"). These freshwater fish provide anglers with a good

fight, thrashing out of the water in an effort to escape. While there is reasonable barra fishing near Darwin, for anglers that are willing to travel to find the best, there are camping tours into the Outback where the prime spots can be found, and 18-kg (40-lb) barra caught. The best time of the year for this is from March to May. Northern Territory Angler Champion, Bryan Sporle from **Land-a-Burra Tours ℂ** (08) 8932-2543, knows the best spots around Darwin for barra fishing, and organizes day trips as well as extended safaris into Victoria River and Arnhem Land for serious fishermen. Expect to pay about AU$200 a day for an all-inclusive tour.

WHERE TO STAY

The **MGM Grand Darwin ℂ** (08) 8943-8888, and the **Beaufort Darwin ℂ** (08) 8943-8888 FAX (08) 8943-8999, in The Esplanade, offer luxury accommodation with ocean views.

Moderately-priced **Poinciana Inn ℂ** (08) 8981-8111 FAX (08) 8941-2440, at 84 Mitchell Street, is in the center of town and close to everything.

There is also a good selection of inexpensive accommodation in Darwin. The **Tiwi Lodge Motel** ((08) 8981-6471 FAX (08) 8981-3285, is at 53 Cavenagh Street. A little out of town, the **Banyon View Lodge** ((08) 8981-8644 FAX (08) 8981-6104, at 119 Mitchell Street, Larrakeyah, is set in tropical gardens and reflects the informality typical of Darwin, where guests can enjoy an evening barbecue.

WHERE TO EAT

Tourists dollars have had a very appreciable influence on the standard of restaurants in Darwin, which have much improved over the last few years. One of the most popular places in town is **Christos on the Wharf** ((08) 8981-8658, on Stokes Hill Wharf (expensive), which offers open-air dining and serves local fish. Their barramundi comes highly recommended. For a menu offering exotica such as buffalo, camel and crocodile, visit **The Magic Wok** ((08) 8981-3332, at 48 Cavenagh Street (moderate), or the **Terrace Restaurant** ((08) 8981-5388, at 122 Esplanade (moderate).

If Darwin weather is not hot enough for you, sample the heat of a Thai curry at the moderately-priced **Hanuman Thai Restaurant** ((08) 8941-3500, at 28 Mitchell Street (moderate).

HOW TO GET THERE

Ansett Australia provides at least one direct daily flight to Darwin from Sydney, Melbourne, Perth, Adelaide and Brisbane. Qantas Australian has fewer services. There are also direct international flights to Bali, Denpasar, Amsterdam, Copenhagen, Frankfurt, Kuala Lumpur, London, Manchester, Paris, Singapore, Zurich and Stockholm.

Driving to Darwin is a major undertaking, as the closest capital city is Adelaide, 3,020 km (1,888 miles) away, and the main highway takes you through Alice Springs — the Red Center of Australia. A detour off the main highway, 244 km (150 miles), is Uluru (Ayers Rock) and other attractions in the Outback. One popular way to see the Top End is driving from Perth, traveling

around the coast by way of Broome, a mere 4,100 km (2,550 miles).

There are bus coaches to Darwin from Brisbane and, via Alice Springs, from Adelaide.

KAKADU NATIONAL PARK

The showplace of the Top End, Kakadu National Park is a spectacular and ancient wilderness, home to hundreds of species of birds and animals and a treasure house of Aboriginal art and lore. It is one of the

world's great parks, justifiably on the highly prestigious World Heritage list.

Located 250 km (156 miles) east of Darwin, a three hour drive, it lies on the western fringe of Arnhem Land. The national park covers 19,000 sq km (7,350 sq miles).

GENERAL INFORMATION

At an information booth at the entrance of Kakadu Park on the Arnhem Highway visitors pay an admission fee of AU$15 that covers a visit of up to 14 days. Children 16 and under are allowed in free of charge. It is a further 80 km (50 miles) to the **Bowali Visitor Centre** ((08) 8938-1120, which provides visitors with a comprehensive collection of *Park Notes*, brochures which explain the ecology of Kakadu Park and maps which locate major Aboriginal art galleries. The center is open from 8 AM to 5 PM. There is also a tourist information center in Jabiru ((08) 8979-2548.

The MGM Grand Darwin Casino.

WHAT TO SEE AND DO

The park includes a broad flood plain and is backed by the high ramparts of the Arnhem Land escarpment. Accessible only in the dry season and by using a four-wheel drive vehicle, majestic waterfalls thunder off the plateau with the 200-m (650-ft) drop of the **Jim Jim Falls** and the smaller **Twin Falls** the most breathtaking. Both are reached off the Kakadu Highway along dirt roads. Throughout Kakadu, during the dry

lightning storms at this time of year, called the "build-up," are an unforgettable sight. During the wet season many regions will not be accessible when roads are washed out.

The Aboriginal people have lived in Arnhem Land for thousands of years; there is evidence of their rich culture in the galleries of rock paintings around Kakadu, a window on the ancient past, a record of Dreamtime myths. More than 300 galleries have been found and it is estimated that at least another 1,000 are known only to local

season the water recedes to a network of lagoons and billabongs which attract thousands of birds. Along the coast, tidal mudflats and mangrove forests provide yet another habitat, and contrast with the rest of the park.

There are both freshwater and estuarine crocodiles in Kakadu. Take heed of crocodile warning signs, and you are strongly advised not to swim or paddle in natural waterways. A better choice is the Olympic-size public swimming pool in Jabiru which is guaranteed to be croc-free.

The best time to see Kakadu is at the beginning of the dry season, between April and August. October and November can be uncomfortably humid, although the savage

Aboriginal clans. Accessible ones are found at **Ubirr** (previously known as Obiri Rock), which is 38 km (24 miles) from Jabiru, and then an easy 45-minute walk from the road. The topography includes a number of overhangs and caves that made natural shelters for Aborigines. Paintings include stick-like figures and "x-ray" drawings of animals showing their internal organs and bone structure. There is also a Tasmanian tiger — a species which died out in the Top End more than 3,000 years ago — drawn on an overhang of the main gallery. Towards a lookout near the main gallery is another site with a series of hunters in motion painted in white on a black wall, and which may be over 1,000 years old. Between April and October guides are available, free of charge, to explain artwork and answer your questions. **Nourlangie Rock**, 28 km (17 miles) south of the Bowali Information Centre, also contains Aboriginal art galleries; the way is clearly signposted.

WHERE TO STAY

The best places to stay in Kakadu are in **Jabiru**, close to the park center. **Gagudju Crocodile Hotel** ((08) 8979-2800 TOLL-FREE 1800 800 123 FAX (08) 8979-2707, in Flinders

Street, is a luxury hotel in the shape of a crocodile. At the other end of the price range is the **Kookaburra Lodge** ((08) 8971-0257, at the corner of Lindsay and Third streets.

HOW TO GET THERE

There are quite a few package tours to Kakadu, with stays ranging from one to six days. Another way to get a view of the park, particularly if you don't have much time, is from the air. **Kakadu Air** TOLL-FREE 1800-089-113 or (08) 8979-2411 FAX (08) 8979-2303, has daily departures from Darwin and Kakadu itself, and the flight covers Jim Jim and Twin falls.

Northern Territory

DOWN THE TRACK

The Stuart Highway, known simply as "the Track," bisects the Northern Territory, from Darwin to Alice Springs 1,530 km (950 miles) to the south and then another 290 km (180 miles) to the South Australian border.

GENERAL INFORMATION

The **Katherine Region Tourist Association** ((08) 8972-2650, is located on the Stuart

Highway on the corner of Lindsay Street. The **Tennant Creek Region Tourist Association** ((08) 8962-3388, is in Peko Road.

WHAT TO SEE AND DO

Driving along the Track can be dry work, so take a detour off the highway and stop at **Daly Waters**, 584 km (365 miles) from Darwin, for an ice cold beer in the oldest pub in the territory.

OPPOSITE: An organized boat tour explores Yellow Waters, a water hole that doesn't disappear during the dry season; it's a popular place to see native wildlife. ABOVE: Beautiful Katherine Gorge LEFT south of Darwin and Standley Chasm RIGHT in the MacDonnell Ranges.

Katherine, 345 km (214 miles) south of Darwin, is the next main town on the highway, and famous for its gorges. It is worth making the arduous journey to see these wonders of nature. **Nitmiluk** (Katherine Gorge) **National Park** is 32 km (20 miles) out of town, and access may be limited during the wet season. The main geological structure is split up into 13 sandstone gorges. On either side of the Katherine River are 70-m (230-ft) walls which change color according to the weather and time of day. The best time to see them is first thing in the morning. In the other direction is the sheer face of Jedda's Leap, where legend has it that a couple jumped to their deaths because they were not allowed to wed. A two-hour boat ride up the first two gorges is probably the best way to appreciate their awesome beauty, although there are longer rides that take in additional gorges. **Katherine Gorge Boat Tours** ((08) 8972-1253 FAX (08) 8971-1044, offers trips ranging from two to eight hours, with the longer trips involving some cross-country hiking.

About an hour and a half south of Katherine is one of nature's little bonuses: If the heat and endless roads become too exhausting for you, jump into the brilliantly clear thermal pool near **Mataranka**, 106 km (66 miles) from Katherine, fed by spring water bubbling to the surface at a warm 34°C (93°F). The spring supports a veritable oasis, a small pocket of palms and lush tropical forest in a landscape otherwise almost bare of vegetation. This region is called the "Never never" — those who live here can never never leave it. The nearby Elsey Station is the location of the Australian classic novel by Jeannie Gunn, *We of the Never Never*, which has been made into a film.

Woodland gives way to the scrub and red earth of the interior at **Renner Springs**, 500 km (310 miles) south of Katherine, this change marking the limit of the monsoons and the beginning of the dry center.

Near **Tennant Creek** is the site of the last gold rush in Australia that started in 1932; even today one mine is still operational. The creek itself is 11 km (seven miles) out of town because many years ago convenience overrode good intentions. In 1933, Joe Kilgariff made his way to the area with a cart carrying supplies and materials for the construction of a pub. Caught in a sudden downpour and bogged in the mud, this publican unloaded his wagon and built the pub on the spot. The thirsty miners chose to build their town next to it rather than near the water supply of the creek, just a few kilometers away!

About 105 km (65 miles) south of Tennant Creek, straddling the highway are the **Devil's Marbles** — hundreds of giant spherical granite boulders, some of which balance precariously on others. Aborigines believe that these are eggs laid by the rainbow serpent during the Dreamtime, so this is a registered sacred site for Aboriginals. The best time to view the Devil's Marbles is at dusk, when the sun's rays bring out the colors of red, yellow and brown minerals present in the granite.

You are more or less at the geographical center of the continent, when you reach **Central Mount Stuart**, a low round hill to the west of the highway, about 65 km (40 miles) past Barrow Creek.

WHERE TO STAY

There is moderately-priced accommodation along the Track, although the smaller places offer less choice.

In Katherine there is the **Pine Tree Motel** ((08) 8972-2533 TOLL-FREE 1800-089-103 FAX (08) 8972-2920, at 3 Third Street, and the **All Seasons Frontier Katherine Motor Inn** ((08) 8972-1744 FAX (08) 8972-2790.

The **Mataranka Homestead Tourist Resort** ((08) 8975-4544 FAX (08) 8975-4580, in Homestead Road, provides moderately-priced accommodation, and guests can relax in the thermal pool filled with natural spring water.

The accommodation choices in Tennant Creek are limited, but **Safari Lodge Motel** ((08) 8962-2207, at 12 Davidson Street, offers both moderately-priced rooms and inexpensive bunkrooms.

THE RED CENTER

Alice Springs, known simply as "the Alice," is widely recognized as the unofficial capital of the Red Center.

In a country where the spirit of the Outback is revered, Australians have a soft spot in their hearts for the Alice.

The area started its life as a link in the first telegraph line across the continent, completed in 1872. Each repeater station was fortified against attacks by hostile Aborigines who hadn't heard that Europeans now "owned" the land which they had occupied for more than 40,000 years.

In 1933 the original name, Stuart, was changed to Alice Springs, after the wife of Sir Charles Todd who was responsible for the

Alice Springs

Alice Springs is at the foot of the **MacDonnell Ranges**, whose ever-changing colors provide an attractive backdrop to the town. There are several points of interest worth exploring before going further afield to the MacDonnell Ranges.

Never have you seen a zoo like the **Alice Springs Desert Park** ((08) 8951-8788, a short 10-minute drive west of town. In the

construction of the Overland Telegraph Line. Sir Charles had the river named after him, no great honor as it is dry most of the year.

Until 20 years ago the population had struggled to reach 4,000, when the Alice survived as a railhead to move cattle southwards. Today the permanent population has grown to about 14,000, supported mainly by tourism which has boomed since the world discovered the "Red Center". The town receives an estimated 150,000 visitors a year.

GENERAL INFORMATION

The **Visitor Information Centre** ((08) 8952-5800, on Gregory Street, is open 9 AM to 6 PM weekdays, 9 AM to 4 PM weekends.

1,300-hectare (3,200-acre) park, four arid habitats have been created, and populated with 120 animals and 320 plants typical of the ecosystem. Seldom seen animals such as the golden bandicoot, Lake Eyre dragon lizard, Western Desert quoll and native cat roam the park. On entering the park stop by the theater where a 20-minute film brings to life the development of desert environments. There are walks through the four different habitats with signs explaining the animals and plants that live in the area. The highlight of the park is the Nocturnal Shed, in which animals that only

An artist's impression of Alice Springs decorates the wall of the market town's shopping center.

come out at night, and are rarely seen by tourists, scurry about.

Built between 1870 and 1872, the **Telegraph Station Historical Reserve (** (08) 8952-3993, on the Stuart Highway, contains a reconstruction of the stone repeater station that was a vital link in the 3,000-km (1,860-mile) Overland Telegraph line. The historic reserve is open daily, and there is a small admission fee charged. There are guided tours from May to September. To get a greater appreciation of the history of central Australia visit the **Old Timer's Folk**

Although his work is universally admired he died a tragic figure in 1959, unable to claim the fundamental human rights white Australians take for granted. You can see works by this great Australian artist in the **Strehlow Art Centre (** (08) 8951-8000, in Larapinta Drive.

The area around the Alice abounds in fascinating and astounding geological features. Certainly the best way to see it is by car or coach; but, be warned that traveling a few hundred kilometers a day is not considered excessive in the Outback. For the

Museum ((08) 8952-2844, on the Stuart Highway south of Alice Springs, which contains displays of relics from the early pioneer days and is open from 2 PM to 4 PM; a small admission fee is charged.

At the **Old Pioneer Cemetery** on George Crescent, only a few headstones remain. Buried here are two men who are part of the Red Center's colorful history — one of them, Harold Lasseter, set out into the desert in 1930 with two camels, never to return. His last diary entry tantalizingly declared that he had found a fabulously rich gold reef, which subsequently, no prospector has ever succeeded in finding. The other, Albert Namatjira, immortalized many features of the MacDonnell Ranges in watercolor paintings.

more adventurous there are camel safaris into the MacDonnell Ranges offered by **Frontier Camel Tours (** (08) 8953-0444 FAX (08) 8955-5015.

MacDonnell Ranges

Fifty kilometers (31 miles) west of Alice Springs in the MacDonnell Ranges is **Standley Chasm**, nine meters (30 ft) wide and 80 m (260 ft) deep. The chasm is on Aboriginal territory and a small entry fee is charged. **Chamber's Pillar** is off the Gap Road, 165 km (102 miles) south of Alice Springs, a protuberance of wind-eroded sandstone over 350 million years old standing 50 m (164 ft) above the surrounding plain, and a landmark visible from afar. **Ormiston**

Gorge is another feature in the MacDonnell Ranges well worth visiting.

For a different view of the MacDonnell Ranges, take to the air for a sunrise balloon ride. **Spinifex Ballooning** TOLL-FREE 1800-677-893 or (08) 8953-4800 FAX (08) 8952-2862, offers a 60-minute flight for AU$140, which includes a champagne breakfast.

Uluru (Ayers Rock)

Uluru (formerly known as Ayers Rock) is the most famous feature of the Red Center. Its domed silhouette is as distinctively Australian as the pyramids are Egyptian or Eiffel Tower French.

Ayers Rock was first sighted by Europeans in 1873, when surveyor William Gosse saw the Rock during an expedition to map the 2,400 km (1,500 miles) of desert between Alice Springs and Perth.

Uluru is on the World Heritage list and part of a 132,566-hectare (327,450-acre) park.

This single rock, the peak of a buried mountain, rises 384 m (1,260 ft) from the surrounding plain; the perimeter is some nine kilometers (5.5 miles) at its base. The flanks of the rock are etched with deep gullies which fill with rushing water when it rains.

The sandstone monolith is rich in the crystalline mineral feldspar, giving the rock its colors which vary with the time and weather. On sunny days it is red to orange; when wet it changes to black, white or shades of purple. Even a novice photographer can take stunning photographs at dawn or sunset when the colors are most vivid.

In 1985 the government handed the Pitjantjantjara and Yankunytjatjara people freehold title over the land which they leased back to the government for 99 years. They did, however, change the name back to its original "Uluru."

Sacred to local Aborigines, Uluru abounds in Aboriginal legends; every crevice and contoured shape has a Dreamtime story attached to it. For example, on the south side the indentations in the rock are where spears scored it in a battle between the poisonous snake people, the Leru, and

Fascinating Aboriginal legends about the crevices OPPOSITE in Uluru (Ayers Rock) are told on a special tour around the rock. RIGHT: The trail to the summit.

Northern Territory

the sleeping lizard people, the Loongardi. Learn more about Aboriginal mythology on trips around the rock with **Anangu Tours** ((08) 8956-2123.

It is possible to climb to the top and there are handrails and guide chains to help climbers on the more difficult sections. The round trip to the summit takes about two hours. About 75,000 people begin the climb each year and most succeed. Some climbers turn back at a place called "chicken rock," so don't be too embarrassed if you don't make it.

If you feel like traveling a bit on the wild side then **Uluru Motor Cycle Tours** ((08) 8956-2019 FAX (08) 8956-2196, will rent you a Harley Davidson for the journey from Ayers Rock Resort to Uluru, or drivers will take you out to the Rock.

The Olgas (Kata Tjuta)

A range of domed rocks called the Olgas (or Kata Tjuta by Aborigines), lies 27 km (17 miles) to the west. **Mount Olga** itself is higher than Uluru, rising 546 m (1,790 ft) above the surrounding plain. The Olgas were best described by their European discoverer, Ernest Giles, who wrote "Mount Olga displayed to our astonished eyes rounded minarets, giant cupolas, and monstrous domes." Driving around the Olgas cannot beat walking through this strange collection of giant rocks, with its gorges and the **Valley of the Wind**.

WHERE TO STAY

Luxury accommodation in the Alice is available from **Plaza Hotel Alice** ((08) 8952-8000, in Barrett Drive. If you want to be close to the casino stay at the **Vista Alice Springs** TOLL-FREE 1800-810-664 FAX (08) 8952-1988, or **Lasseter's Hotel Casino** TOLL-FREE 1800-808-975 FAX (08) 8953-1680, at 93 Barrett Drive.

For real Outback accommodation try **Ross River Homestead** ((08) 8956-9711 FAX (08) 8956-9823, on the Ross Highway, 80 km (50 miles) out of Alice Springs, where you stay in slab timber cabins. There are several adventure trips organized out of the Homestead, and if you have always wanted to learn to throw a boomerang, then lessons are provided by Mike Turner at 10 AM every day.

The quiet **Outback Motor Lodge** TOLL-FREE 1800-896-133 FAX (08) 8953-2166, at South Terrace, is moderately priced as is the nearby **Gapview Resort Hotel** ((08) 8952-6611 TOLL-FREE 1800-896-124 FAX (08) 8952-8312, at the corner of Gap Street and South Terrace.

HOW TO GET THERE

Uluru is approximately 470 km (290 miles) southwest of Alice Springs and reached by taking the turnoff from the Stuart Highway onto the Lasseter Highway.

There are daily flights into Uluru from Alice Springs, Cairns, Melbourne, Sydney and Perth.

There are daily bus services between Alice Springs and Uluru, and many commercial package tours of Uluru and the Olgas are available.

NATIONAL PARKS

The oldest river in the world carved **Finke Gorge**, 155 km (96 miles) west of Alice Springs, into the surrounding plain. It is noted for its cabbage palms, a vestige of when the area was much wetter, and can only be reached by four-wheel drive vehicles.

The **Henbury Meteorite Conservation Park**, 150 km (93 miles) southwest of Alice Springs, contains a series of craters formed 4,700 years ago when a shower of meteorites struck the Earth at about 40,000 kph (25,000 mph). The largest is 183 m (600 ft) wide and 15 m (50 ft) deep.

Simpsons Gap National Park, 22 km (14 miles) west of Alice Springs, features several gaps. Access is easy with several walking tracks as well as a 17-km (10-mile) cycle track through the park.

National parks information can be obtained in Darwin ((08) 8999-3881 FAX (08) 8981-0653, Alice Springs ((08) 8951-8211 FAX (08) 8951-8268 and Katherine ((08) 8973-8770 FAX (08) 8972-2373.

Best seen at sunrise and sunset, Uluru (Ayers Rock) rises out of the desert displaying an astonishing variety of colors.

South Australia
Hidden
Treasures

SOUTH AUSTRALIA has lived under a heavy historical disability. As the one state that never accepted convicts, South Australia has no notable prisons, guard houses, police barracks or courthouses with which to interest tourists. To compensate, the industrious free settlers built churches and beautiful colonial sandstone buildings. In its capital, Adelaide, extensive parklands were established along the sluggish Torrens River.

In the twentieth century a love for culture was added, with the inauguration of the Adelaide Arts Festival, the first such event in Australia. To complete the picture of an entirely civilized place, South Australians acquired an appreciation of fine wines. The best, as any South Australian will quickly tell you, are made exclusively in this state's Clare Valley, McLaren Vale and Barossa Valley.

ADELAIDE

Adelaide is set out on a grid pattern with broad avenues and immaculate streetscapes which reflect its graciousness. Just across the Torrens River lies North Adelaide, both the city's first suburb and one of the more elegant in Australia. Surrounding Adelaide are 668 hectares (1,650 acres) of parklands, the pride and joy of the city. They are made for strolling through, playing on or just looking at.

Beyond the city, the suburbs stretch to the low sand dunes of the Gulf St. Vincent in the west, and up into the green folds of the Adelaide Hills to the east.

Once known as the "City of Churches," Adelaide's respectable exterior hides a more risqué underside.

BACKGROUND

Founded in 1836, South Australia was a reaction by its liberal founders to the convict base of other colonies. Social theorist, Edward Gibbon Wakefield, believed that colonies could grow on the capital raised from the sale of Crown land to free settlers. He argued that a civilized community could only thrive with such colonists. Ironically, Wakefield hatched his scheme while in spending time in Newgate Prison for abducting a fifteen-year-old heiress. His proposal was initially

rejected by the government. By the time it had been accepted in a modified form Wakefield had lost interest, but his supporters remained committed to his plan. On August 15, 1834, Westminster passed an Act for the Establishment of the Colony of South Australia.

In 1836 Colonel William Light, the first Surveyor-General, chose the location for Adelaide. Later that year Governor Hindmarsh arrived to administer the new colony. A raging quarrel erupted between the two men who disagreed on where Adelaide

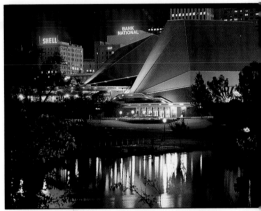

should be sited. To an onlooker this squabble was out of place in the civilized colony both men wished to found. The volatile Hindmarsh followed his run-in with Colonel Light with petty disputes with land developers, and was recalled by the Imperial Government in 1838.

Surviving without convict labor proved difficult. It was only economic stimulation provided by copper discoveries, in Kapunda in 1842 and Burra in 1845 that allowed Adelaide to embark on an ambitious building program. Fortunately many of these churches, public buildings and houses built in the late nineteenth century survive today, adding to the city's charm.

GENERAL INFORMATION

The **South Australian Tourism Commission Travel Centre** ((08) 8212-1505 TOLL-FREE 1800-882-092, located at One King William

OPPOSITE: Adelaide's Rundle Mall is a pedestrian-only shopping precinct. The Festival Centre ABOVE is home to the best arts festival in the country.

Street, is open weekdays from 9 AM to 5 PM and provides information, books accommodation and can arrange tours throughout the state. It is open every day although on weekends it closes at 2 PM. The **Royal Automobile Association of South Australia** ((08) 8202-4540, at 41 Hindmarsh Square, sells maps, offers information about road conditions and makes reservations for accommodation. In Glenelg there is a **Tourist Information Centre** ((08) 8294-5833, on the foreshore at Bayworld Museum, which is open daily.

Information about Adelaide's public transport can be obtained from the **Passenger Transport Information Centre** ((08) 8210-1000, on the corner of King William and Currie street open 7 AM to 8 PM. For information on country and interstate trains phone ((08) 8231-4366 from 8:30 AM to 5:30 PM weekdays.

WHAT TO SEE AND DO

Central City

The easy way to explore Adelaide is on the **Adelaide Explorer Bus**. The two-and-a-half hour journey, starting at the travel center at One King William Street, is a round trip of Glenelg and the city. Passengers can get on and off the tram as often as they like on the same ticket. However, Colonel Light's urban layout for Adelaide and its flat topography makes it a walker's delight.

After exiting the travel center, turn into **North Terrace**, Adelaide's most charming boulevard. Along its dignified tree-lined length are South Australia's seats of political power, learning and culture. I'm uncertain into which of these categories to put the **Adelaide Casino** ((08) 8218-4111, which is also in North Terrace and housed in a renovated railway station, undoubtedly the most elegant in Australia. Its interior is crowded with tables set for blackjack, craps, baccarat and roulette, while video poker machines are located on the first floor of the casino. Between Monday and Thursday it is open from 10 AM to 4 AM. The closing hour is extended to 6 AM at weekends and on holidays. Dress requirements are for smart casual clothes. Jeans are acceptable; running shoes and T-shirts are not.

East along North Terrace is the **Old Parliament House** ((08) 8226-8555, built in 1855, which has now been turned into a constitutional museum with constantly changing exhibitions.

Nearby is the **Art Gallery of South Australia** ((08) 8207-7000, with an excellent collection of Australian art. While there, make sure you see works by Hans Heysen who painted the rocks of the Flinders Ranges and mighty ghost gums.

The **University of Adelaide** is crammed between North Terrace and the river. The overcrowding, however, has not robbed the predominantly neo-Gothic campus of its academic repose. While on campus drop into the **Museum of Classical Archaeology** ((08) 8303-5239, on the first floor of the Mitchell Building off North Terrace, which exhibits artifacts from ancient Rome, Greece and Egypt, some dating back 5,000 years. The museum is open weekdays from noon to 3 PM.

Further along North Terrace are the **Botanic Gardens and State Herbarium** ((08) 8228-2311, a relaxing 30 hectares (75 acres) of shady lawns and promenades. Down the center of the gardens magnificent 120-year-old Moreton Bay fig trees line the avenue to the Main Lake. Near the Plane Tree Drive entrance is the **Bicentennial Conservatory**, a giant glasshouse in which a fine spray of water nourishes lush rain forest, beautiful flowers and waterside plants. While in the gardens, open daily, it is hard to imagine that a major city is just a few hundred meters away.

Ayers House at 228 North Terrace, just opposite the Royal Adelaide Hospital, was built in 1855. Home to Sir Henry Ayers, who was elected Premier of South Australia for a record seven times, the stately mansion is open to the public Tuesday to Sunday.

Turn right after Ayers House into East Terrace, and after a couple of minutes' walk is the **Tandanya Aboriginal Cultural Institute** ((08) 8224-3200, at 253 Grenfell Street. The institute supports Aboriginal culture, art and dance, and its activities and exhibitions are open to the public. Authentic Aboriginal art and artifacts can be purchased from the center, which is open from 10 AM to 5 PM. Grenfell Street leads into **King William**

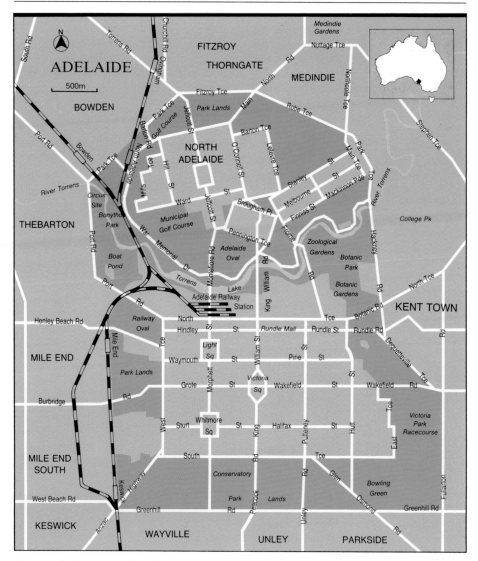

Street, which, at 42 m (140 ft), is the widest of any Australian city thoroughfare, bisecting the city and continuing into North Adelaide.

The center of Adelaide is marked by **Victoria Square**, located at the junction of Grote, Wakefield and King William streets. Just north of Victoria Square is the **Post Office**, built in 1867, and the imposing Renaissance-style **Town Hall** built between 1863 and 1866, inspired by public buildings in Florence and Genoa. There are one-hour tours of the interior of the Town Hall every Tuesday and Thursday at 10:30 AM and 2:30 PM.

Festival Centre

The **Festival Centre**, overlooking the Torrens River, is located off King William Street north of the city. Opened in 1973, the same year as the celebrated Sydney Opera House, the Centre is the focus of Adelaide's cultural life. Its admirers assert that while the Festival Centre cost one tenth of the Opera House it is ten times more successful. Spite may have motivated this claim, but what is indisputable is that the Festival Centre is made for comfort, its concert halls have excellent acoustics and its stages are functional. The superb complex houses the Festival Theatre, an experimental theater, the

Playhouse, an amphitheater for outdoor performances and a plaza for informal cultural gatherings, such as poetry readings.

The Festival Centre is the main venue of Adelaide's well-known **Arts Festival** which attracts top performers from overseas and Australia to sing, act, and dance for enthusiastic audiences. This was mainly a hometown affair when it started in 1960 but today visitors attracted by its reputation pack Adelaide for the 10-day festival, a benchmark by which cultural festivals in other states are measured.

Port Adelaide

The port was established in 1840 and boasts some of the finest historic buildings in South Australia. Solid stone warehouses, workmen's cottages and wharves are a reminder of an era when the port was home to clippers and steamships. Explore the area bounded by Nelson Street, St. Vincent Street, Todd Street and McLaren Parade for intact nineteenth-century streetscapes. The area's history is on display in the **Maritime Museum** ((08) 8240-0200, at 126 Lipson Street.

Glenelg

The first settlement in Adelaide was at Glenelg, which today is a pleasant seaside suburb. To get there take Adelaide's only tram, which starts at Victoria Square and is a pleasant 30-minute ride to Jetty Road, Glenelg's main thoroughfare.

In Macfarlane Street, Glenelg North, a plaque marks where Governor Hindmarsh proclaimed South Australia a British colony. The plaque can be seen next to the arched remains of an ancient gum tree. Nearby, in the **Patawalonga Boat Haven** ((08) 8294-2122, in Adelphi Terrace, is a replica of Hindmarsh's ship, the *Buffalo*, which has been converted into a museum and eating establishment.

ADELAIDE AFTER DARK

The liveliest spot in the city is Hindley Street, with its many pubs and restaurants. It also includes one of the more infamous strip joints in Australia called the **Crazy Horse** at 141A Hindley Street.

There are also some good nightclubs in and around Hindley Street. The **Cartoons Nightclub** at 145 Hindley Street has live music most nights of the week and a dance club, while **Rio's International** at 111 Hindley Street is more upmarket. The daily newspaper, the *Adelaide Advertiser*, is a good source of information on what is happening in Adelaide. On Thursday the Guide section provides information on theater and band venues. The free newspaper *Rip It Up* is left lying around pubs and music shops, and contains a wealth of information on the local

music scene. *The Adelaide Review* provides an excellent and critical guide to theater, concerts and dance and is distributed free of charge at better bookshops.

WHERE TO SHOP

Rundle Mall is lined with department stores, coffee shops and cinemas. Colorful flower stalls and a fountain make it a pleasant setting to shop, or to sit back in an outdoor café and be entertained by buskers. There are a number of arcades leading off the mall for those seeking even greater shopping variety. The **Myers Centre** fronts the mall and it is worth dropping into its international food hall on the lower ground floor.

The **Central Market** has operated from its site in Grote Street for over 120 years and specializes in fresh foodstuffs. Kangaroo and emu meat can be purchased in the meat section. In Rundle Street near Frome Street is the **East End Market**, open weekends. It has an enormous food hall that can seat 150 people, and offers a choice of Chinese, Italian and other cuisines from around the world, but its main attraction is its stalls selling crafts, clothing and souvenirs.

Opals are a popular souvenir. A form of silica, quality opals come in various colors

and Design Centre ((08) 8410-0727, at 19 Morphett Street, is a government project. Some of the best examples of local pottery, paintings, sculpture, weaving and glassware can be seen in its gallery, which exhibits contemporary works. There is also a retail shop that sells crafts, with many pieces being produced by craftspeople who work in studios on the premises. Visitors are free to visit the studios to see artists at work, either in furniture design, ceramics, glass and metal. There are also some very good private galleries in Adelaide. Original Australian hand-

— orange, red, yellow and the rare blue. The best opals have large areas of uniform color and have no fractures or flaws. South Australia's come in light colors. The best place to learn more about them is **Opal Field Gems** ((08) 8212-5300, at 33 King William Street, where you can see them being cut; they also have a video running on the history of opal mining. Opal jewelry can be purchased from **Olympic Opal** ((08) 8267-5100, at 142 Melbourne Street in North Adelaide, and black opals from **Bartram Opals** ((08) 8223-3684, at 30 Gawler Place.

Adelaide supports a lively community of craftspeople. Turn a corner and more likely than not you will come across the works of local artists. The **Jam Factory Craft**

made arts and crafts can be purchased from **L'unique** ((08) 8231-0030, in the City Cross Arcade off Rundle Mall, while in North Adelaide **Greenhill Galleries** ((08) 8267-2887, at 140 Barton Terrace (west), has regular exhibitions of paintings by Australian artists.

Outside the central shopping precinct are several streets in the suburbs with much to offer. **Melbourne** in North Adelaide is a lively avenue of trendy restaurants, boutiques and gift shops, while for antiques **Unley Road** and **Goodwood Road** should be explored.

ABOVE and OPPOSITE: Outdoor art at Adelaide's Festival Centre.

SPORTS

South Australia supports a good basketball team, the National Basketball League Adelaide 36ers. When they play at home the venue is the Clipsal Powerhouse in William Street, Beverley.

Football is taken seriously, and **Football Park** in Turner Drive, West Lakes, is usually filled with quite a partisan crowd whenever the Adelaide Crows or Port Power play at home. Cricket and football are played at the Adelaide Oval off King William Road.

The **City of Adelaide Golf Links** ((08) 8267-2171, has two 18-hole courses.

WHERE TO STAY

Luxury

The **Grosvenor Vista** ((08) 8407-8888 TOLL-FREE 1800-888-222 FAX (08) 8407-8866, at 125 North Terrace, is conveniently located across from the casino. The **Adelaide Meridien** ((08) 8267-3033 TOLL-FREE 1800-888-228 FAX 8239-0275, at 21–37 Melbourne Street, North Adelaide, has spacious rooms and executive suites are available with separate lounge and bar.

For something a little different try out the **North Adelaide Heritage Apartments** (/FAX (08) 8272-1355, which offer a choice of historic cottages dating from the turn of the century. Many of the apartments are fitted with colonial antique furnishings and the rooms are scented with fresh flowers.

There are rooms with great ocean views at the **Stamford Grand Hotel** ((08) 8376-1222 TOLL-FREE 1800-882-777 FAX (08) 8376-1111, in Moseley Square, Glenelg. The hotel is also handy for access to the airport, just five minutes away.

Moderate

Largs Pier ((08) 8449-5666, at 198 The Esplanade, Largs Bay, is an impressive three-story hotel with wide colonial verandahs. When built in 1883 it was able to offer the luxury of sea water and hot and cold fresh water on tap. These days it retains its stylish reputation but not the sea water on tap. Attached to the main building are 17 motel-style units. In North Adelaide, the **Old Adelaide Inn**

((08) 8267-5066 TOLL-FREE 1800-888-378 FAX (08) 8267-2946, at 160 O'Connell Street, is only about 20 years old — its name is misleading. Ask for a quiet room if the noise from the main road is likely to bother you.

Inexpensive

Princes Lodge ((08) 8267-5566, located at 73 Lefevre Terrace, North Adelaide, offers budget accommodation within walking distance of the city. At Glenelg there is **St. Vincent** ((08) 8294-4377, at 28 Jetty Road, and a few blocks away is the **Norfolk Motel** ((08) 8295-6354, at 69–71 Broadway.

WHERE TO EAT

Any visitor to Adelaide is dared by locals to try South Australia's national dish — the pie floater — a meat pie sitting in green pea soup. Should you feel both peckish and brave, **Cowley's Pie Cart** (inexpensive) opens after 6 PM outside the Post Office on Franklin Street, while **Balfour's** (inexpensive) is outside the casino on North Terrace.

There are also more conventional places to eat. Adelaide has many good restaurants where meals can be enjoyed with a bottle of wine from the admirable vineyards of the Barossa and Clare valleys or McLaren Vale.

At the western end of Hindley Street there are good, inexpensive and moderately-priced restaurants which are noisy and full of life. As this is also the entertainment center of the city, the restaurants keep filling with customers during the evening and meals can be obtained from late afternoon; alternatively, have a later supper after a show. For Lebanese food try **Quiet Waters** ((08) 8231-3637, at 75 Hindley Street (inexpensive), or **Jerusalem Sheshkabab** ((08) 8212-6185, at 131B Hindley Street (inexpensive). A tasty Sri Lankan meal, amazingly cheap, is available from the **Ceylon Hut** ((08) 8231-2034, at 27 Bank Street. This simple café is located just off Hindley Street and is not open on Sunday. Run by Vietnamese Buddhists, the **Blossom's Vegetarian** ((08) 8212-7805, at 167 Hindley Street (inexpensive), takes the humble bean curd and serves it in an amazing variety of interesting dishes.

Restaurants in North Adelaide are more upmarket. Overlooking the city, perched on the top floor of the Hotel Adelaide International, is **The Brougham (** (08) 8267-3444, at 62 Brougham (expensive), specializing in seafood. Fine Italian cuisine is served in **Casa Mia Restaurant (** (08) 8267-2410, at 141 Melbourne Street (moderate). If you like Cajun fish and the exotic flavors of Creole cooking try **Bacall's (** (08) 8267-2030, at 149 Melbourne Street (moderate). Another restaurant area is in Gouger Street, which has a wide selection of Asian and

berra. Adelaide is a fine starting point for exploring the Outback and there are good services to Alice Springs, Uluru (Ayers Rock), Broken Hill, Ceduna, Coober Pedy, Katherine, Mount Gambier and Tennant Creek.

There are regular bus services from Alice Springs, Canberra, Darwin, Perth, Sydney and Melbourne.

The *Indian–Pacific* train, linking the Indian and Pacific Oceans, passes through Adelaide on its journey from Perth to Sydney. The *Ghan* makes the 20-hour journey

European-style restaurants. There is even a restaurant that serves indigenous Australian food: kangaroo, yabbies and (you lucky people!) witchetty grubs, when they can get them. The **Red Ochre Grill (** (08) 8212-7266, at 129 Gouger Street (moderate), has a café that opens up into a formal restaurant. For a simply delicious meal try the chargrilled emu medallions or Murray cod garnished with bush herbs.

HOW TO GET THERE

A number of international flights include stopovers in Adelaide, and from other states there are direct flights from Melbourne, Sydney, Darwin, Perth and Can-

from Alice Springs easy going, as the train is equipped with excellent dining facilities and a bar.

DAY TRIPS FROM ADELAIDE

ADELAIDE HILLS

The Adelaide Hills rise out of the central plain and provide a perfect view of the city to the west. Being so close, a day trip to the hills is an agreeable weekend activity (see SHORT BREAKS in YOUR CHOICE).

Adelaide is renowned for its open spaces, such as here on the waterfront promenade at Glenelg Beach around the Ramada Grand Hotel and town hall clock tower.

There are many picturesque villages and hamlets in the Adelaide Hills worth visiting. One of the most popular destinations is **Hahndorf**, just thirty minutes away from Adelaide.

In 1838, 52 Lutheran families fleeing Prussia settled on 60 hectares (150 acres) of farmland in the hills 30 km (19 miles) east of Adelaide. The settlement was named Hahndorf after the Danish captain of the *Zebra*, the ship that brought them to South Australia. The community prospered; however, when the First World War broke out German-

German. In Hahndorf many of the original structures have been preserved and the German heritage of the gabled village is evident everywhere.

As the township was founded by Lutherans it follows that their religion was manifested in two fine old churches — **St. Michael's** constructed in 1858, and **St. Paul's**, constructed in 1890. Both churches are still used by the local community. The **Blacksmith's Shop** and neighboring buildings were also built in the nineteenth century. There are also German restaurants in the

speakers encountered hostility from other Australians. For a while Hahndorf changed its name to Ambleside to disguise its origins, but reverted to its original name in 1935. Other German villages in the Adelaide Hills also changed names but not all reverted to their original names after the war.

General Information

The **Adelaide Hills Tourism Information Centre** ((08) 8388-1185, at 41 Main Street, Hahndorf, provides brochures on attractions in the Adelaide Hills.

What to See and Do

The architecture of many buildings and cottages in the Adelaide Hills is typically

town, and best of all, the **German Cake Shop** at Two Pine Street, which serves the sweet sacher torte.

Numerous other villages are scattered around these hills where many interesting galleries can be found. In Clarendon you will find **The Old Clarendon Gallery** ((08) 8383-6219, with regularly changing exhibitions, while in the town of Meadows the **Paris Creek Pottery** ((08) 8388-3224, offers local craftware.

The unique **Warrawong Sanctuary** ((08) 8370-9422, on Stock Road, Mylor, is home to an assortment of smaller indigenous animals such as brush-tailed bettongs, tammar wallabies and rainbow lorikeets. Its main claim to fame is its breeding colony of platypuses, the only such colony in existence. The best time to see the wildlife is at dusk, and the management has organized walks each evening at sunset. Reservations are required.

Where to Stay

Rather than staying in Adelaide many travelers prefer one of the charming guesthouses or bed-and-breakfast places in the Adelaide Hills.

The **Apple Tree Cottage** ((08) 8388-4193, at Oakbank, is a secluded self-contained and moderately-priced settlers' cottage set in 70 hectares (170 acres) of farmland. At Aldgate there are some pretty bed-and-breakfast spots tucked away in the hills. The **Adelaide Hills Nation Ridge Country Retreat** ((08) 8370-9119 FAX (08) 8370-9484, at 11 Nation Ridge Road, provides elegant lodging on a one-hectare (two-acre) property; dinners are available on request at this luxury-priced accommodation. Within easy reach of good restaurants, art galleries and wineries is the moderately-priced **Aldgate Lodge Bed & Breakfast** ((08) 8370-9957 FAX (08) 8370-9749, located at 27 Strathalbyn Road.

Also in the moderate price range is the conventional **Hahndorf Inn Motor Lodge** ((08) 8388-1000 TOLL-FREE 1800-882-682 FAX (08) 8388-1092.

How to Get There

The Adelaide Hills region is about 30 km (19 miles) from the city and can be reached by taking the signposted turn-off on the South-Eastern Freeway. Several coach companies offer tours of the hills which show you the main sights.

BAROSSA VALLEY

German Lutherans fled their native land because they found religious persecution by the King of Prussia intolerable. In an expedition lead by Pastor August Kavel, 468 Prussians and Silesians and Pomeranians arrived in Australia from their homeland in 1838.

These immigrants had a profound influence on the new colony, and its architecture. The Barossa Valley is dotted with many

Prussian villages. The origin of the valley's name is Spanish but the local German population referred to it as "New Silesia" for many years.

The German immigrants brought with them considerable agricultural knowledge. When in 1847 grape vines were found to thrive in the valley many farms became vineyards. Today approximately 9,000 hectares (22,200 acres) of vineyards are under cultivation. The Barossa Valley produces approximately one third of Australia's total wine output, and is well-known among

those who have discovered that Australia produces excellent wines.

GENERAL INFORMATION

Information can be obtained at the **Barossa Valley Tourist Information & Wine Centre** ((08) 8563-0600, in Coulthard House at 66 Murray Street, Tanunda, at the northern end of the Barossa Valley. In Adelaide, information can be obtained from the **Gawler Visitor Centre** ((08) 8522-6814, at Two Lyndoch Road.

OPPOSITE: Wine tastings are offered at the historic Bridgewater Mill in the Adelaide Hills. ABOVE: Autumnal tones at Chateau Reynella winery.

WHAT TO SEE AND DO

The valley is more than 40 km (25 miles) long and 11 km (seven miles) wide and is easily accessible from Adelaide, just 50 km (31 miles) away.

The main destinations in the Barossa Valley are indeed its wineries, many of which are open for tours and tastings. More than 50 are situated in the area; usually signs along the road are sufficient to direct visitors. The main ones are concentrated

kilometers to the west you can walk down the shady street of **Bethany** — the valley's oldest village which was founded in 1842 — and pass by the thatched barns and pretty rustic cottages of an earlier, more romantic period.

WHERE TO STAY

For luxurious accommodation stay at the **Woodlands Vineyard Homestead (** (08) 8524-4511, at the corner of Barossa Valley Way and Altona Road in Lyndoch.

along the Barossa Highway between Lyndoch and Nuriootpa.

Penfolds on Tanunda Road, Nuriootpa, and **Seppeltsfield Winery** in Seppeltsfield are two of the oldest vineyards in the region and they invite visitors to come taste their wines.

One of the more picturesque towns in the Barossa Valley is **Tanunda**, which features old buildings and cottages built in architectural styles common in Germany in the mid-nineteenth century. Traditional games such as German skittles are still a favorite pastime. Other evidence of the region's German heritage can be seen in the **Barossa Historical Museum (** (08) 8563-0507, at 47 Murray Street; open daily. A few

In the heart of the Barossa in Nuriootpa are the **Nuriootpa Vine Inn (** (08) 8562-2133 FAX (08) 8562-3236, at 14–22 Murray Street, and the **Karawatha Guest House (** (08) 8562-1746, in Greenock Road, both of which are moderately priced.

Located in Tanunda, the luxury-priced **Stonewell Cottages (** (08) 8563-2019, in Stonewell Street, are full of character. Very close in price is the **Lawley Farm (**/FAX (08) 8563-2141, on Krondorf Road, run by Bruce and Sancha Withers who do everything they can to make their collection of nineteenth-century stone cottages comfortable for guests whom they invite into their elegant farmhouse each morning for a hearty breakfast.

HOW TO GET THERE

The Barossa Valley can be reached from Adelaide by taking the Main North Road to Gawler, and then turning right towards Lyndoch. The first wineries appear along the road within 70 minutes' driving.

FLEURIEU PENINSULA

The Fleurieu Peninsula is just south of Adelaide, and has long been a favorite family holiday area with fishing and water sports the main activities.

GENERAL INFORMATION

The **Victor Harbour Tourist Information Centre** ((08) 8552-5738, at 10 Railway Terrace, **Strathalbyn Tourist Information Centre** ((08) 8536-3212, in South Terrace, and the **Goolwa Tourist Information Centre** ((08) 8555-1144, in Cadell Street, provide general information about the Fleurieu Peninsula.

WHAT TO SEE AND DO

At the northern end of the peninsula is **McLaren Vale**, a lesser-known wine making region than the Barossa Valley. There are more small vineyards here that produce quality wines with character. The roads around McLaren Vale are not clogged with tour coaches, and at the smaller vineyards the winemakers are more likely to take time to chat about their favorite topic — making wine. These vineyards are scattered in the hills around the township of McLaren Vale, and most have tastings and sales on the premises.

Seaview Winery in Chaffey's Road is one of the best known in the area. Take some time to search out the smaller vineyards which survive on their reputations and sell wine from their own premises; they are able to produce some quite remarkable wines which shame the more established brands. One is **Noon's** ((08) 8323-8290, tucked away on Rifle Range Road, where tastings are in a shed off the main homestead, and Drew Noon is more than happy to talk about his

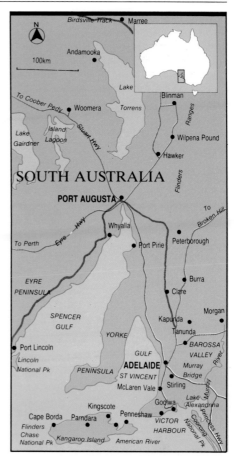

produce over a plate of cheese, biscuits and a glass of his best Shiraz. There is also a barbecue area in the vineyard where visitors can have a picnic and perhaps try out a Noon's Riesling.

Low hills run down the center of the peninsula, where historic towns dot the landscape. Their placid appearance belies their past; smugglers once worked the region, evading customs officials as they landed spirits and tobacco illicitly. Many a gang of contraband runners have rowed their illegal merchandise up the Onkaparinga River and hidden in Old Noarlunga, where the old Horseshoe Inn was a favorite hideout.

About 40 km (25 miles) from McLaren Vale is the seaside town of **Victor Harbour**, a popular destination for vacationers from

Western River Cove provides a safe haven for boats exploring the Kangaroo Island Coast.

Adelaide. A causeway connects the town to **Granite Island** and visitors can take a horse tramway across the bridge. The service runs daily from 10 AM to 4 PM.

Another way to explore the peninsula is to take the **Cockle Train** ((08) 8391-1223, along the coast from Goolwa to Victor Harbour. The train runs every Sunday and holiday periods. The 16-km (10-mile) journey takes about 30 minutes.

Victor Harbour overlooks **Encounter Bay** where southern right whales can be seen swimming close to shore. The best time to

How to Get There

An enjoyable way to reach the Fleurieu Peninsula is aboard the **Southern Encounter** ((08) 8391-1223, a steam train that winds its way from Mt. Barker in the Adelaide Hills, and then onto Strathalbyn, Goolwa and Victor Harbour. Advance reservations are recommended; the train operates from May to November. Premier Roadlines ((08) 8415-5555, runs coaches to Goolwa daily, departing from 111 Franklin Street, Adelaide.

see them is from May to September. More information can be obtained from the **South Australian Whale Centre** ((08) 8552-5644, at Two Railway Terrace.

Where to Stay

In Victor Harbour **Smugglers** ((08) 8552 5684, located at 16 Crozier Road, is a warm, friendly guesthouse. The luxurious **Whalers' Inn** ((08) 8552-4400 FAX (08) 8552-4240, at The Bluff overlooking Encounter Bay, welcomes guests with a complimentary bottle of champagne on their arrival; the view, from its waterfront seafood restaurant, of the bayside and Granite Island is quite splendid.

KANGAROO ISLAND

At the tip of the Fleurieu Peninsula is Cape Jervis, where the ferry connects each day with Kangaroo Island, Australia's third largest island — 140 km (87 miles) long and about 60 km (37 miles) wide. There is an abundance of native wildlife and its beaches provide good viewing of penguins and seals (see WALK WITH THE ANIMALS in TOP SPOTS).

Background

Kangaroo Island was first sighted in 1802 when Matthew Flinders was circumnavigating the continent. He sent crew members ashore to shoot kangaroos for food when supplies ran low. The French, for a while, were also interested in southeast Australia and in 1803 Kangaroo Island was visited by their navigator, Nicholas Baudin, after whom several landmarks around the island were named.

Its early history is also closely connected with the sealing and whaling industries in the southern waters off Australia. Since these were banned the seal population is thriving and sightings of whales in the southern oceans are frequent.

The island abounds with indigenous wildlife. Kangaroos are everywhere, and in the **Flinders Chase National Park** at the western end lives a colony of **koalas** and Cape Barren geese.

A good place to see **fairy penguins** is along the beach at **Penneshaw**. During May and June ungainly fluffy chicks wait in burrows for their mothers' return with fish for dinner. Arrive at sunset and take a flashlight, but don't use a flash on your camera because it upsets the birds. As the night approaches they tumble out of the surf and

GENERAL INFORMATION

Tourist information can be obtained from the **Kangaroo Island Gateway Information Centre (** (08) 8553-1185, in Howard Drive, Penneshaw, which is open seven days a week; or the **National Parks and Wildlife (** (08) 8553-2381, which supplies information on camping and nature tours.

WHAT TO SEE AND DO

The best way to travel is by car; you can take your own automobile over on the ferry. Bike rental is also available but the number of unpaved roads on the island makes cycling less attractive.

dash to their burrows along the cliff to feed their hungry offspring.

At **Seal Bay**, a 45-minute drive from the main settlement of **Kingscote**, lives a colony of sea lions. Arrangements to see them must be made with the park ranger (** (08) 8559-4207. From a distance, the sea lions have the appearance of large boulders scattered along the clean white sand. They lie immobile on the beach, exhausted by their fishing expeditions. Occasionally one of these large mammals annoys a neighbor, a short altercation takes place, and then lethargy returns

OPPOSITE and ABOVE: Two views of a weather-sculpted granite boulder near Cape du Couedic overlooking the Southern Ocean.

with the two combatants losing interest and returning to their solitary contemplation. If disturbed by human beings they can become aggressive, and the park ranger whose hut is above the beach will advise visitors as to a safe distance from which to view them.

There is also some good surf fishing off **Emu Bay**, where bull salmon of up to five kilograms (11 lb) have been caught; and river fishing in **Middle River** and **Cygnet River** where bream, salmon trout and mullet may be hooked.

WHERE TO STAY

The best place to stay on the island is the renovated, luxury-priced **Ozone Seafront Hotel** ((08) 8553-2011 FAX (08) 8553-2249, on the foreshore at Kingscote, which is both comfortable and stylish, and has a nice bar and bistro downstairs overlooking the Western Cove.

Ellson's Seaside Guest House ((08) 8553-2030 FAX (08) 8553-2368, on Chapman Terrace, is a moderately-priced old-fashioned guesthouse in Kingscote, which also has modern motel rooms.

The moderately-priced **Wanderers Rest of Kangaroo Island** ((08) 8553-7140, in Bayview Road, overlooks American River from its hillside perch. This place is very relaxed and secluded; the only noise is native birds welcoming the dawn.

Wilderness Lighthouse Accommodation offers inexpensive cottages in heritage buildings located away from the towns, in Cape du Coudic, Cape Borda, Rocky River and Cape Willoughby. It is run by the National Parks and Wildlife Service ((08) 8559-7235 FAX (08) 8559-7268. The **Kangaroo Island Holiday Letter Agents** (/FAX (08) 8553-2340, have all types of accommodation on its books, from host farms, motels to backpacker hostels.

HOW TO GET THERE

The **Kangaroo Island Sealink** (131-301 and **Kangaroo Island Ferry Connections** TOLL-FREE 1800-018-484, run ferries between Cape Jervis and Penneshaw in a trip taking 30 minutes. The **Kangaroo Island Fast Ferries**

((08) 8295-2688, link Glenelg with Kingscote in a two-hour trip.

Emu Air TOLL-FREE 1800-182-353, and **Kendell Airlines** TOLL-FREE 1800-338-894 have flights from Adelaide to Kingscote.

BURRA

Many of the original buildings remain intact in Burra, 156 km (97 miles) north of Adelaide, one of Australia's oldest mining towns.

Approximately 50,000 tons of copper were extracted from the hills around Burra between 1845 and 1877. The boom attracted miners from Wales, Scotland and Cornwall; even small communities of Germans and

Chileans came. In the mid-nineteenth century Burra was in fact the largest inland town in Australia.

Burra is one of the undiscovered gems of South Australia, and deserves more attention than it has received. The very fact, however, that it has been ignored means that its nineteenth-century town and village streetscapes are intact and have not been tampered with by well-meaning tourism promoters trying to make them appealing.

GENERAL INFORMATION

The **Tourist Information Centre (** (08) 8892-2154, at Two Market Square, has a wealth of historic information on the town. There are organized tours by the center when enough people show interest.

WHAT TO SEE AND DO

For the visitor who doesn't mind wearing out some shoe leather, the 11-km (seven-mile) **Heritage Trail** around Burra is the best way to see most of the points of interest such as historic churches, the graveyard, colonial buildings and the copper mines. Some of the sites are out of town, and can be reached by car. A map can be bought from the Tourist Information Centre.

Decked out in formal wear, fairy penguins frequent beaches around Kingscote, Kangaroo Island at dusk.

To familiarize yourself with its history pay a visit to the National Trust of South Australia **Market Square Museum** ((08) 8892-2154, at 9 Market Square, which includes a re-creation of a general store and post office of the 1870s. A more extensive museum on the mining history of Burra is located in the **Bon Accord Mine Complex** ((08) 8892-2056, in Railway Terrace, once a working mine.

The scars of open cut mines are all around Burra, the water in them stained green by copper salts. The miners lived

within their own ethnic communities; for example, the row of stone houses along Kingston Street is where the Cornish miners lived, and **Paxton Cottage Number 1** has had its original furnishings restored and is open to the public on weekends and public holidays. Other cottages in Paxton Square have been modernized and converted into visitors' accommodation (see WHERE TO STAY, below).

The Cornish miners also lived along the river, in caves dug into the bank. Extensions to accommodate additions to the family were easily accomplished by simply excavating another room. Best of all, the miners had no rent to pay. It is estimated that 1,800 of these thrifty people lived along a

five-kilometer (three-mile) stretch of river, where several of the dwellings remain intact and can be visited as part of the Heritage Trail tour.

Another highlight of the Heritage Trail is **Hampton**, an English village built in 1857 which remained unchanged until it was abandoned in 1960. Ruined houses in various states of disrepair line its single street, and cows graze about its outskirts.

WHERE TO STAY

For a taste of the real Burra stay at **Paxton Square** ((08) 8892-2622 FAX (08) 8892-2555, in Kingston Street, which provides, refurbished 1850 miners' cottages at moderate tariffs. Other accommodation is at the moderately-priced **Tivers Row** ((08) 8892-2461, in Truro Street, or the inexpensive **Burra Caravan and Camping Park** ((08) 8892-2442, which has powered sites and on-site vans available.

HOW TO GET THERE

From Adelaide you can get to Burra by car along the Main North Road and Barrier Highway. **Bute Buses** ((08) 8826-2110, provide regular service from Adelaide Wednesday to Sunday; and **Greyhound Pioneer** (132-030, services the same route departing daily at 8 AM.

FLINDERS RANGES

Seen from Adelaide on a hot day, the Flinders Ranges shimmer in the distance, changing color — from reds and orange to blues and purple — depending on the time of day and the distance. These jagged mountains are not high but in places have a rugged beauty accentuated by the plain surrounding them. They begin south of Adelaide and stretch north into the desert interior of South Australia — a distance of around 800 km (500 miles).

The Flinders Ranges: Purple plains OPPOSITE lead into the rugged hills... but watch for crossing 'roos. The ranges ABOVE stretch into the desert interior of South Australia, a popular area for walks and drives among ochre cliffs and along rocky stream beds.

The geological history of the Flinders Ranges is complex. Formed 500 million years ago, the mountains gradually eroded to low lying hills. About 50 million years ago new disturbances pushed up the old range, resulting in a profile of saw-tooth ridges together with the rounded hills of the earlier phase.

GENERAL INFORMATION

Tourist information and maps of walking trails can be obtained from the **Peterborough Tourist Information Centre** ((08) 8651-2708, in Main Street, **Port Augusta Tourist Information Centre** ((08) 8641-0793, at 41 Flinders Terrace, and **Quorn Tourist Information Centre** ((08) 8648-6419, at 3 Seventh Street.

WHAT TO SEE AND DO

Not far from Port Augusta is **Quorn**, which was an important junction for trains servicing inland South Australia. One way to get a feel for the romance of the long-past era of the steam train is to take the **Pichi Richi Railway** ((08) 8648-6598 or (08) 8395-2566, through the Pichi Richi Pass to Woolshed. The round trip takes about three hours but the train only runs between March and November on the second and fourth Sunday, although it is worth phoning because additional trips are arranged during the tourist season.

Hawker is the gateway to the northern Flinders Ranges. Ten kilometers (six miles) south of Hawker are the **Yourambulla Caves**, which contain fine Aboriginal rock paintings and carvings.

A singularly interesting place in the district is **Wilpena Pound**, a natural amphitheater whose rocky walls and cliffs encircle an oval bowl, 20 km (12 miles) long and eight kilometers (five miles) wide. The only way in is along a track through the gap in the ramparts of the northeast corner. The bowl itself is covered with scrub, and in spring wildflowers grow in profusion. Five walking tracks snake across the basin, which although fairly flat will take a good day's hiking for the return trip. There are also shorter walks on marked tracks. If you are

willing to clamber up **St. Mary's Peak** (1,170 m or 3,840 ft) there is a marvelous view of Wilopena Pound from the top.

The Flinders Ranges are split by a number of gorges through which dirt roads wind; the sides are rich in yellows and ochres broken by the greens of the eucalypts that sprout mysteriously from the walls. **Kangaroos** inhabit the area, and you may be lucky enough to see a mountain kangaroo or a rare yellow-footed rock wallaby hopping up steep slopes or stopping to graze on the ledges.

The area is rich in Aboriginal lore: legend has it that Akurra the serpent created the ranges and formed the gorges by wriggling across the countryside. He then slithered westward to Lake Frome and drank it dry, which explains the absence of water there. He now sleeps in the Yacki water hole in the Gammon Ranges.

Interesting walks abound along the ranges' 700-km (434-mile) length, with a variety of landscape types and ecosystems. Walking maps can be obtained from the ranger's office located in Hawker, in the Port Office building.

WHERE TO STAY

The **Rawnsley Park Tourist Park** ((08) 8648-0030, in Hawker Road, provides moderately-priced cabin accommodation in the heart of the Flinders Ranges National Park. At nearby Hawker inexpensive accommodation is offered by the **Hawker Hotel-Motel** ((08) 8648-4102 FAX (08) 8648-4151, at 80 Elder Drive, and the **Outback Chapmanton Motel** ((08) 8648-4100 FAX (08) 8648-4109, at One Wilpena Road.

At Quorn there is the inexpensive **Mill Motel** ((08) 8648-6016, at Two Railway Terrace.

HOW TO GET THERE

The most scenic routes to the Flinders Ranges are north through Burra to Quorn or via the Clare Valley, through Melrose and Wilmington to Quorn. It is 66 km (45 miles)

Generations of Aboriginal artists decorated rock outcrops, which can be seen throughout the Flinders Ranges.

to Hawker, which is a good place to base yourself. The **Flinders Ranges National Park**, which protects some of the wilder sections of the mountain range, is 30 km (13 miles) from Hawker. The coastal road along Spencer Gulf to the Flinders Ranges is swampy and monotonous and is not recommended. Hawker is about 400 km (250 miles) from Adelaide.

There are good roads leading through the Flinders Ranges but many are unpaved; a four-wheel drive vehicle is recommended for a self-drive tour.

NULLARBOR PLAIN

Most people traveling from Adelaide to Perth prefer to fly, in order to avoid the flat featureless Nullarbor Plain, but not all (see THE OPEN ROAD in YOUR CHOICE).

The Plain runs along the Great Australian Bight, between **Ceduna** in South Australia toward the mining town of **Norseman** in Western Australia.

WHAT TO SEE AND DO

The 1,300-km (800-mile) Nullarbor Plain is an empty expanse of absolutely flat terrain. Its rust-colored earth is tinged grey-green by bluebush and saltbush and punctuated by one-house towns that exist solely to service the train and passing traffic.

WHERE TO STAY

Most of the accommodation in the Nullarbor Plain is on the Eyre Highway. Overlooking Murat Bay is the moderately-priced **Ceduna Community (** (08) 8625-2008, on the corner of O'Loughlin and South Terraces. Over the border into Western Australia, is the town of **Madura**, where the only accommodation is the moderately-priced **Madura Pass Oasis Motel** TOLL-FREE 1800-998-228, on the Eyre Highway. Further west the old mining area of Norseman has a reasonable range of accommodation: the **Great Western (** (08) 9029-1633, in Princep Street, is centrally located and moderately-priced. The **Norseman Hotel (** (08) 9039-1023, at 90 Roberts Street, is an inexpensive alternative; also centrally located.

HOW TO GET THERE

Coaches between Adelaide and Perth regularly travel along the Eyre Highway. Further inland is the railway, which is the last leg of the *Indian-Pacific* from Sydney. With few barriers to circumnavigate, the train track runs in an straight line for 478 km (300 miles).

COOBER PEDY

Coober Pedy, 863 km (535 miles) northwest of Adelaide, is an opal mining town on the edge of the Great Victoria Desert and makes a fascinating stopover on the way to Alice Springs.

To start a conversation with a local just mention the weather, and watch him or her wax lyrical on whether the next day will be baking hot, blistering hot, scorching, or just hot. Such conversations are preferably held over an ice cold beer, the local antidote to the heat.

Despite any boasts from its denizens, Coober Pedy is not the hottest place in Australia. That honor goes to Cloncurry in Queensland which reached 53.1°C (127°F) in 1889. Nevertheless in a town where the temperature is often over 40°C (105°F) the quality of the heat is a topic worthy of very serious discussion; when the temperature drops below 30°C (85°F) locals are known to reach for a jacket.

The town was built on the wealth of opals, discovered in the area in 1915. With a permanent population of just over 2,000, it remains the largest opal mining town in Australia (see NOODLE FOR OPALS IN THE OUTBACK in TOP SPOTS).

GENERAL INFORMATION

The **Coober Pedy Tourist Information Centre (** (08) 8672-3474, is in the Council Office in Hutchison Street, and is open 9 AM to 5 PM weekdays, 9 AM to noon Saturday and 2 PM to 5 PM Sunday.

TOP: A tourist mine. Many people in the remote opal mining town of Coober Pedy have carved out underground houses BOTTOM to avoid the heat.

WHAT TO SEE AND DO

To escape the heat and wind many miners chose to live underground in caves or dug-outs, where the temperature is a steady 24°C (75°F). Approximately 40 percent of the population live underground.

On the surface the landscape is desolate; mines and diggings cover a radius of 50 km (31 miles) around the town. Thousands upon thousands of small pyramids of white sand two to three meters (six to nine feet) in height are piled up beside old diggings. Care should be taken walking around Coober Pedy because old mines have been known to collapse in drops of up to 30 m (100 ft).

While not as close to the Almighty as they could be, the **Catacomb Church** in Cata-comb Street and **Church Saints Peter and Paul**, are both underground and a good deal cooler than had they been built along more traditional lines, soaring to the heavens. Both can be inspected daily and services are con-ducted on Sunday. In 1993 the **Serbian Church** opened in Potch Gully; its walls are covered in fine religious carvings by Norm Ashton.

Also underground is the **Umoona Opal Mine and Museum** ((08) 8672-5288, in Hutchison Street, which is a complex of chambers. Incorporated is a museum with exhibitions on opal mining and Aboriginal culture as well as an impressive display of opals. The **Old Timer's Mine** ((08) 8672-5555, in Crowder's Gully Road, is another museum which gives an intriguing insight into opal mining and includes an original 1918 miner's home. Across the road is **The Big Winch**, a giant mine winch overlooking the town. Below it is an opal and art gallery, displaying famous black opals. Another way to explore Coober Pedy is to take the **Gem City Opal Tours** ((08) 8672-5333, where Trevor McLeod, a crusty ex-miner himself, shows you around the surrounding countryside.

In the **Breakaway National Reserve** is the **Painted Desert**, which draws visitors to its ever-changing colors. You can get there by taking the Alice Springs Road for 28 km (17 miles) out of Coober Pedy.

WHERE TO STAY

Very sensibly, there are several underground hotels in Coober Pedy. **Opal Inn** ((08) 8672-5054 FAX (08) 8672-5911, on Hutchinson Street, and the **Desert Cave** ((08) 8672-5688 TOLL-FREE 1800-088-521, on Hutchinson Street, are both moderately priced.

HOW TO GET THERE

Most coaches between Alice Springs and Adelaide which take the Stuart Highway stop over in Coober Pedy. **Kendall Airlines** has one flight a day from Adelaide.

Native pearls and the national gemstone adorn an opal-encrusted rock cut in a familiar shape.

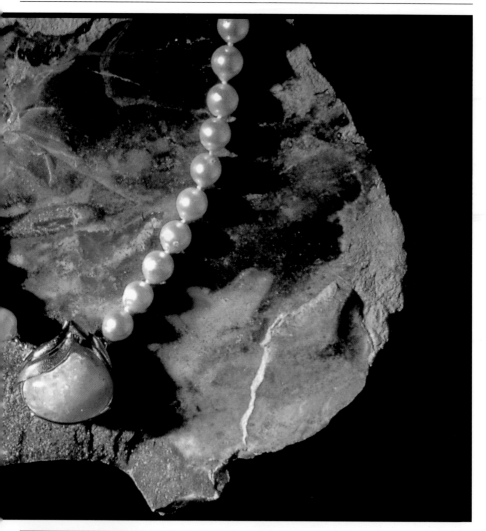

NATIONAL PARKS

The **Simpson Desert Conservation Park** covers 692,680 hectares (1,710,920 acres) and access is only by four-wheel drive vehicles. This is a desert of sand dunes, their subtle colors seen at their best at dusk and dawn.

The **Tantanoola Caves Conservation Park** ((08) 8734-4153, is 21 km (13 miles) southeast of Millicent. Caves honeycomb the ancient limestone cliffs, where there is a walkway through the main cavern.

In the district are two lakes, each different in its own way, which merit a visit.

Near the border of Victoria is the **Blue Lake** which in November changes color from its winter-grey to a startling blue; to date science has been unable to explain this. **Lake Eyre** blooms after rain, a rare event in this region which is the driest in Australia with an average rainfall of 100 to 150 mm (four to six inches). Once it was thought to be the edge of a great inland sea, but many explorers have been disappointed by what they found, a very large dry pan containing an estimated 500 million tons of salt.

Visitors to the Simpson Desert Conservation Park or Lake Eyre National Park require an AU$15 Overnight Pass or an AU$50 Desert Pass, both of which include maps of the area. For national parks information contact the **Nature Conservation Society of South Australia** ((08) 8223-6301, at 120 Wakefield Street, in Adelaide.

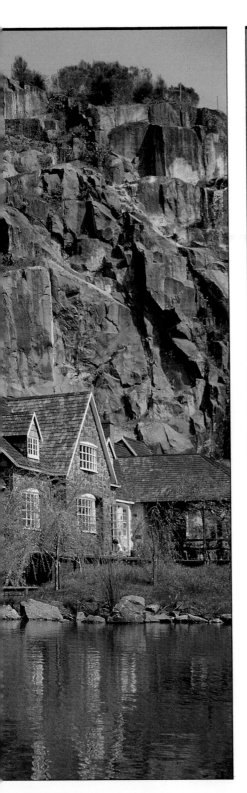

Tasmania
The Holiday Isle

A VISIT to Tasmania is not advised for the indecisive traveler, who will be faced with a mind-numbing list of choices of things to see and do. Australia's smallest state has it all. And more.

Tasmania is blessed with countryside which changes from rolling hills in the north, reminiscent of picturesque English counties, to the rugged majesty of its west coast. It has cool untouched rain forests and wildernesses where you can walk for days and never see another soul. The state is quite compact, taking just two and half hours to drive from north to south; many of its attractions can be reached without having to travel great distances.

Tasmania is sparsely populated with just under half a million people in an area approximately the size of Ireland. In the largely undisturbed countryside, much of it reserved as national parks, are numerous opportunities to see animals in their natural setting. It is common for wallabies and possums to feed around the country cottages where you may be staying. Tasmania is also home of the Tasmanian devil, extinct on the mainland, an animal usually about 30 cm (12 inches) tall, although males can grow to 90 cm (35 inches) and weigh up to 90 kg (200 lbs). The Tasmanian devil, named because of its fierce appearance, is shy, but with luck you may see one feeding at night in the remoter parts of the northwest and central regions of the island. The Tasmanian tiger is believed to be extinct, although sightings have been reported occasionally in remote regions.

Australia's second oldest colony, Tasmania retains many fine Georgian buildings and largely unchanged village streetscapes. Many colonial cottages provide accommodation, acquainting tourists with the history of the state. To complete the holiday experience, dine at the fine restaurants which concentrate on local ingredients such as Tasmanian smoked salmon, King Island Camembert and freshwater and saltwater fish.

So self-contained is the island that Tasmanians refer to other Australians as "mainlanders" or remind them when they visit that they come from "Tasmania's northern island."

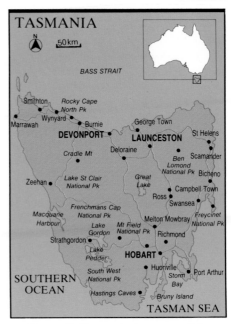

Above all, Tasmania does everything to cater to tourists' needs. The state is known around Australia as the Holiday Isle.

HOBART

Hobart is confused by simple concepts such as time and place. It knows that it is near the end of the twentieth century, but insists on giving the outward appearance of a nineteenth-century city although the occasional luxury hotel or high rise building breaks the skyline as a gesture to modernity. The population of Hobart knows that it lives in the capital of a state but insists on maintaining the friendliness and intimacy of a country town, where everyone knows everyone else and nothing is rushed.

The climate is mild in summer but decidedly chilly in winter, and is the only state capital that has any winter snow, albeit rarely. Above the city is Mount Wellington, its summit often hidden in cloud or dusted with snow, while the majestic River Derwent divides the city from surrounding green farmland and outlying suburbs. Hobart's landscape more closely resembles the European countryside than any other part of Australia.

OPPOSITE: Sunset at Bicheno, busy little fishing port and charming old holiday resort.

GENERAL INFORMATION

The **Tasmanian Travel and Information Centre** ((03) 6230-8233, at the corner of Elizabeth and Davey streets, can handle all your tour reservations and answer any queries. There are free counter copies of *Treasure Islander* and *Tasmanian Travelways*, newspapers which provide up-to-date information about attractions around Tasmania, and useful information about accommodation and tours.

Information is also on the web at http://www.tas.gov.au/tourism/tasman.html, which provides up-to-date information on attractions and events throughout the island.

BACKGROUND

Hobart, Australia's second oldest city, was started only 16 years after Sydney, with the intention of thwarting French designs on Tasmania.

Governor Macquarie, when he gave instructions to build the settlement on the River Derwent, wanted to avoid repeating the chaotic street plan of Sydney so the city center is laid out on a grid.

When prisoner transportation ended in the Australian colonies, Hobart became a backwater. Even today, Australia's second city is the country's smallest state capital with a population of just 180,000 people. However, being bypassed by progress has meant that Hobart retains much of it Georgian elegance and heritage.

WHAT TO SEE AND DO

The best place to start an exploration of Hobart is **Constitution Dock**, where fresh fish are sold straight off the boats.

Adjacent is **Franklin Wharf** where river cruisers set off each day for a tour of the River Derwent. A trip on the *Emmalisa* ((03) 6223-5893, provides an opportunity to travel on an original vintage ferry. The boat runs a lunch cruise that lasts about one and a half hours, departing at 11:30 AM and 1:30 PM.

South of the wharf area are the graceful lines of **Parliament House**, built by convicts in 1827 and originally used as a Customs

House (although many additions and alterations have since been made). When Parliament is in session visitors can view proceedings from the public gallery, while on non-sitting days, if you are fortunate, an attendant will show you around.

Back down the hill, east of the Parliament House, is **Salamanca Place**. In the nineteenth century Salamanca was a busy area, with Clydesdales pulling drays along the cobbled street to load wool clippers and other vessels. Most of the warehouses along the street have been preserved but rather than storing wool, they now house galleries, restaurants and souvenir shops. On Saturday mornings Salamanca Place is abuzz with a colorful market catering to locals and tourists alike.

On the high ground at the back of Salamanca Place is **Battery Point**, a colonial-era village looking much as it did a century and half ago, with many fine Georgian cottages and houses. The point took its name from the battery of cannons that in 1818 were placed on high ground to repulse the French should they try and take Hobart. Invaders never came, and the cannons were never fired in anger.

As Hobart's first suburb, the winding narrow streets of Battery Point were home for the merchants, seamen, boat builders and fishermen who worked at the docks. The **Shipwright's Arms** at 27 Trumpeter Street, is a reminder of the kind of public house that served the locals. In the center of Battery Point is **Arthur Circus**, a charming little park surrounded by tiny stone cottages. The **National Trust** ((03) 6223-7570, has an organized walking tour of Battery Point which leaves every Saturday from the Wishing Well in Franklin Square and is good value at AU$8.

To learn a little more about the seafaring history of Hobart visit the **Maritime Museum** ((03) 6223-5082, at Secheron House at 21 Secheron Road, with a unique collection of memorabilia from the colony's early seafaring days. The museum is open daily and an admission fee is charged. Another attraction in Battery Point is the **Narryna Folk Museum** ((03) 6234-2791, at 103 Hampton Road, housed in an historic Georgian house built in 1836. It is Australia's oldest folk museum, featuring furniture, clothing and prints from the penal colony's earliest days, and is open daily with an admission fee charged. On your return to the city, observe that backing onto Hampton Road is **Anglesea Barracks**, Australia's oldest military establishment, built in 1811 and still used by the army. The barracks are open daily and a narrated tour is conducted every Tuesday at 11 AM.

Mt. Wellington, towering 1,270 m (4,165 ft) above the city, provides great views of the surrounding countryside. From the

top it is possible to see parts of the southwest corner of Tasmania. Choose your weather, however, as the peak is liable at any time of year to be wreathed in cloud. At the bottom of Mt. Wellington, should you have developed a thirst, drop into **Cascade Brewery** ((03) 6224-1144, on Cascade Road, South Hobart. Established in 1832, it is the oldest brewery in Australia. Visitors can learn more about the art of making beer in the museum attached to the brewery before walking through the colonial gardens at **Woodstock** which is included in the tour, across the road from the brewery. There are tours of the brewery, museum and gardens conducted on weekdays at 9:30 AM and 1 PM; reservations are essential.

HOBART AFTER DARK

For such a small place, Hobart has a lively nightlife. On the weekend there are more than 30 nightspots and pubs that provide live music.

Starting at about 10 PM, **Round Midnight**, at 39 Salamanca Place, dances the night away, as does **Infinity Nightclub** on the first floor at 251 Liverpool Street, a recent addition to Hobart's nightlife. The **St. Ives Brewery Hotel** has three bars that provide entertainment that caters for every taste. At **Club Surreal** you can dance into the early hours, and the decor is... well... surreal. Dali, eat your heart out! The other bars are the **Hazard Zone**, with a DJ keeping the proceedings going and **Caf Eye** where there are live bands downstairs Wednesday, Thursday and Friday, while the three upstairs bars rock through the night Friday and Saturday.

There is a gig guide in *The Mercury* newspaper every Thursday, which lists live music venues for the coming week.

The brightest lights shine at **Wrest Point Casino** at 410 Sandy Bay, a five-minute taxi

Hobart's busy Franklin Wharf. From here river cruisers set off for tours of the Derwent.

ride from the city. There are live bands playing in various bars around the complex most nights, and the gaming rooms offer all the usual gambling variations from poker machines to roulette.

WHERE TO SHOP

Salamanca Place has a good selection of craft shops. Popular souvenirs are products made from local woods: Huon pine is particularly prized, being an almost indestructible wood growing only in the remote

SPORTS

The highlights of the sporting calendar are the Sydney–Hobart and Melbourne–Hobart yacht races. Both end around New Year's Day and the town turns to celebrations and the usual intemperate drinking. The **Royal Yacht Club of Tasmania ℂ** (03) 6223-4599, can provide additional details of the races.

There are four 18-hole golf courses within a few kilometers of the city center and numerous nine-hole country courses

regions of the southwest today, although once it was common. The honey-yellow wood contains a pleasant-smelling resinous oil which preserves it and retains a distinctive scent for decades. There are many shops offering wooden crafts such as "eggs" and salt and pepper shakers, but for better quality wooden products, have a look around the **Handmark Gallery** at 77 Salamanca Place. Finely crafted glassware and woodwork can be seen in **The Tasmanian Shop** at 108 Elizabeth Street. The **Crafts Council of Tasmania ℂ** (03) 6245-0545, at 17 Cambridge Road, has compiled a directory of other craft shops worth visiting; it can be purchased from most craft shops.

beyond the city limits. The **Royal Hobart Golf Club ℂ** (03) 6248-6161, at Seven Mile Beach, welcomes visitors and clubs and bag can be hired. The *Guide to Tasmanian Golf Courses* is available for AU$1.50 from any Tasmanian travel center.

WHERE TO STAY

Luxury
Just above Salamanca Place in Battery Point is the imposing **Lenna of Hobart ℂ** (03) 6232-3900 FAX (03) 6224-0112, a stately mansion at 20 Runnymede Street, once the home of whaling magnate Alexander McGregor. Its sumptuous interior recalls how well one with some initiative could live in the colony.

Tantallon Lodge (/FAX (03) 6224-1724, at Eight Mona Street, Battery Point, combines colonial decor with luxury accommodation, while the very modern **Hotel Grand Chancellor** ((03) 6235-4535 FAX (03) 6223-8175, at One Davey Street, fronts the wharf area. The **Wrest Point Hotel Casino** ((03) 6225-0112 FAX (03) 6225-3909, at 410 Sandy Bay, towers above Hobart offering unsurpassed views of the city and easy access to the gaming rooms.

Moderate

The place to stay for a taste of the real Hobart is at Battery Point where there is a good choice of colonial cottages providing bed and breakfast. The best rooms in **Cromwell Cottage** ((03) 6223-6734, at Six Cromwell Street, are on the top floor and overlook the River Derwent. **Colville Cottage** ((03) 6223-6968 FAX (03) 6224-0500, at 32 Mona Street, is set in a beautiful English garden, while **Barton Cottage** ((03) 6224-1606 FAX (03) 6224-1724, at 72 Hampden Road, provides spacious accommodation in a two-story colonial building. There are quite a few other cottages to choose from. Make further inquires at the **Cottages of the Colony** TOLL-FREE 1800-804-613, or **Tasmanian Colonial Accommodation Association** TOLL-FREE 1800-815-610.

Inexpensive

The **Waratah Motor Hotel** ((03) 6234-3685 or (03) 6234-3501 FAX (03) 6234-3502, at 272 Murray Street, offers modest accommodation close to the city center.

WHERE TO EAT

Hobart has several excellent seafood restaurants which draw on the local catch. **Mure's Upper Deck Restaurant** ((03) 6231-1999 (expensive), at Victoria Dock, is a Hobart institution and provides good quality seafood meals and wonderful views of the dock area. **Mure's Lower Deck Restaurant** (moderate) is a less formal bistro. Nearby is the **Drunken Admiral Restaurant** ((03) 6234-1903, located at 17–19 Hunter Street (expensive), which serves an excellent bisque, its interior a maze of nets and seafaring memorabilia.

There are several good restaurants in Salamanca Place which cater to tourists. At the far end N°87 is a seafood and steak restaurant, the **Ball and Chain Grill** ((03) 6223-2655 (moderate), serving generous portions from its charcoal grill. In summer there is nothing nicer than sitting outside in its courtyard. **Panache** (N°89) ((03) 6224-2929 (inexpensive), is a simple café in an historic sandstone building; here also, the outdoor dining area is very pleasant.

There is a wide choice of restaurants in Elizabeth Street, North Hobart, of which the

most popular is **Mit Zitrone** ((03) 6234-8113, at N°333 (moderate), which is casual but serves some sensational food, in fact, some of the best in Australia. For cuisine made of the freshest Tasmanian ingredients try **Dear Friends** ((03) 6223-2646, located at 8 Brooke Street, Sandy Bay (moderate), four kilometers (two miles) from the city, near the Wrest Point Casino. At the Wrest Point Casino itself on the seventeenth floor is the **Revolving Restaurant** ((03) 6225-0112 (expensive). **Prosser's on the Beach** ((03) 6225-2276, on Beach Road, Long Point (expensive), overlooks the River Derwent and the chili prawns invite the accompaniment of a cool Riesling from the restaurant's excellent cellar of Tasmanian wines.

Less expensive meals can be obtained in the city from **Bertie's Pasta Restaurant** ((03) 6223-3595, at 115 Collins Street (inexpensive), and **Battery Point Brasserie** ((03) 6223-3186, at 59 Hampton Street (moderate),

OPPOSITE: Restaurants, galleries and craft shops, which now line Salamanca Place were once wool warehouses. ABOVE: A Hobart seafood restaurant.

which has an emphasis on local game. For dessert try the homemade ice cream.

HOW TO GET THERE

The only direct Ansett and Qantas flights are from Melbourne and Sydney, through which passengers from other departure points need to connect.

The **Spirit of Tasmania** ferry leaves Melbourne at 6 PM on Monday, Wednesday and Friday, arriving at Devonport the next morning. The bus connections arrive in Hobart at 1:15 PM the next day.

DAY TRIPS FROM HOBART

PORT ARTHUR

Port Arthur was started as a penal colony in 1830. In 1979 the Tasmanian and federal governments spent nine million dollars to make the site a premier tourist attraction by restoring parts of the penal settlement itself.

The Port Arthur Historical Site is 102 km (63 miles) southeast of Hobart. Visitors usually make a day trip from Hobart to see it, although accommodation is available locally (See UNFORGETTABLE PORT ARTHUR in TOP SPOTS).

General Information
Tourist information can be obtained from the **Port Arthur Information Office** ((03) 6250-2363 in Port Arthur.

What to See and Do
Now surrounded by pleasant lawns, the four-story **Penitentiary** is still ominous. The last prisoners were released in 1877 but ghosts remain of men sentenced to the hideous conditions from which some died or were driven insane. Other buildings open to tourists are the **Model Prison** and the **Lunatic Asylum.**

Also worth a visit is the **Isle of the Dead**, a colonial cemetery that is reached by a ferry which leaves the jetty at Port Arthur daily at noon and 3 PM.

How to Get There
Organized tours to Port Arthur are available from Tiger Line ((03) 6234-4077 or

(1800) 030-620, leaving Hobart Monday, Wednesday, Friday and Sunday at 9:15 AM and returning at 5 PM. Transport, lunch and entrance into Port Arthur cost AU$49 for adults.

RICHMOND

Richmond — 20 minutes from Hobart — is a fine example of an early nineteenth-century village. Many of the original buildings are still intact and at night the streets are lit by gas lamps.

The Coal River is spanned by the **Richmond Bridge**, the oldest in Australia, dating back to 1823. Its setting is quite beautiful as ducks swim in the placid waters under the bridge, and weeping willows shade its banks. A backdrop to the bridge is **St. John's Church**, built in 1824 and still used by parishioners. In town visitors can see **Old Hobart Town** on Bridge Street, a scale model of Hobart as it was in the 1820s. See the restored jail house, built in 1825. It once held Ikey Solomons who was sent to Australia as a guest of His Majesty. This petty criminal is believed to have been the model used by Charles Dickens to create the character Fagin in *Oliver Twist*.

Prospect House ((03) 6260-2207, is one of the nicest settings for a restaurant you could wish. Meals are served in the front rooms of this Georgian dwelling built in 1830 by convicts. Accommodation is also provided at the back in airy rooms with louvered French doors opening on a peaceful courtyard.

How to Get There
Richmond is 26 km (14 miles) northeast of Hobart and a regular weekday bus service takes 30 minutes to make the journey. There are four buses a day, two in the morning and two in the evening.

BRUNY ISLAND

About 35 km (22 miles) south of Hobart, in the tranquil waters of D'Entrecasteaux

All that is left of the brutal Port Arthur penal colony are picturesque ruins set in clipped green lawns and gardens.

Channel is Bruny Island, which is divided by a very narrow isthmus; at high tide it is not much wider than the road. Driving along the isthmus at night requires much care because fairy penguins occasionally walk across the road.

Bruny Island was first sighted by Abel Tasman in 1642 and has been visited by a veritable "who's who" list of Australian sea explorers, such as Cook, Furneaux and Bligh.

It is also a place of great sadness to Aborigines: there is a memorial on the island to Truganini, believed to be the last tribal Tasmanian Aborigine, a fact since disputed. True or not, the tragedy of the Tasmanian native inhabitants remains a painful fact, so effectively were they exterminated by the white man's diseases and barbarism. There is a poignant verse to the people of Truganini at **Big Hummock**. It says, "They roam no more upon this isle, so stay and meditate awhile."

There are minibus tours provided by **Bruny Island Venture Tours (** (03) 6273-2886 TOLL-FREE 1800-124-835 FAX (03) 6273-0269, for small groups of people. Meals are included and a full-day tour costs AU$90. Peter Watson, whose association with the island spans 45 years, introduces visitors to its rugged beauty and explains the history he obviously loves dearly. One of the highlights of this tour is a visit to Resolution Beach, where two 300-year-old blue gums stand, as they did when Captain Cook visited the island.

If your time is limited at least take a look at the **lighthouse**, built in 1836, and still in operation.

There are few good eating places on Bruny Island; but, at **Penguin (** (03) 6293-1352, in Venture Bay you can try local delicacies such as Atlantic smoked salmon, smoked trout and crayfish, in season. During spring many orchards on the island sell delicious sweet black Tasmanian cherries from their front gates.

How to Get There

Bruny Island is 34 km (21 miles) south of Hobart and can be reached by ferry from Kettering. The crossing takes about 15 minutes and the ferry takes cars across to the island.

THE WEST COAST

The trip down the west coast is popular as it takes in some of the most spectacular scenery in Tasmania, with majestic mountains, fast flowing rivers and still lakes.

WHAT TO SEE AND DO

Tarraleah
Tarraleah is perched on the Central Highland Plateau, and is a convenient stop when touring the west coast or the lake region to the north. The town was planned and built by the Hydroelectric Commission, a major employer in Tasmania and a power unto itself, which has payed little attention to the government.

Typical of those settlements built by the Hydroelectric Commission, simple timber houses are provided for its workmen.

One of the best maintained nine-hole golf courses in Tasmania is here with an indoor swimming pool, also maintained by the Hydroelectric Commission.

In days gone by the guesthouse was reserved for the top brass of the Commission and a whole suite of rooms was kept ready in case the Commissioner should drop in for a breath of country air, but today the town has been privatized.

The guesthouse **Tarraleah Chalet** ((03) 6289-3128 FAX (03) 6289-3177, was sold to private owners and is now open to all comers. See it before it is renovated, because it is a classic artifact of the 1930s. Rooms have

quaint names such as Lake Echo, Laughing Jack Lagoon and Clumy Dam; the lounge is comfortable and the glass-enclosed verandahs are wonderfully warm on sunny winter days.

Queenstown

Queenstown, on the west coast, is one of the most desolate places on earth. Its lunar landscape is man-made by polluted fallout from the copper smelter.

Both approach-roads to the town wind through bare red-brown clay, as all the topsoil has been washed away. Before mining began the steep hills were covered with

Cradle Mountain is the island's most popular destination, especially for hikers.

dense rain forest. For 78 years the copper smelter in Queenstown belched sulfuric acid into the atmosphere, killing those trees not felled to feed the furnaces. Topsoil eroded off the bare hills, making the current attempts at regenerating the vegetation exceedingly difficult. A proposal by environmentalists to resoil and revegetate the bare Queenstown hills was successfully opposed by locals, who perversely saw their lunar landscape as a tourist attraction.

If the ozone layer finally decides to give up the ghost, atomic fission gets out of hand and sparks a nuclear winter or the greenhouse effect fries the earth, then I imagine the rest of the world will start to look like Queenstown. The place is a timely warning, and for that alone it is worth a visit, albeit a brief one.

Strahan

Strahan, standing on the shore of Macquarie Harbour, was once a major coastal port. Huge Huon pine logs were floated down the **Gordon River** for milling in Strahan and then export.

This small unassuming town is the starting point for cruises along the Gordon River, which runs through part of the World Heritage area. The **Gordon River Cruises (** (03) 6471-7187, depart from the main wharf every day at 9 AM and return at about 1:30 PM. The cruise moves up the Gordon River, past ancient Huon pines until at Heritage Landing there is an opportunity to get off and explore some of the 2,000-year-old rain forest, via a walkway designed to prevent damage to the delicate ecosystem. The availability of day trips down the Gordon River is limited; to obtain an idea of the richness of the scenery, **Wilderness Air (** (03) 6471-7280 FAX (03) 6471-7303, provides flights over the Southwest Heritage Area. The seaplane touches down on the Gordon, 40 km (25 miles) upstream, and a walk to **St. John Falls** allows visitors to experience the rain forest.

Cradle Mountain

The **Cradle Mountain-Lake St. Clair National Park** is one of the most popular destinations in Tasmania, particularly with hikers.

It is possible to walk from Lake St. Clair to Cradle Mountain on the **Overland Track**, an 85-km (53-mile) hike that is both challenging and rewarding. The journey takes five to six days and the path is well signposted. It is important that walkers are fit because there are no access roads and the only way out in an emergency is by helicopter. There are huts along the way to provide shelter from bad weather, which can come upon the mountain quite suddenly. The best time to visit the area is from December to April. Before starting out all walkers must register with the park ranger; a fee is charged.

There are also shorter walks around Lake St. Clair and Cradle Mountain for less experienced walkers that vary between one and eight hours, and provide a surprising variety of scenery within a short distance.

WHERE TO STAY

Once the only accommodation in mining towns was in pubs. In Queenstown three hotels still provide inexpensive accommodation. In Orr Street there are the **Empire Hotel (** (03) 6471-1699, **Hunters Hotel (** (03) 6471-1531, and the **Commercial Hotel (** (03) 6471-1511, on Driffield Street. The **Queenstown Motor Lodge (** (03) 6471-1866, at 54–58 Orr Street, is moderately priced.

At Strahan, **Franklin Manor (** (03) 6471-7311 FAX (03) 6471-7267, overlooking Macquarie Harbour, offers comfortable colonial accommodation in a gabled guesthouse built in 1897. The restaurant attached to Franklin Manor gives preference for reservations to guests. **Sharonlee (** (03) 6471-7224 FAX (03) 6471-7375, offers moderately-priced self-contained cabins.

The **Cradle Mountain Lodge (** (03) 6492-1303, offers luxury accommodation in log cabins, which are a perfect base for exploring the national park. Each cabin has a potbellied stove, and in the evening potaroos, small wallabies, graze around the back of the cabins. There are also the **Cradle Mountain Campgrounds (** (03) 6492-1395, nearby which offer an inexpensive option.

Craggy peaks surround the tranquil waters of Lake St. Clair TOP and Cradle Mountain Lodge BOTTOM provides a comfortable sanctuary for bush walkers.

HOW TO GET THERE

About 165 km (102 miles) from Hobart, along Lyell Highway is **Derwent Bridge**, a pub and no much else. It is the turn-off for the Lake St. Clair entrance to Cradle Mountain-Lake St. Clair National Park. The Cradle Mountain entrance can be reached by turning off the Bass Highway at Wilmont and continuing south along a 58 km (36 miles) stretch of road, the last section of which is unpaved.

Tasmanian Wilderness Travel runs a daily bus to Cradle Mountain from Devonport and Launceston on Saturday, Tuesday and Thursday, with weekday service from Hobart between November and April. A bus to Lake St. Clair departs every Tuesday from Hobart, Launceston and Devonport between May and October and daily for the rest of the year. Tiger Line buses run from Hobart to Strahan via Queenstown and Derwent Bridge on Tuesday, Friday and Sunday, and from Strahan to Devonport on Wednesday and Friday. Transport from Derwent Bridge to Lake St. Clair operates on demand and the charter service can be contacted at ((03) 6492-1431

UP THE MIDDLE

The **Midlands Highway** runs 198 km (123 miles) between Hobart and Launceston, and is Tasmania's main artery. It bypasses many of the historic villages along the route, allowing them a peace that was lost elsewhere with the advent of motor cars. Most townships which are just a short distance off the highway, have early histories as coaching stops and military depots and are rich in colonial character. The trip takes about two hours by car but there are sufficient places of interest for it to be worth taking your time.

The route was first surveyed in 1807 by Surveyor-General Charles Grimes, and towns sprang up along its length, radiating out from the two major population centers. By 1830, there were 16 inns along the route providing refreshment for travelers between Hobart and Launceston. The road, built using convict labor, was not com-

pleted until 1850. At the time it was the best highway in the country on which the latest methods of road-making were used.

WHAT TO SEE AND DO

Ross

Ross, 122 km (76 miles) from Hobart, is situated on the Macquarie River. The village is splendidly preserved, and indeed a living museum of nineteenth-century architecture. Its streets are lined with historic homes and public buildings, many of which have been restored and now house hotels, museums, and shops catering for tourists.

Spanning the river is the **Ross Bridge**, which is not quite as old as the one at Richmond, having been built only in 1836 with convict labor. It is, however, certainly one of the most beautiful in Australia. Over the sandstone arches the convicts added 186 carved stones which took their inspiration from Celtic folklore. It is rumored that some of the figures are caricatures of local colonial "deities."

The main intersection of Bridge and Church streets, was known locally as the "four corners of Ross" — Damnation (one corner was occupied by a women's prison, now gone), Recreation (the Town Hall), Salvation (**Lady of Sacred Heart Catholic Church**) and Temptation (**Man O'Ross Hotel**). While not all four buildings remain, fortunately the 1817 hotel survives, its interior richly paneled with Tasmanian oak and blackwood.

Ross itself, with its leafy streets has the feeling of an English village. Opposite St. John's Church on the main street is the **Village Bakery and Tea Room** that serves light refreshment; and a display of fine Tasmanian craft gives visitors an opportunity to purchase a quality souvenir.

Evandale

Take the turn off the main highway at Breadalbane for Evandale, 20 km (12 miles) from Launceston. The village provides an excellent example of an intact Georgian streetscape. Off the main road eight kilometers (five miles) from town is **Clarendon House**, which was built in 1838 by wealthy wool grower and merchant James Fox on his

5,700-hectare (14,000-acre) property. Approaching the house down the long drive it is difficult not to be impressed by the first appearance of the two-story mansion, its façade supported by huge Ionic columns and an architectural style which would not have been out of place on a grand plantation in old Virginia. The house is furnished in the style of the period and is open for visits.

True to its nineteenth-century origins, in February the streets of Evandale are transformed as cyclists precariously balance on

good or rapid as the Midlands Highway, but the scenery more than justifies getting off the beaten track to see this seldom-visited area, which is the largest alpine habitat in Australia.

From Launceston drive along the Bass Highway to Deloraine and then turn onto the scenic Lake Highway, which takes you onto the windswept central plateau with its scurrying clouds, gnarled pencil pines, moorland and mountains. The terrain is pockmarked with glacial lakes, some of them so shallow that it is possible to walk

penny farthing bicycles, for an annual race. The week includes a parade and country fair.

Perth

Perth, on the highway only 20 km (13 miles) south of Launceston, also has strong nineteenth-century connections. The historic **Leather Bottell Inn** ((03) 6398-2248, has been converted into an excellent restaurant, and is open daily for morning and afternoon teas, lunch, and for dinner from Thursday to Saturday.

Central Highland

An alternative route through the center of Tasmania takes you to the **Land of Three Thousand Lakes**. The roads here are not as

across, and others no larger than a football field.

The lakes in this rarely-visited part are teeming with wild brown trout, much prized by fly-fishermen (who are trying to keep this great fishing ground a secret). Buy a fishing license — which can be purchased from most sport store — and visit one of the 40 major lakes or hundreds of creeks, tarns or highland rivers and cast a line for a wild Tasmanian trout. Fishing in the region is of world standard, as was recognized in 1988 when the World Fly Fishing Championship was held on the Central Highlands. Reeling

ABOVE: Hobart and wintery Mt. Wellington. The Tasman Bridge is one of 5,000 bridges on the island.

in a two-kilogram (four-and-a-half-pound) trout is an everyday event and in some lakes four-kilogram (nine-pound) trout are not uncommon. Brown trout dominates throughout the region. Some of the best places to fish are **Arthurs Lake, Macquarie River, Bronte Lagoon, Little Pine Lake** and **Great Lake**. Sea-run trout are found in estuaries. The best times to fish is from the beginning of October to late March. Organized tours by locals who know the best places to fish are available from **Peter Hayes Guided Fishing,** that operates out of the **Compleat Angler Lodge (** (03) 6259-8295, in Miena, and **Ausprey Tours (** (03) 6330-2612, which is organized out of Launceston and specializes in fly fishing.

WHERE TO STAY

Ross has quite a good selection of colonial accommodation. The **Man O'Ross (** (03) 6381-5240, is inexpensive and feeds you a hearty breakfast. There are several charming, moderately-priced self-contained cottages, dating back as early as 1850, which can be reserved through the **Colonial Cottages of Ross (** (03) 6381-5354 FAX (03) 6381-5408, in Church Street. Each is furnished with furniture from the mid-nineteenth century.

There are few places to stay along the Lake Highway, but some moderately-priced accommodation is available in Bothwell. **Whites Cottages (** (03) 6259-5651, in Queens Street, provides bed-and-breakfast accommodation while eight kilometers (five miles) out of town is the quaint **Mrs. Woods Farmhouse (** (03) 6259-5612.

The **Compleat Angler Lodge (** (03) 6259-8179, on Haddens Bay, and **Great Lake Hotel (** (03) 6259-8163 FAX (03) 6259-8147, on Swan Bay, are moderately priced. These hotels cater to fishermen.

HOW TO GET THERE

Tasmanian Redline Coaches run a daily service between Hobart and Launceston along the Midlands Highway. There are no regular buses for transportation along the Lakes Highway, so the only way to explore this area is by car.

LAUNCESTON

The first test any visitor has in gaining acceptance from the locals is if he or she pronounces the city's name correctly. *Lawn*-ceston will be greeted with hoots of protest, while *Lon*-ceston will elicit a sigh of satisfaction. Casually refer to the town as "Lonny" and you will be accepted as an honorary local and invited home for dinner to meet the family.

Despite its small size with a population of about 93,000, Launceston has an intense rivalry with Hobart. Both cities once reported separately to Sydney. In 1812, much to Launceston's horror, it came under the control of the colonial administration located in Hobart.

GENERAL INFORMATION

In Launceston the **Tasmanian Travel and Information Centre (** (03) 6336-3122, at the corner of St. John and Paterson streets, is open from 8:45 AM to 5 PM weekdays, and from 9 AM to noon weekends.

WHAT TO SEE AND DO

Tasmania's second largest city is otherwise known as the garden city because of its numerous parks in which European trees such as ash, oak and elm thrive. It also has some marvelous Victorian streetscapes to enjoy. It is an excellent base for exploring the northern part of Tasmania, with its historic villages, fine wineries and national parks, and has enough attractions in its own right to justify staying there a couple of days.

Launceston's most outstanding natural beauty spot, only a few minutes' walk from the center of the town, is the **Cataract Gorge and Cliff Grounds**, set in a 160-hectare (395-acre) reserve where the Esk River spills. The park that provides access to the gorge is an splendid setting for a picnic. Cataract Gorge itself is a canyon through which the South Esk River plunges, with spectacular ferocity after heavy rain, into the Tamar River. A walking path follows the cliff face and a 300-m (985-ft) chairlift, the world's largest single-span lift, offers a breathtaking ride over the waters.

The natural beauty of Launceston — founded just a few months after Hobart — is complemented by a variety of historic buildings, a number of which line St. John and George streets.

Visit the city's **Queen Victoria Museum and Art Gallery (** (03) 6331-6777, in Wellington Street, which houses one of the finest colonial art collections in the nation, as well as fascinating relics from Tasmania's past including the famous Tasmanian tiger.

The best known commercial attraction is the **Penny Royal (** (03) 6331-6699, on Paterson Street, which recreates colonial industrial practices. A watermill has been restored to working order, along with a cornmill, windmill, cannon foundry and arsenal.

Grindelwald, 15 km (nine miles) north of Launceston, is a Swiss village transported to the Antipodes. This does not appear as out-of-place as it may seem, as the landscape in this part of Tasmania with its green rolling hills resembles the foothills of the Swiss Alps.

WHERE TO STAY

Luxury

Eight kilometers (five miles) southwest of Launceston is the **Country Club Casino (** (03) 6344-8855 FAX (03) 6335-5788, at Prospect Vale . The hotel offers guests access to its 18-hole, par-72 golf course, dining in its classy restaurant, and at night live entertainment at the casino or gambling at its gaming tables.

For an agreeable stay **Grindelwald Resort (** (03) 6330-0400 FAX (03) 6330-1607, on Lake Louise is a good choice.

Moderate

Launceston was founded in 1805 and many of its splendid nineteenth-century houses and cottages have been converted into self-contained accommodation. A large weeping willow shades **The Shambles (** (03) 6334-2231 at 121–129 Balfour Street, where visitors can lay themselves down at night on an old-fashioned four-poster bed. Other nineteenth-century cottages that provide accom-

modation are **Airlie (** (03) 6334-2162 FAX (03) 6334-3195, at 89 Margaret Street, **Thyme Cottage (** (03) 6398-5129 FAX (03) 6398-5164, at 31 Cimitiere Street, and just a few minutes' walk from Cataract Gorge is the imposing Federation-style **Turret House (** (03) 6334-7033 FAX (03) 6331-6091, located at 41 West Tamar Road. At the corner of Margaret and York streets is the **Old Bakery Inn (** (03) 6331-7900 FAX (03) 6331-7756, which has been restored to its nineteenth-century condition, and some of the original ovens remain.

Inexpensive

For comfortable motel-type accommodation try the **Great Northern Hotel** TOLL-FREE 1800-030-567 FAX (03) 6331-3712, at 3 Earl Street, or **North Lodge** TOLL-FREE 1800-006-042 FAX (03) 6334-2810, at 7 Brisbane Street.

WHERE TO EAT

The **Gorge Restaurant (** (03) 6331-3330, in Cliff Ground (moderate), is perched in the grounds of Cataract Gorge. The view from the restaurant is of the surrounding cliffs, which at night are illuminated. During the

A jolly boat ride at Penny Royal World takes visitors back to nineteenth-century Tasmania.

day, light meals and afternoon tea are served on outside tables, where peacocks strut, oblivious of diners.

You can dine in great style at **Fee & Me** ((03) 6331-3195 (expensive), at the corner of Fredrick and Charles streets, located in an elegant two-story mansion built in 1835, well known for its excellent cellar of Tasmanian wines. Nearby is **Elm Cottage** ((03) 6331-8468, at 168 Charles Street (moderate), a quaint restaurant near the middle of Launceston. **Quigley's Balfour Terrace** ((03) 6331-6971, at 96 Balfour Street (moderate), is notable for its game and fish dishes.

HOW TO GET THERE

Ansett and Australian Airlines have flights from most state capital cities to Launceston, although direct service is only available from Melbourne and Sydney. **Airlines of Tasmania** TOLL-FREE 1800-030-550, provide flights between Hobart and Launceston.

The **Spirit of Tasmania** ferry leaves Melbourne at 6 PM on Monday, Wednesday and Friday, arriving at Devonport the next morning. A bus connection arrives in Launceston at 10 AM the next day.

THE EAST COAST

Tasmania is not well endowed with the Australian trinity of sun, surf and sand; the nearest you get to it is on the east coast, where there is a string of small, pretty resort towns. The coast has secluded beaches on which to swim, or there are scenic walks along the magnificent coastline.

The Tasman Highway runs 435 km (270 miles) between Hobart and Launceston. From Launceston it loops through the northeast corner of the island, skirting the rocky bastion of the Ben Lomond plateau and reaching the coast at **St. Helens**.

WHAT TO SEE AND DO

Bicheno

Once boats left Bicheno to harpoon whales in the Tasman Sea or kill seals on the islands off Tasmania. Now the only quarry are crayfish, oysters and abalone.

This seaside village, a popular holiday destination, attracts surf fishermen. Bicheno is also a good base for exploring the nearby **Douglas-Apsley National Park**.

Just north of town is the **East Coast Bird Life and Animal Park** ((03) 6375-1311, on the Tasman Highway, where native animals such as wombats, pademelons and Tasmanian devils can be seen, and friendly wallabies can be hand fed.

Coles Bay

Coles Bay is located at the neck of the peninsula that constitutes the **Feycinet Peninsula National Park**, with its pink granite peaks and vertical cliffs dropping straight into the sea. A 25-km (16-mile) walking circuit takes in coastal scenery, and tracks lead to **Wineglass Bay** and the **Lighthouse**.

Swansea

Located on Oyster Bay, Swansea was settled in the 1820s and many of its original buildings are still standing. The **Swansea Bark Mill and East Coast Museum** ((03) 6257-8382, at 96 Tasman Highway, was built in 1886 and today is a museum which shows visitors the early industries in the area. Of particular interest is the display of how leather was tanned using black wattle bark. An entrance fee is charged and the museum is open daily. The bay has safe sheltered beaches and is, therefore, popular with families.

WHERE TO STAY

There is a good range of accommodation in Bicheno, a dedicated holiday town. The oldest building was built in 1845: the jail house. Following a long tradition of offering free accommodation to guests cunningly invited by the Crown, the **Bicheno Gaol House** ((03) 6375-1430 FAX (03) 6375-1368, has upgraded standards and service, and now seeks paying guests. For the curious, some of the original cells remain. The cottages are on the corner of James and Burgess streets.

The modest **Wintersun Lodge Motel** ((03) 6375-1225, at 35 Gordon Street, is inexpensive while the **Diamond Island Resort** ((03) 6375-1161, at 69 Tasman

Highway, is moderately priced and has a restaurant attached.

Freycinet Lodge ((03) 6257-1010, near Coles Bay, is located in the national park and provides moderately-priced accommodation. Vans can be hired at the **Coles Bay Caravan Park** ((03) 6257-0100, at very reasonable rates.

In Swansea the historic **Oyster Bay Guesthouse** ((03) 6257-8110, at 10 Franklin Street, built in 1836, and **Schouten House** ((03) 6257-8564, offer moderately-priced accommodation.

For information on national parks contact the Tasmanian Conservation Trust ((03) 6234-3552.

Convenient to Hobart is the **Mt. Field National Park**, 80 km (50 miles) west of the capital on the Lyell Highway. Its forests contain many ancient trees — Huon Pines, gums and sassafras. Several walking tracks through the national park are popular in summer and there is good skiing in winter at higher altitudes.

The **South-West Wilderness** is a World Heritage Area and features rugged terrain

HOW TO GET THERE

Redline Coaches run buses along the east coast between Hobart and Launceston with stops at St. Helens, Bicheno and Swansea. Suncost, Peakes Coaches and Tiger Line run less frequent services to the east coast towns on weekdays.

and a remote, untouched coastline. While **Federation Peak** is only 1,425 m (4,675 ft), scaling it challenges the best climbers; the last section goes up a steep rock face. Watch out for the weather which can change suddenly in the mountains.

NATIONAL PARKS

About 28 percent of Tasmania is protected under the National Parks Service. Some of this land is further designated as World Heritage areas. There is an entry charge for all 14 national parks in Tasmania. A daily pass is AU$5 and a monthly pass is AU$30.

The Ringarooma River in Tasmania's northeast.

me for a Carlton.

Victoria
Fit for a Queen

MELBOURNE

Queen Victoria never visited Australia but had she done so, I'm sure that she would have gravitated towards Melbourne where many of its public buildings and houses would have looked so familiar, built as they were during her glorious reign.

As Melbourne went through cycles of boom and bust, the city's skyline and suburban streetscapes were shaped by architectural styles of the Victorian period — neo-Gothic, Italianate and Classical.

Writing about the Melbourne of 1856, a contemporary admired "its wide and spacious thoroughfares, fringed with edifices worthy of the wealth of its citizens, and corresponding in architectural pretensions to their occupants." Fortunately much of Melbourne's architectural heritage remains intact, and although skyscrapers line the streets of the central city many fine buildings have not been sacrificed to the developers' passion for high rise boxes of steel and glass.

Walking around Melbourne and its suburbs it is still possible to see lavishly embellished buildings from the mid-1850s, a taste which became more outrageous during the boom years of the 1880s and 1890s. All of this, I'm sure, would please the fickle Queen Victoria who was notoriously difficult to "amuse."

GENERAL INFORMATION

Tourist information covering Melbourne is available from the **City Experience Centre** ((03) 9658-9658 FAX (03) 9654-1054, located in the Melbourne Town Hall on the corner of Swanston and Collins streets. Opening hours are 9 AM to 7 PM weekdays, and 10 AM to 5 PM weekends and public holidays. Next door is the **Victoria Visitor Information Centre**, which offers information for country areas from 8:30 AM to 5:30 PM Monday to Friday, and from 9 AM to 5 PM on weekends. The RACV office ((03) 9642-5566, at 360 Bourke Street, can also help with information and reservations.

The City of Melbourne publishes the monthly *Melbourne Events*, available free of

charge from most hotels. There is also a phone information service on (0055-30-000. Calls to this service are time-charged.

For information on Melbourne's public transport call the **Met Information Centre** (131-638 or visit its office in the city at 103 Elizabeth Street. For information on country trains phone **V/Line** (132-232.

BACKGROUND

Melbourne was "bought" by John Batman in 1834 from the Aboriginal landowners.

After handing over what he thought was a fair price, namely 20 blankets, 30 knifes, 12 red shirts, four flannel jackets and the like, he was able to boast that "I am the greatest landowner in the world." What the local tribal people thought of this bargain, involving 243,000 hectares (600,000 acres) of prime real estate, is not recorded. If they had any regrets they could have put the 50 handkerchiefs Batman provided as part of the price to use and wiped their eyes.

The colonial government, unimpressed with Batman's business acumen, did not recognize his land claim.

The monumental architecture of Melbourne's Exhibition Building.

The outline of Melbourne was devised by Robert Hoddle in 1836. His vision for what was then only a village of a few makeshift houses and muddy streets, was of a city with wide avenues laid out in a neat grid.

Melbourne grew slowly at first, but when gold was discovered in Bendigo in 1851 the city boomed and Hoddle's vision became a reality. Within a few years the population quadrupled to 80,000 and the government embarked on a civic building program which established Melbourne as a great nineteenth-century Victorian city. In

1853 alone 1,000 buildings were erected in the city area, and this growth continued in fits and starts until early into the twentieth century. At the height of this construction activity the city was justifiably known as Marvelous Melbourne.

WHAT TO SEE AND DO

The central city area has much to offer during the day, although at night and at the weekend it quiets down considerably. After sunset, activity focuses on the theater area of Bourke Street, between Swanston and Exhibition streets, in Chinatown along Little Bourke Street, and Southgate on the Yarra River.

At night and weekends the main action moves to the inner suburbs, each of which has its own character and is worth visiting. Melbourne has an extensive tram system making the suburbs easily accessible.

To get a perfect view of Melbourne from the bay along to the Dandenong Mountains, take an elevator ride up to the 55th floor of the tallest building in the city, the **Rialto** ((03) 9629-8222 TOLL-FREE 1800-677-441, at 525 Collins Street.

City Strolls

The city's architectural character was set in the mid to late nineteenth century. Unfortunately, over the last 30 years Melbourne has lost some fine buildings to developers. Many beautiful old buildings, however, remain.

The city is set out in a grid, making it easy to move around. Start at the corner of Flinders and Swanston streets at **Flinders Street Station**. Before the underground train loop was built, this was the hub of Melbourne. When the railway management threatened to remove the clocks over the entrance that announced the arrival of trains, the city blew its collective stack because meeting "under the clocks" had become a tradition.

Walk north along Swanston Walk, a failed pedestrian mall. Beware of street trams and bikes — they are still allowed along the mall. At the corner of Collins Street is the **City Square** with water cascading around its boundary. During weekday lunchtime, free entertainment is often provided in the square, at weekends daredevil skateboard riders turn the square into an unofficial acrobatics track.

Turn left into Collins Street and walk two blocks to Queen Street where you are surrounded by the buildings which once housed Melbourne's financial institutions, built during the land boom of the 1880s and early 1890s when each building society tried to outdo its neighbor in ostentation. Many have spires and turrets more suited to a Bohemian castle, and interiors resplendent with ceiling paintings and gold trim. Buildings at the corner of Collins and Queen streets are well worth visiting; at 388 Collins Street griffins guard the entrance of what was once the **E.S.&A. Bank**, built in 1883. Its embellishments pushed it to the limits of outrageousness, even for a neo-Gothic building.

In the block past Williams Street, between 471 and 483 Collins Street, are four buildings that will give you some idea what Melbourne's streetscape looked like a 100 years ago.

Take a tram back along Collins Street to Spring Street, facetiously known as the Paris end of the street, shaded by plane trees and at night lit up with fairy lights. Ahead of you is the **Old Treasury Building** (1858), in classical Renaissance style, which now houses an exhibition on Melbourne's history.

Turn left at Spring Street and walk a block to Bourke Street; off to your right is the state **Parliament House**, built in stages between 1856 and 1930. The original design included plans for a dome on top of the building, which unfortunately failed to materialize. The interior is richly adorned, the highlight being the Legislative Council Chamber with its ornately painted vaulted ceiling. There are **guided tours (** (03) 9651-8911, on weekdays when Parliament is in recess. For the very hardy it is possible, when the House is sitting, to endure the public gallery when Parliament is in action.

Opposite Parliament is the **Windsor Hotel**, one of Melbourne's institutions with a colorful history. In 1886 it was bought by the Honorable James Munro, president of the Temperance Party who ceremoniously burned his liquor license and renamed the hotel the Grand Coffee Palace. Under the guidance of the temperance philosophy the Grand went into a decline until 1921, when a new owner obtained a new liquor license. Today the Windsor has several bars but it has not turned its back on more sober beverages. In the lounge from 3 PM to 5:30 PM Monday to Saturday, and from 3:30 PM to 6 PM Sunday, afternoon tea is served on a full silver service, cucumber sandwiches (with the crusts trimmed off), cakes and fresh tea or coffee. This Melbourne institution is popular with wealthy farmers and their wives down to the city "for a spot of business." It also has the Grand Dining Room with a stained-glass dome. Ease back into the leather chairs and relax in the company of Melbourne's Establishment.

Nearby is the **Princess Theatre**, at which such blockbusters as *Phantom of the Opera* and *Les Miserables* were shown recently. Built in 1887, this is a thoroughly vulgar piece of Victoriana with ludicrous decoration; its façade includes figures of the Muses, urns, lions and a golden angel tooting a trumpet.

Catch a tram down Bourke Street and alight at Swanston Walk. This is the beginning of the **Bourke Street Mall**, usually crawling with buskers who will importune you with every means at their disposal.

As well as the Met tram service, the free City Circle Tram can be used to reach many of the city's main attractions. It travels in both directions along Spencer, LaTrobe, Spring and Flinders streets every 10 minutes from 10 AM to 6 PM.

Melbourne's Art Complex

Just outside the central city area as you head south along Swanston Street over the Yarra River is the **Victorian Arts Centre (** (03) 9281-8000, which consists of three buildings. There is always a full program of plays, dance and ballet, details of which are listed in the daily newspapers. The **Theatres**

The mogul façade of a theater OPPOSITE and St. Paul's Cathedral and Civic Square ABOVE

Building, recently recapped with a new illuminated spire, which glows blue at night. Along the walls of the foyer are 800 tiles, entitled **"Paradise Gardens,"** commissioned from the late Sidney Nolan, which you must see. The building also contains the **Westpac Gallery**, almost opposite the entrance. Exhibitions are varied and always interesting; entry is free. There are guided tours of the Victorian Arts Centre ((03) 9281-8152, which start at noon and at 2:30 PM weekdays and at 10:30 AM and noon on Saturdays. Tours of the backstage are con-

ducted on Sunday at 12:15 PM and 2:15 PM, and last around an hour and a half.

Next to the center is the **Concert Hall**, an unadorned building with a functional interior where the main auditorium has excellent acoustics. Within the building is the **Performing Arts Museum** ((03) 9281-8263 with eclectic exhibitions dealing with all aspects of entertainment, past and present.

On the other side is the **National Gallery of Victoria** ((03) 9208-0222, which has a permanent exhibition of Australian works as well as regular exhibitions from overseas. Open daily from 10 AM to 5 PM, entrance is free, but admission fees apply for special exhibitions. There is also an excellent collection of Chinese robes and ceramics.

Just below the complex beside the Yarra River is **Southbank**, with its outdoor cafés and shops. On a sunny Sunday afternoon, this is the liveliest place in town. With swarms of people promenading along the Yarra river, shopping at the weekend outdoor craft market, sightseeing, or just sipping a cappuccino while watching the world go by. Bliss.

Queen Victoria Market

At the edge of the city at the intersection of Elizabeth and Victoria streets is the Queen Victoria Market ((03) 9658-9600, which was inaugurated in 1878 and has the largest stock of fresh produce in Melbourne: over 1,000 stalls spread over seven hectares (17 acres). A few similar markets remain around Melbourne, and are popular despite the proliferation of dreary multi-story shopping complexes, supermarkets and malls in the suburbs.

The market is divided into four sections: meat and fish; fruits and vegetables; the delicatessen; and finally a section containing miscellaneous clothing, souvenirs, footwear, toys, kitchenware and hardware.

The first customers arrive as early as 6 AM to pick out the best of the fresh produce, followed by a coffee (and if the stomach is up to it, a *bratwurst* from shop 99–100 in the delicatessen section where Irene and Nino Greco have been catering to this early morning craving for over 25 years). **Le Croissant des Halles** (corner of Elizabeth and Therry streets) offers a more traditional choice for breakfast — a croissant, just out of the oven, and fresh coffee. The market provides an ideal source of inexpensive food for a picnic on the Yarra River or in one of the many parks that ring the city. **Tina's Deli** (shop 33–35) is a wonderful source of Australian cheeses, while bread baked in wood-fired ovens can be bought from **Andrew's Bread Shop** (shop 29–30).

On Saturday at midday the pace becomes frenetic as shoppers rush for bargains before closing time at 1 PM. Stallholders stand in the aisle shouting out special deals. Bags of beans

ABOVE: Flinders Street Railway Station—a good place for buskers to attract passersby. OPPOSITE: Diners enjoy a leisurely meal overlooking the Yarra River and city skyline.

or trays of glistening trout are offered for a few dollars, and a box of fruit can be bought for under AU$5.

On Sunday no fresh food is sold and the Victoria Market is given over to serving tourists looking for a sheepskin coat, a cheap cuddly plush koala for their children or a T-shirt with a local design. The regulars, with a keen eye for a bargain, are also out in droves.

St. Patrick's Cathedral and District

Behind Parliament House is St. Patrick's Cathedral, built between 1858 and 1897. Gargoyles guard its bluestone exterior, and it is possible to visit the inside of the church during the day.

Other denominations built their places of worship nearby. The sturdy **Lutheran Church** (24 Parliament Place) was built in 1853, **Baptist Church House** (486 Albert Street) was built between 1859 and 1863 and **East Melbourne Synagogue** (488 Albert Street) was finished in 1877. It is worth wandering around the streets behind Parliament where there remain lovely examples of late nineteenth-century houses and public buildings.

Melbourne's Stately Houses

The National Trust owns a number of stately homes in the suburbs, open to the public and providing an insight into a more gracious era in the history of Melbourne.

Built between 1869 and 1887, **Rippon Lea (** (03) 9523-6095, at 192 Hotham Street, is a grand house located in suburban Elsternwick. The Romanesque building is surrounded by five and a half hectares (14 acres) of garden, considered the best surviving nineteenth-century example in Australia. On a fine day, picnickers flock to its grounds.

Como ((03) 9827-2500, in Como Avenue, South Yarra, was built in the 1840s and retains its original furnishings. This beautiful house overlooking the Yarra River, contains a ballroom and has a delicacy, elegance and lightness quite out of place in Australian society.

Just a 30-minute drive from Melbourne, **Werribee Park (** (03) 9741-2444, is an imposing 60-room Italianate mansion built in 1874

with 12 hectares (30 acres) of gardens including an ornamental lake. Adjacent to it is the Werribee Zoo (** (03) 9742-7933, where lions, hippos, giraffes, rhinoceroses and other animals can be seen close up during an exciting safari bus ride.

Carlton

Carlton is adjacent to the city and can be reached by tram (N°1 or N°15) north along Swanston Street, but it is close enough to be walkable.

The south end of Drummond Street which intersects LaTrobe Street in the city has many wonderful terrace houses dating back to 1864. Most of the nineteenth-century streetscape remains intact. Other streets in Carlton contain many more examples, shaming boring modern suburbs with their

mediocrity, sameness and lack of inspiration. Through the center of Carlton runs Lygon Street which has acquired an Italian character. Many postwar immigrants settled here, and Melbournians should be grateful to them for introducing cappuccino, good pasta and outdoor cafés into their city.

Although many Italian families have moved out of Carlton to more affluent suburbs, their children return to promenade along Lygon Street on warm summer evenings and dine in its numerous cafés.

Brunswick Street

Brunswick Street starts at Victoria Parade in Fitzroy, and can be reached by taking any tram east along Collins Street. The beginning of the street takes in Melbourne's first suburb

— Newtown — established in the 1840s and later absorbed into the municipality of Fitzroy. The oldest houses in the street are **Mononia** at N°21, built in 1851, and **Dodgshun House** at N°9, which is now a medical center.

Located at the city end of the street is **Roar 2 Gallery** (N°115A), which has become a Melbourne institution among avant-garde artists. Started in 1981 by a group of art school graduates, it provided them with a place to show works rejected by mainstream galleries. Many artists from Roar 2 have gained recognition and moved on, but a new generation has taken their place. The **Sutton**

Like many cities, Melbourne's skyline has been dramatically elevated with glossy twentieth-century skyscrapers; however, some fine buildings remain from the nineteenth-century growth period.

Gallery, a little further north at N⁰254, is open Tuesday to Saturday from 11 AM to 6 PM. Some of the best artworks can be seen in the open air — brightly painted street furniture and whimsical statues fill Brunswick Street with color. Just beyond Johnston Street is the **Brunswick Street Bookshop** (N⁰305), which stays open late. They have a good selection of novels and art books; arm chairs are provided for serious browsers. On fine evenings buskers enliven this part of the street, which is always crowded at weekends.

For a little piece of heaven, pig out on rich ice creams at **Charmaine's** (N⁰370).

Down by the Beach

St. Kilda is a bayside suburb just eight kilometers (five miles) from the city. Its fortunes have fluctuated, having started as an affluent suburb in the mid-nineteenth century with white mansions lining its Esplanade, where families "took the sea air" on weekends.

The twentieth century has not been gentle to St. Kilda, and as the gentry have fled for Kew, Toorak and South Yarra, art deco apartment buildings invaded and mansions were subdivided into boarding houses. St. Kilda is undergoing a rebirth and hopefully the sparkle will return to this seaside suburb.

The best place to survey St. Kilda is from the end of the pier. From the vantage point of the historic **St. Kilda Pier Kiosk**, the skyline looks Moorish with its domed buildings and a foreshore fringed with palm trees.

There is a walking track and bike lane running parallel to the beach. One way to view St. Kilda beach at high speed is to hire roller blades from **Rock 'n' Roll** at 11A Fitzroy Street. Val Guerra will help the inexperienced with an impromptu lesson.

South of the pier is Acland Street, the main meeting place for the Jewish community. If you want to flirt with hyperglycemia try the rich confections of **Monarch Cake Shop** at N⁰103 Acland Street, or you can sit down with cake and coffee at **Acland Cakes** at N⁰97. Further up the road is **Linden**, at N⁰26, a stuccoed brick mansion built in 1870 and converted into an art gallery, where admission is free.

Luna Park, between the Esplanade and Acland Street should not be missed with its gaudy four-meter (24-ft) entrance in the shape of a laughing clown. Unfortunately the interior is now shabby and rundown, as the public's taste in amusements has changed from Ferris wheels and roller-coasters to Space Invaders and Nintendo.

On Sunday there is an art and craft market along the Upper Esplanade, which is popular with tourists.

From the pier it is possible to take a ferry over to **Williamstown** on the other side of the city. The ferry departs from St. Kilda every hour on weekends. Williamstown still has the feeling of a village rather than a suburb, despite its proximity to Melbourne. It started life as a port town in 1837 but as the Port of Melbourne developed, fell into disuse. Its streets are lined with Edwardian laborers' cottages, and a stroll around is well worthwhile. On the last Sunday of every month a market is held in the park opposite Nelson Place.

MELBOURNE AFTER DARK

At night the action concentrates on the strip between the Bourke Street Mall and Exhibition Street, the location of theaters and cinemas.

For live music the pubs provide a choice of jazz, folk, heavy metal and good old rock and roll. For most of these gigs there is no entrance fee but check beforehand. For the coolest blues and jazz put on your shades for the **Night Cat** at 141 Johnston Street or **Bennetts Lane** at 25 Bennett Lane, Melbourne. With a name like the **Blarney Stone**, at the corner of Bay and Crockford streets, Port Melbourne, all you are likely to hear in this pub is Irish folk music. For something a little noisier try rock and roll at the ultra chic **Esplanade Hotel** on the Upper Esplanade at St. Kilda. **The Lounge** at 243 Swanston Walk in the city offers an eclectic selection of music on most nights and its food is very good. In Carlton, Brunswick, Prahran and Fitzroy there are quite a few establishments where aspiring bands perform.

New Australian plays are often staged at **La Mama** at 205 Faraday Street, Carlton. This theater has become renowned as the launch pad for some of Australia's better-known playwrights and actors. The audience seldom exceeds 50 people and in winter a fire blazes in one corner. The actors and the playwright usually stay around afterwards to chat and sip coffee. There are also several upmarket theaters in the Arts Centre on Swanston Street.

The free newspapers *In Press* and *Beat* are available in most entertainment venues and provide an excellent guide to music, films and bands. *Beat* also produces a gig guide on the web at http://www.ozonline.com.au:80/beat/m_giggui.htm. *Beat* caters mainly for young people, but on Fridays the daily newspaper *The Age* has a lift-out section, *Entertainment Guide*, which is the most comprehensive source of information on what's happening in Melbourne. The *Entertainment Guide* is also on the web at http://www.theage.com.au.

WHERE TO SHOP

Melbourne Central is the city's newest shopping complex, dominated by the **Daimaru** department store, and containing over 150 specialty shops. Entertainment is often provided at lunchtime under its conical skylight that covers a shot tower built in 1889. Old and modern have been successfully integrated and this area is always crowded with lunchtime shoppers.

Several galleries here sell Aboriginal paintings. The **Gallery Gabrielle Pizzi** at 141 Flinders Lane sells works from major Aboriginal artists and has taken many of its exhibitions on overseas tours. A wide range of paintings and artifacts from central Australia can be purchased from the **Gallery of Dreamings** at 73 Bourke Street; overseas shipment can be arranged.

A good selection of stores selling souvenirs are usually clustered around the larger hotels. For something out of the ordinary try the **Maker's Mark** at 85 Collins Street, where every month exhibitions of Australia's foremost craftspeople are held — and everything is for sale. This is an opportunity to buy jewelry or a gift of the best natural materials available in Australia, such as Broome pearls, Argyle champagne diamonds and native woods.

The **Meat Market Craft Centre** located at 42 Courtney Street, North Melbourne is just a short walk from Victoria Market. Its name hardly conjures up a craft shop, but as it was indeed a meat market this eccentricity may be forgiven. It offers pottery, handpainted fabrics, woodcrafts and leatherwork by contemporary artists and has regular exhibitions of other crafts, also for sale.

Toorak Road and Chapel Street in South Yarra are lined with trendy boutiques stocked with the latest fashions. For antiques, go to High Street, Armadale, where

a large selection of colonial and Edwardian artifacts and furnishings will be found.

SPORTS

Melbourne has some of the best sporting facilities in the country.

From March to September Melbourne goes football crazy. There are league football games on Friday nights and Saturday afternoons. The best stadiums to go to see a game and soak up the atmosphere are the Melbourne Cricket Ground (MCG) in Brunton Avenue, Jolimont, and Waverley Park in Wellington Road, Mulgrave. Special trains and buses are brought in to service for these games. There is horse racing at Flemington, Caulfield and Moonee Valley all year long, with the main season coming in spring. The highlight of the Spring Racing Carnival is the Melbourne Cup in which everyone seems to take an interest, even if they may not during the rest of the year.

A night match at Melbourne Cricket Ground.

Many punters get no further than enjoying chicken and champagne in the car park, a sensible diversion.

The Australian Tennis Open is held at Melbourne Park, where, for two weeks each January, the world's top players compete in this Grand Slam tournament. In March, car racing enthusiasts flock to Albert Park in Melbourne for the Australian Grand Prix, the first event in the annual FIA World Championship.

WHERE TO STAY

Luxury

At the top end of the market there has been an encouraging growth in boutique hotels in Melbourne, combining luxury with intimacy. These are small establishments, so book well ahead.

An easy walk from the city, **Magnolia Court** ((03) 9419-4222 FAX (03) 9416-0841, at 101 Powlett Street, East Melbourne, has an old world charm. Ask for a room in the older Victorian buildings dating back to 1858 and 1862, rather than in the extension added in the 1960s.

Located in the ritzy suburb of South Yarra is another small gem of a hotel. **The Tilba** ((03) 9867-8844 FAX (03) 9867-6567, at the corner of Toorak Road West and Domain Street, is an old Victorian house filled with sunshine from its leadlight windows and skylight.

The **Beaumont** ((03) 9853-2722 TOLL-FREE 1800-338-578 FAX (03) 9853-3773, located at 7 Studley Park Road, is in Kew, one of Melbourne's leafier suburbs, five kilometers (three miles) from the city. The building is modern with a good restaurant, **Sequins**, attached to the hotel. Guests can also hire bicycles to go riding at the track along the Yarra River.

Another place a little way out from the city is the new **Novotel Bayside** ((03) 9525-5522 FAX (03) 9525-5678, at 16 The Esplanade, St. Kilda. This hotel is just above the beach and its 224 rooms provide excellent views of Port Phillip Bay on one side and the city skyline on the other. Its postmodern architecture raised a few eyebrows when it was first built, but now the design seems compatible with the beach environs.

In the city are several luxury hotels with some character. **Le Meridien** ((03) 9620-9111 TOLL-FREE 1800-331-330 FAX (03) 614-1219, at 495 Collins Street, is in a renovated late-Victorian building brilliantly converted into a top hotel. Downstairs are bars, restaurants and coffee lounges. **The Windsor** ((03) 9653-0653 FAX (03) 9654-5183, is at the corner of Spring and Bourke streets. The hotel has been classified by the National Trust.

For those who like their accommodation fresh off the drafting board, there is the very

new **Grand Hyatt** ((03) 9657-1234 or 131-234 FAX (03) 9650-3491, at 123 Collins Street, with potted palms and pseudo-antique statuary in the lobby, or the **Centra** ((03) 9629-5111 TOLL-FREE 1800-335-590 FAX (03) 9629-5624, located at the corner of Flinders and Spencer streets, overlooking the Yarra River.

Moderate

The Victoria ((03) 9653-0441 FAX (03) 9650-9678, located at 215 Little Collins Street, is an unpretentious hotel in the center of the city which is more interested in providing comfortable and affordable accommodation than dressing its lobby in oceans of marble and deploying armies of bellhops.

In elegant East Melbourne, the **Georgian Court Guest House** ((03) 9419-6353 FAX 9416-0895, 21–25 George Street, offers comfortable and friendly bed-and-breakfast accommodation only a few minutes from the middle of town, and the staff are only too willing to help with information on what to see and do.

Outside the city there are good motels which are not too expensive. The **Ramada Inn** ((03) 9380-8131 TOLL-FREE 1800-222-431 FAX (03) 9388-0519, at 539 Royal Parade, is quite reasonable, while a little further up

communal lounge because it stifles conversation, and this friendly bed and breakfast is a great place to meet other travelers and swap traveling tips. In St. Kilda there is **Olembia Private Hotel** ((03) 9537-1412, at 96 Barkly Street, which is also a bed-a-breakfast place, while **Leopard House** ((03) 9534-1200, at 27 Grey Street, and **Enfield House** ((03) 9534-8159 FAX (03) 9534-5579, at Two Enfield Street, cater to backpackers.

There are two YHA hostels in North Melbourne, the enormous, modern **Queensberry Hill Hostel** ((03) 9329-8599, located

the road you'll find **Princes Park Motor Inn** ((03) 9388-1000 TOLL-FREE 1800-335-787 FAX (03) 9387-3749.

For a quiet, intimate atmosphere, try the **Avoca Bed and Breakfast** ((03) 9696-9090 FAX (03) 9696-9092, at 98 Victoria Avenue, Albert Park, an elegant Victorian terrace close to the beach.

Inexpensive

One of the most remarkable budget hotels in Melbourne is **The Nunnery** ((03) 9419-8637 FAX (03) 9417-7736, at 116 Nicholson Street, Fitzroy, located in a beautiful terrace building. Rooms vary from six-bed dormitories, to single rooms which once were the cells of nuns. Television is discouraged in the

at 78 Howard Street, and a quieter and more intimate youth hostel ((03) 9328-3595, at 76 Chapman Street.

WHERE TO EAT

Melbournians love to eat out, and the number and variety of restaurants is mind-boggling. The choices range from inexpensive places which reflect the numerous nationalities who have chosen to make their home in Melbourne to the more formal restaurants of the Establishment. Between these extremes are sidewalk cafés and informal bistros.

Taking in the panoramic view of the city skyline from St. Kilda's pier.

Restaurants tend to congregate in districts, offering a scale from one end of the price range to the other. Some included in this section are away from these precincts but are listed because they offer an exceptional setting or outstanding cooking.

Richmond has become the home of the Vietnamese community which is served by unpretentious establishments congregated along Victoria Street, just 10 minutes from the city. Although you may have to queue, which is a good sign in itself, try **Thy Thy 2** ((03) 9428-5914, located at 116 Victoria Street, (inexpensive) or for the best *pho* (beef or chicken soup) in Melbourne go to the **Van Mai** ((03) 9428-7948, at 372 Victoria Street (inexpensive).

For an inexpensive feed in the city try **Ong International Food Court**, at 265 Little Bourke Street (inexpensive), which is in the basement of the Welcome Hotel. The food of eight different Asian cuisines can be ordered from stalls, and no dish costs more than AU$8. Little Bourke Street and the lanes leading off it between Swanston and Spring streets, comprise **Chinatown**, with its many good restaurants. Inexpensive meals are available from the **Supper Inn** ((03) 9663-4759, upstairs at 15 Celestial Avenue (inexpensive), where the adventurous can try duck's tongues (recommended) or congee, a Chinese rice gruel (not recommended). You decide! In the higher price bracket is the **Flower Drum** ((03) 9662-3655, at 17 Market Lane (expensive), rated as one of the best Chinese restaurants in Australia. Choose from a wide variety of fresh seafoods such as prawns, scallops and abalone, or try their justifiably famous Peking Duck.

Brunswick Street in Fitzroy started as the place for the avant garde. There are still a few restaurants which reflect its early days, such as the **Black Cat** (Nº252) ((03) 9419-6230 (inexpensive). This modest café is decked out with 1950s memorabilia. Try its widgie spider, a scoop of ice cream in crimson lemonade, which I have never encountered elsewhere. The decor of the **Babka Bakery Café** ((03) 9416-0091, at Nº358 (moderate), may be modern, but in the mornings it is filled with the good old-fashioned smell of freshly baked bread, and

with dozens of early morning patrons enjoying a delicious breakfast and the best coffee in town.

There are some superb moderately-priced Thai restaurants in Melbourne. If you don't mind sitting cross-legged at a low table, there is the **Thai Thani** ((03) 9419-6463, at 293 Brunswick Street (moderate).

The **Café Provincial** ((03) 9417-2228, at 299 Brunswick Street (moderate), boasts a wood-fired oven and makes the best pizza in Melbourne. I strongly recommend the *calazone di prosciutto*, which is a pizza pastry filled with Parma ham, eggplant, spinach, onions and cheese.

In St. Kilda the **Tolarno Bar and Bistro** ((03) 9525-5477, at 42 Fitzroy Street (expensive), offers innovative Australian food, with lots of Mediterranean and Asian influence. Iain Hewitson's menu is always changing to reflect the availability of ingredients according to the season. His signature dish is roasted blue swimmer crabs, but the task of eating them with dignity is beyond me.

Overlooking St. Kilda beach is the **Stokehouse** ((03) 9525-5555, at 30 Jacka Boulevard. Its **downstairs** area (moderate) offers meals and snacks. You can have pizza made in their wood-fired oven, and then enjoy one of their delicious cakes. **Upstairs** (expensive) is more formal. Just before sunset is the best time to enjoy its panoramic view of the southern end of Port Phillip Bay.

Madame Joe Joe ((03) 9534-0000, located at 9 Fitzroy Street, St. Kilda (expensive), is definitely a chic place to be seen. The cuisine is "modern Australian", and includes some wonderfully exotic dishes, wicked deserts and good coffee.

If love good Italian food then head for Lygon Street in Carlton. **Trotter's** ((03) 9347-5657, at Nº400 (inexpensive), is a small friendly restaurant with most dishes under AU$10. It also does breakfast from 8 AM, and has the best poached eggs and hash browns in Melbourne. Across the road is **Tiamo** ((03) 9347-5759, at Nº303 (moderate), which is small, smoky, and a favorite haven for generations of college students looking for a hot meal and really good coffee. Established in 1952 the **Universita Bar and Ristorante** ((03) 9347-2142, located at Nº257 (inexpensive), is also frequented by students in search of good Italian regional food, as well as Italians who enjoy the student atmosphere. It has maintained its reputation and excellent value, and there is no main dish costing over AU$15

Donnini ((03) 9347-3128, located at 312 Drummond Street, Carlton (moderate), specializes in northern Italian cuisine, but its flag-bearer is Donini's pasta, reputed to be the best in Melbourne.

The **Great Australian Bite (** (03) 9329-9068, at 18 Molesworth Street, North Melbourne (expensive), has a reputation for experimenting with indigenous foods and unusual combinations. While the menu changes to reflect seasonal produce, one thing is constant: the chef, Karl Ferrern's, specialty that was placed in the Gourmet Olympics a few years back — rack of salt and sugar cured lamb, smoked over gum leaves.

For a meal either before or after a concert or performance at the Arts Centre, the **Treble Clef (** (03) 9281-8264 (moderate), provides simply prepared food which is moderately priced.

The **Colonial Tramcar Restaurant (** (03) 9696-4000 (expensive), is a converted 1927 tram that allows diners to watch Melbourne pass by, while enjoying their repast. The cost of the five-course meal and drinks on Friday and Saturday night is AU$90, justified more by a pleasant experience than the standard of food. The Tramcar is booked well ahead, so a reservation is essential.

Borsalino's ((03) 9459-1771, at 57 Cape Street, Heidelberg (expensive), serves a combination of Italian and French food. The restaurant is located in a two-story house built in 1898, with many of its original fixtures remaining. The menu changes frequently and the chef always ensures a good selection of vegetarian dishes on the menu.

Expensive restaurants in Melbourne often have a clubbish atmosphere, as behooves the home of the Establishment. Fortunately Melbourne's upper crust have discerning palates and demand the best food and service from their preferred restaurants. The chefs at **Chinois (** (03) 9826-3388, at 176 Toorak Road, South Yarra (ex-

pensive), have successfully combined the flavors of Western and Eastern cuisines to produce memorable dishes; their Sunday "adventure" lunch is quite popular. Melbourne's most highly reputed French restaurant is **Jacques Reymond (** (03) 9525-2178, at 78 William Street, Prahran (expensive). They offer an extensive range of game and fish dishes, as well as a good vegetarian selection.

HOW TO GET THERE

Tullamarine is an unimaginatively conceived but major international airport, and certainly better than Sydney's. Regular flights arrive from Asia, Europe and North and South America. Melbourne is also a major stop on bus routes along the southeastern seaboard.

By car, the trip from Sydney takes about 12 hours; allow 10 hours from Adelaide.

DAY TRIPS FROM MELBOURNE

THE DANDENONG RANGES

Taking the family for a drive to the Dandenong Ranges is a favorite day trip for Melbournians. They hardly justify the grand name of "ranges," at their highest point 630 m (2,060 ft) above sea level. In the hamlets and villages of these hills European trees have been introduced, providing colorful displays in autumn and away from built-up areas large tracts of native forest remain.

General Information
At the foot of the Dandenongs, is the entrance of the **Ferntree Gully National Park**. The **Dandenong Ranges Tourist Information Service (** (03) 9758-7522, at 1242 Burwood Highway, Upper Ferntree Gully, provides walking maps of the area free of charge, as well as a wealth of useful information. It is open 9 AM to 4:30 PM every day.

What to See and Do
Before white settlers established themselves in the Dandenongs, it was an important area for Aborigines. The Yarra Yarra tribe hunted here in summer. Monbulk,

corrupted from the Aboriginal word *Mon-bolloc* and meaning "hiding place in the hills," was reputed to contain healing springs.

In 1935, sculptor William Ricketts obtained two hectares (four and a half acres) of bushland, upon which he retired to live as a hermit. On his allotment he carved native animals and Aboriginal figures from clay. Ricketts' property was acquired by the Victorian Government in 1964, extended to six hectares (15 acres) and opened to the public. The **William Ricketts Sanctuary** ((03) 9751-1300, is at 92 Mt. Dandenong Tourist Highway, just past Kalorama, an enchanted place where sculptures have been molded into rocks or set into fern-lined nooks and grottos where water trickles over carved possums and kangaroos. Ricketts' vision was of a harmony between man and the universe; he believed that no one understood this relationship better than the Aborigines.

Dotted among the hills are a number of Bavarian and Swiss-style restaurants, such as the **Cuckoo** ((03) 9751-1003, in Olinda, moderately priced. For something special, dine in the nearby **Kenloch** ((03) 9751-1008.

There are also many tearooms in the Dandenongs. Just outside **Sassafras** there is **Henry the Eighth** ((03) 9755-1008, with its open fires in winter, and in town is **Miss Marple's Tearoom** ((03) 9755-1610, with its quaint English interior. Devonshire tea consisting of scones, fresh cream and jam is best enjoyed on a clear autumn or winter's day in front of a fire. Such an indulgence can only be justified after a brisk walk in the nearby **Sherbrooke Forest Reserve**. In its shady glades the very lucky may be rewarded by the sight of a lyrebird, always retiring and shy. The lyrebird is flightless and the male displays its large tail (resembling a lyre, surprise!) during the mating dance.

There are also many small galleries in the villages in the Dandenongs where the artists have a fixation on gum trees.

At Belgrave you can catch **Puffing Billy** ((03) 9754-6800, a narrow gauge railway running 13 km (eight miles) to **Emerald Lake Park** through beautiful fern glades, over ancient wooden bridges and across farmland. The line closed in 1954, but was restored by steam enthusiasts.

How to Get There

Trains leave Flinders Street for Belgrave Station every hour or so, where the train connects with buses which visit all the main attractions.

PHILLIP ISLAND

Phillip Island has long been a favorite summer vacation place for Melbournians. It has the advantage of being close by, with beaches less dreary than the sluggish waters of Port Phillip Bay. Phillip Island has, more recently, gained an international reputation for its **penguins**.

General Information

The **Phillip Island Tourist Information Centre** ((03) 5956-7447, is in Newhaven and is open daily, providing visitors with maps of the island and taking reservations for the penguin parade. Most of the coach companies and hotels can give you information on tours to see the penguins.

What to See and Do

As night falls over **Summerland Beach**, fairy penguins make their way to their burrows further up the shore, watched by hundreds of tourists on terraces built along the foreshore. Photographers are asked not to use electronic flash because it upsets the birds whose number varies from just handful to a few hundred, depending on the season. There could be better places to see penguins in Australia, but none more convenient.

Fortunately, there are other things to do on Phillip Island while waiting for the penguins to arrive. For some great walks try **Churchill Island** which is connected by a walkway to the main island. Explore its historic buildings and gardens established in the 1860s. Just to the south of Newhaven is the **Cape Woolamai State Fauna Reserve**, which has good walking tracks and is an important nesting ground for mutton birds. Care should be taken not to disturb them. Migratory travel may have carried these birds some 30,000 km (19,000 miles), in a

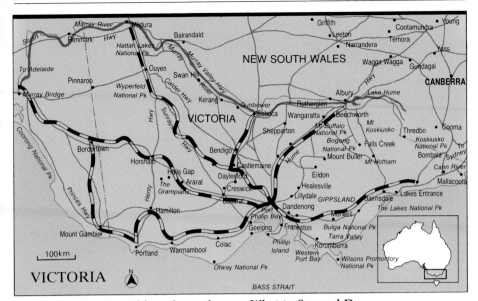

VICTORIA

round trip voyage to and from the northern hemisphere.

SPA COUNTRY

A short hour-and-a-half drive from Melbourne are the spa towns of **Daylesford** and **Hepburn Springs**, where for years people came to "take the waters." Therapeutic treatment provided included taking baths in spring water claimed to provide relief for a variety of complaints. Today these twin towns have added to their natural assets by providing visitors with a chance to heal the body with spa baths (complete with aromatic oils), massage and walking tracks. Afterwards the digestion is challenged by tantalizing restaurants and the rest cure completed in a guesthouse that caters to every need.

While the Spa Country is an easy day trip from Melbourne, a longer stay is strongly recommended (see SHORT BREAKS in YOUR CHOICE). This will allow sufficient time to feel the full benefit of the restorative powers of this restful region.

General Information

Information is available from the **Daylesford Tourist Information Centre** ((03) 5348-1339, in Vincent Street, which is the main thoroughfare in Daylesford. The center is open seven days a week.

What to See and Do

On Wombat Hill in Daly Street is a Catholic convent which has been imaginatively converted to a restaurant–gallery. The **Convent Gallery** exhibits pottery, paintings and jewelry from top Victorian artists and craftspeople.

There are two artificial lakes in Daylesford — **Jubilee Lake** and **Lake Daylesford**, and it takes about an hour to walk around both. An alternative way to take your exercise is to hire a boat or canoe from the **Boathouse Café** ((03) 5348-1387.

If the weather lets you down drop into the **Bookbarn** next to Lake Daylesford, which has a wide selection of books. Its owner, Kerry Bolton, invites browsers to sit around the potbellied stove and dip into any books they are thinking of purchasing.

Where to Stay and Eat

There are several excellent restaurants in Daylesford, of which the most stylish is **Lake House** ((03) 5348-3329, in King Street, where reservations are essential. It also offers luxury-priced accommodation overlooking Lake Daylesford. For an inexpensive meal try **Sweet Decadence** ((03) 5348-3202, at 57 Vincent Street, named after the chocolate made on the premises. In Hepburn Springs, the **Cosy Corner Café** ((03) 5348-3825, at 3 Tenth Street, has a friendly ambiance and an open fire in winter.

Luxury accommodation is available in Hepburn Springs at the **Linton House** ((03) 5348-2331, 68 Central Springs Road, while the comfortable **Dudley House** ((03) 5348-3033, located at 101 Main Road is moderately priced.

How to Get There

Daylesford is 109 km (68 miles) northwest of Melbourne, off the Midland Highway. Hepburn Springs is a further four kilometers (two miles) north.

GOLD FIELDS

Marvelous Melbourne was founded on the wealth of the gold fields which sprang to life in the rush in 1851, centering around Ballarat and Bendigo. In the following decade 1,000 tons of gold were extracted, worth 110 million pounds and accounting for 40 percent of the world's total production. The find attracted miners who had tried their luck on the Californian fields and adventurers hoping to get rich quickly. Some did, but most didn't.

To help the successful prospectors spend their hard earned money, townships such as Ballarat, Bendigo, Castlemaine and Maldon sprouted like toadstools, satisfying the needs of the miners with banks, stores hotels and brothels. Satisfying parched throats, bars and grog shops did a bustling trade everywhere.

Many of the gold mining towns continued to prosper after the gold ran out, although their populations today are a fraction of what they were during the rush.

GENERAL INFORMATION

There are tourist information centers in all of the major towns. They are: **Castlemaine Tourist Information Centre** ((03) 5470-6200, Duke Street, **Bendigo Tourist Information Centre** ((03) 5444-4445, Pall Mall Centre, **Ballarat Visitor Information Centre** ((03) 5332-2694, 39 Sturt Street, and **Maldon Visitor Centre** ((03) 5475-2569, High Street.

The gold rush days live on at Sovereign Hill, a reconstructed mining town at Ballarat.

WHAT TO SEE AND DO

Ballarat

The state's largest inland metropolis, with a population of 63,800, Ballarat lies 112 km (70 miles) from Melbourne. It has matured from a rough tent city during the gold rush into a provincial center with pretensions to style and graciousness with its mid- to late nineteenth-century architecture. The National Trust is kept busy in Ballarat where over 60 buildings have been classified for their historical importance. Wherever you go you can see decorative cast iron verandah friezes and balustrades common to all British colonial architecture from Calcutta to Cape Town. Take a look in the shops at the north end of Lydiard Street for some typical examples of lacy embellishments.

Sovereign Hill Gold Mining Township ((03) 5331-1944, at the corner of Main Road and Bradshaw Street, is a re-creation of a gold rush township. The main drag represents the Main Street of Ballarat as it was 150 years ago. It is a living museum, with over 40 buildings housing a forge, bakery, confectioner and hotel — all operational and open for business. At Red Hill Gully in the township you can pan for gold or take a look at the underground mine nearby. In the evening there is a sound and light show *Blood on the Southern Cross* which relates the melodrama of the rumpus at the Eureka Stockade. Sovereign Hill is great fun for adults and children alike, and has won national awards for its living history museum.

If the prospect does not make you weep or sink into a coma and you insist on seeing where a rebellious rabble at the **Eureka Stockade** was dealt with, a replica of the "fortification" stands at the corner of Stawell and Eureka streets. There is also a memorial in the park to the 22 troublemakers and five soldiers who died during the rebellion.

Bendigo

North of Ballarat is Bendigo, queen city of the goldfields. The former wealth of the city is obvious when you arrive at the center of town where the magnificent **Alexandra**

Fountain stands at the crossroads. Nearby is the elegant **Shamrock Hotel**, at the intersection of Pall Mall and Williamson Street which once served hooch to the many Irish miners of Bendigo. It was said that the owner of the hotel would earn himself another £4 each day by sweeping the floor and collecting gold dust brought in on his customers' boots. On a warm night there is still no nicer place to be than on the balcony of this fine hotel enjoying a tall cold ale. Almost across the road, on the Pall Mall is the old Post Office, built in 1887, which is now the tourist bureau. It is well worth a visit, as the interior has been lovingly restored to its former splendor.

Chinese indentured laborers also left their mark on Bendigo. The **Chinese Joss House** ((03) 5442-1685, in Finn Street, Emu Point, is a temple built in the 1860s by the lonely men of See Yup to honor their ancestors in the China of their youth. The best way to get there is on the vintage **Talking Tram** ((03) 5443-8070, which is not much at small talk but waxes lyrical about Bendigo's history. It starts in the center of town.

The tram takes you on a visit to the **Central Deborah Mine** ((03) 5443-8322, in Violet Street, which operated in the 1940s and 1950s and is linked to shafts sunk a century earlier. The gold mine is 422 m (1,385 ft) deep with 17 levels; tours are conducted daily and the conditions of mining may be viewed and pondered.

Maldon

Gold was mined at Maldon from 1854 until the 1930s and the town retains much of its gold rush streetscape, protected by the National Trust. Visitors to the **Blacksmith and Wainwright Shop** in High Street will see a blacksmith working at restoring nineteenth-century wagons.

To experience what the miners must have seen when they were underground, there is a candlelit tour of **Carmans Tunnel** ((03) 5475-2656, a 570-m (1,870-ft)-long horizontal shaft two kilometers (one mile) from town, off Parkin's Reef Road; open only on weekends and public holidays.

At Hornsby Street is the Maldon Station. The **Maldon Tourist Railway** ((03) 5475-2966, offers a delightful steam train to Muckleford on weekends and during national and school holidays.

Castlemaine

The rush at Castlemaine started about a year after the first diggings at Ballarat.

Castlemaine today is a leisurely country town, justifiably proud of its gardens and galleries. The **Art Gallery and Museum** ((03) 5472-2292, at 14 Lyttleton Road, has a good collection of art dating from the late nineteenth century to the mid-twentieth. It is open from 10 AM to 5 PM. In Mostyn Street you will find the **Market Museum** ((03) 5472-2679, built in 1861, which has exhibitions and audio-visual displays telling the story of the Castlemaine gold rush. Daily opening hours are from 10 AM to 5 PM. There are also good private galleries showing contemporary arts and crafts, such as the **Federation Fine Art Gallery** ((03) 5472-2025, at 8 Parker Street.

The **Buda Historic Home and Garden** ((03) 5472-1032, at the corner of Hunter and Urquhart streets, is open for inspection daily. The house was built in 1861 on two hectares (five acres) of beautiful gardens, and has been furnished to re-create the nineteenth-century colonial style; on display is silverware by the Hungarian silversmith Ernest Leviny, who once owned Buda.

WHERE TO STAY

The best places to stay on the gold fields are in historic hotels and cottages which provide bed and breakfast. In Main Street, Maldon, **Lemonwood Cottage** ((03) 5475-2015, offers historic cottage accommodation at moderate prices. In Castlemaine the luxury-priced **Midland Private Hotel** ((03) 5472-1085, at Two Templeton Street, retains much of its late nineteenth-century interior, while the **Coach and Rose** ((03) 5472-4850, located at 68 Mostyn Street, is a small and cozy moderately-priced bed-and-breakfast establishment.

For a bit of luxury and a glimpse of history spend your night at the **Shamrock** ((03)5443-0333, at the corner of Pall Mall and Williamson Street in Bendigo, which also serves excellent meals in its dining rooms.

For something a little more romantic and with a lot of tranquillity, the moderately-priced **Nanga Gnulle** (/FAX (03) 5443-7891, located at 40 Harley Street, has open fires and a beautiful garden. Eight kilometers (five miles) out of Bendigo is one of my favorite getaways, the moderately-priced **Skye Glen Llama Farm** ((03) 5439-3054 FAX (03) 5441-5051, which overlooks the peaceful Mandurang Valley, where Ron and Heather McLeod have taken their Scottish background to extremes, serving hearty highland breakfasts, and shortbreads for afternoon tea; they've even given the llamas Scottish names. Also in the moderate category, in Ballarat **Craigs Royal Hotel** ((03) 5331-1377, at 10 Lydiard Street South, was built in 1867 and is classified by the National Trust. Rooms at the high end of the moderate range have spa baths.

There are also a number of moderately-priced motels along the highways out of Ballarat and Bendigo.

HOW TO GET THERE

The gold fields are about two hours from Melbourne, and driving around them provides an opportunity to take in a good deal in a relatively short time. There are regular bus and train services to Bendigo and on weekdays bus services between the main towns in this area.

GREAT OCEAN ROAD

Drive down the **Great Ocean Road** for coastal scenery that is both varied and spectacular (see THE OPEN ROAD in YOUR CHOICE). This is one of the great scenic drives in Victoria.

GENERAL INFORMATION

There are information centers in most of the towns along the Great Ocean Road. They are: **Great Ocean Road Visitor Information Centre** ((03) 5237-6529 FAX (03) 5237-6194, 155 Great Ocean Road; **Lorne Tourist Information Centre** ((03) 5289-1152 FAX (03) 5289-2492, 144 Mountjoy Road, open Monday to Wednesday 9:30 AM to 4 PM, Thursday and Friday 9 AM to 5 PM and weekends 10 AM to

3 PM; **Warrnambool Information Centre**
((03) 5564-7837 FAX (03) 5561-2133, 600 Raglan Parade, open weekdays, school and
public holidays 9 AM to 5 PM and weekends
10 AM to 12 PM and 1 PM to 4 PM; and **Port
Fairy Information Centre** ((03) 5568-2682
FAX (03) 5568-2833, in Bank Street, open weekdays 10 AM to 4 PM and weekends 10 AM to
12:30 PM and 1:30 PM to 4 PM.

WHERE TO STAY

The holiday towns along the Great Ocean
Road have a good range of moderately-
priced accommodation, from motels to self-
contained flats and holiday houses rented
by the week. Reservations are essential
during school holidays, and over summer
most places are filled with vacationing
families.

The **Surf City Motel** ((03) 5261-3492
FAX (03) 5261-4032, is off the highway at
Torquay opposite Zeally Bay, while **Just
June's** ((03) 5289-1147, at 12 Casino Court,
is a pleasant bed-and-breakfast place.

On the Mountjoy Parade at Lorne are the
Kalimna Motel ((03) 5289-1407, and the
Anchorage Motel ((03) 5289-1891. Bed and
breakfast accommodation is provided at the
Otway Homestead ((03) 5289-1147, on
Erskine Falls Road.

Princetown is a perfect place to stay to be
near the most spectacular attractions of the
Great Ocean Road. **Apostle's View** ((03)
5598-8277, in Booringa Road, and **Macka's
Family Farm** ((03) 5598-8261, on Princetown
Road, are moderately priced.

At the very end of the Great Ocean Road,
15 km (nine miles) from Warrnambool is the
historic village of **Koroit**. At the center of
this charming little dairy town is **Bourke's
Koroit Hotel** ((03) 5565-8201, a classic bush
pub authentically restored by Mick Bourke
and filled with nineteenth-century furnishings.

HOW TO GET THERE

Take the Princes Highway out of Melbourne
to Geelong, then turn off to Torquay on the
Coast Highway, eventually intersecting with
the Great Ocean Road. There are also package coach tours along the Great Ocean Road.

MURRAY RIVER PORTS

The golden days of the riverboats, between
1850 and 1880 is a chapter often forgotten in
Australia's history but the romance of those
adventurous and colorful times lingers on
along the Murray River.

Just over a century ago before railways
and paved roads, the Murray was the nation's trading highway with hundreds of
riverboats plying its 2,590-km (1,610-mile)
length. With its tributary, the Darling, it

formed a commercial artery for the entire
southeast of the continent.

GENERAL INFORMATION

You will find tourist information centers in
most of the main towns along the Murray.
The **Swan Hill Regional Tourist Information Centre** ((03) 5032-3033, at 306 Campbell Street, Swan Hill, **Echuca Moama
Tourism** ((03) 5480-7555, in Heygarth Street,
Echuca, and **Mildura Tourism** ((03) 5021-

OPPOSITE: Whorls of the plow stretch across
the vast wheatland of Victoria's Wimmera.
ABOVE: Dunes at Croajingolong, which runs along
38 km (68 miles) of wild ocean. OVERLEAF: The
Murray Princess steams its way up river.

4424, on Deakin Avenue, provide information on the Murray River and attractions to be found nearby.

WHAT TO SEE AND DO

The Murray River is often little more than a muddy trench these days because the level of its waters are manipulated by the Snowy Mountain scheme to provide hydroelectric power and irrigation for southeastern Australia. It only meanders slowly westward towards South Australia, running along side the Murray Highway on its southern bank.

Echuca, an hour's drive north from Bendigo, is the patriarch of all the great Murray River ports. Flourishing and strutting Echuca was once the greatest inland port and second only to Melbourne in Victoria. The wooden wharf, preserved in the Port of Echuca area, has three different levels to allow for the 10-m (30-ft) variation in river heights which once plagued this stretch of the Murray. The **Historic Port** of Echuca is now a tourist precinct, housing a number of museums, as well as **Gumnutland**, a model village and railway, and **Sharp's Magic Movie House and Penny Arcade**. The **Star Hotel** has an underground bar, and features an escape tunnel once used by those patrons wishing to avoid the attention of the local constabulary.

While visiting Echuca, a cruise on an **paddle steamer** is a must. The *P.S. Pevensey* ((03) 5482-4248, offers a one- hour heritage cruise, while the *M.V. Mary Ann* ((03) 5480-2200, boasts a fully-licensed restaurant, and runs lunch and dinnertime cruises.

A half-an-hour drive from Echuca, the road passes by **Gunbower Island**, a 50-km (31-mile)-long rookery, 53 km (33 miles) later reaching **Kerang**, an agricultural town at the end of a chain of lakes with the largest breeding grounds in the world for ibis and certain other species of waterfowl.

Swan Hill was the other great river port of last century. On three hectares (seven acres) at Horseshoe Bend is the **Pioneer Settlement** ((03) 5032-1093, centered around the *Gem*, in its day the biggest and most powerful vessel on the river. The streets are lined with shops, a forge, a bakery and coach offices which recall a lost era.

Another 250 km (155 miles) downstream is **Mildura**, garden city of the river and center of the Sunraysia fruit-growing district.

WHERE TO STAY

A novel place to stay is on a houseboat; these self-contained units are a great way to tour the Murray River. Reservations can be made through **Echuca Rich River Houseboats** ((03) 5480-2444 TOLL-FREE 1800-132-643. There is some fine bed-and-breakfast and cottage accommodation in Echuca. The **River Gal-**

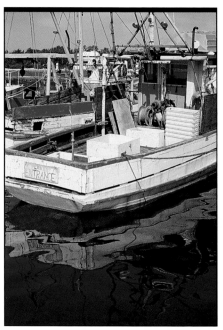

lery Inn ((03) 5480-6902, at 578 High Street, has an old world charm where guests are invited to breakfast in its sunny courtyard. **Murray House** ((03) 5482-4944 FAX (03) 5480-6432, at 55 Francis Street, has an open fire and a guest's library.

In Swan Hill two motels in the moderate price range are the **Swan Hill Motor Inn** ((03) 5032-2728, at 405 Campbell Street, and **Paruna Motel** ((03) 5032-4455 TOLL-FREE 1800-810-445, at 386 Campbell Street.

WHERE TO EAT

The paddle steamer, the *Gem* in Swan Hill has a restaurant aboard, where local yabbies and fish are offered with wine. For a sense of history enjoy a light lunch or afternoon tea at the **Murray Downs Homestead**, one and a half kilometers (one mile) from Swan Hill, and afterwards take a walk around this 1866 mansion.

Carriages ((03) 5032-2017, at the Pioneer Motor Inn, 421 Campbell Street, Swan Hill, has a good varied menu. **Silver Slipper** ((03) 5032-2726, at the Swan Hill Motor Inn, specializes in fresh river fish.

HOW TO GET THERE

There are direct flights into Mildura from Adelaide, Broken Hill, Melbourne and Renmark. V/Line runs train service from Melbourne to Swan Hill and a rail/coach service provides access to Echuca. The Vinelander MotoRail runs to Mildura.

Coach tours to Echuca itself are operated by Australia Pacific and Australian Colonial tours. Tour operators offer extended tours of the Murray region. Greyhound buses bound for Broken Hill pass through Echuca and Swan Hill, and Greyhound Pioneer buses to Deniliquin stop at Echuca.

NATIONAL PARKS

Information about national parks can also be obtained from the **Victoria Visitor Information Centre**, in Swanston Street, Melbourne, or from local tourist bureaus. The **Victorian National Parks Association** ((03) 9650-8296 FAX (03) 9654-6843, organizes walks every weekend around Victoria's parks. Non-members pay AU$5 and transport to the park can usually be arranged. Reservations, however, need to made two to four weeks ahead.

The **Organ Pipes** ((03) 9390-1082, 25 km (15 miles) north of Melbourne, is off the Calder Highway. This national park features dramatic 20-m (60-ft)-high basalt columns recalling — wait for it — organ pipes.

The **Point Nepean National Park** ((03) 5984-4276, stretches along 40 km (25 miles) of scenic coastline and contains several rare plants and animals; between November and March dolphins can be seen cavorting in the waters off the coast. Approach via the Mornington Peninsula, 100 km (62 miles) south of Melbourne.

Its many walking tracks make the **Little Desert** ((03) 5391-1275, 375 km (230 miles) northwest of Melbourne, ideal for hikers. The park supports a wide range of ecosystems and is the home of the mound-building mallee fowl. In spring wildflowers color the landscape. You can reach the park from the Western Highway, near Dimboola.

A walking holiday of Victoria is not complete unless **Wilson Promontory** ((03) 5680-9555, 250 km (155 miles) southeast of Melbourne is part of the itinerary. It is a mixture of picturesque beaches and a wide

range of natural vegetation including forest, heaths, coastal areas and wetlands. This national park is one of the most popular in Victoria and reservations for accommodation are essential during holiday periods.

ABOVE: Mildura Post Office. OPPOSITE: Fishing boats at Lakes Entrance.

Western Australia

The Irrepressible State

WESTERN AUSTRALIA has always been somewhat set apart from the rest of the country. Even though it is not much younger than the other states it has a feeling of newness. Its citizens have a nationalism that is parochial — more Western Australian than Australian.

Its geographical isolation required Western Australia to be self-reliant, a task made easier by its healthy mining industry. More than any other place in Australia, Western Australia sees its future in Asia, hardly surprising when you consider that Perth is closer to Singapore than Sydney.

Perth is the fastest-growing city in Australia. Over the last few decades its skyline has shot up, reflecting the state's confidence. Unfortunately many of the new developments were promoted by homegrown entrepreneurs, who in the 1980s used borrowed money to take over companies. The bubble finally burst in the early 1990s and thousands of small investors lost their savings.

There have been other booms and busts in the state's history. Each time the irrepressible Western Australians bounced back to new heights.

The state covers a third of the continent, most of it is a desert which comes alive each spring with a carpet of wildflowers. The northern portion of the state is watered by monsoons, receiving between 500 and 1,000 mm (20 to 40 inches) of rain between December and April.

PERTH

Perth exudes confidence and lauds financial success. While sections of "old Perth" remain, it is its newness that strikes the visitor, its numerous office towers which dominate the skyline.

Just as the people of Perth are willing to work hard, they also expect to play hard. The temperate climate makes Perth an outdoor city: each night its streets are alive while on the weekends Perth's beaches, boardwalks, tennis courts and sidewalk cafés are crowded.

Western Australians enjoy their spare time to the full, eschewing formality yet insisting on the best when they go out.

BACKGROUND

The Swan River Colony was founded in 1829 by Captain James Stirling; its growth was retarded by its disadvantages of remoteness from the colonies on the eastern seaboard, and the virtual unnavigability of the Port of Fremantle for seagoing vessels.

It began as a free settlement but grew slowly because of a labor shortage. In 1850 the colonial government requested convict labor to boost its flagging economy.

Western Australia's next growth spurt occurred when gold was discovered in Coolgardie and Kalgoorlie in the early 1890s. After Federation locals were able to boast that their state was the "Golden Gate of Australia."

There were other discoveries of mineral wealth, with enormous reserves of natural gas off the northwest coast and iron ore in the Pilbara.

The state's relationship with the rest of Australia has not always been harmonious. On April 8, 1933, Western Australian held a referendum on whether to secede from the rest of the country. There was overwhelm-

OPPOSITE: Sand patterns at Eucla. ABOVE: View across the Swan from the Royal Perth Yacht Club.

ing support for the proposal, with 138,653 voting "yes" and just 70,706 voting "no." Western Australians objected to the federal government's high tariff policy which disadvantaged their state's exports. In particular the high price of sugar to protect Queensland's growers raised their ire. To dramatize their point the Fremantle Sugar Party was held to emulate the famous Boston Tea Party, threatening to dump sugar into Fremantle Harbour. This not very original act of defiance never took place and the west soon lost its enthusiasm for secession.

WHAT TO SEE AND DO

Perth is situated on a broad stretch of the Swan River of almost lake-like proportions, which gives a feeling of spaciousness; sailing boats provide an attractive backdrop to the city.

Overlooking the Swan River is **King's Park**, 400 hectares (1,000 acres) of gardens and bushlands on the western edge of the central business district. The park was reserved by explorer/politician John Forrest in

GENERAL INFORMATION

The **Western Australian Tourist Centre** ((08) 9483-1111, at the corner of Forrest Place and Wellington streets, has a good selection of brochures and can arrange accommodation and tours. The **tourist booth** in Fremantle ((08) 9336-6636, is located in the Town hall Arcade.

Getting around the city is free within the bounds of Kings Park Road, Thomas Street, Newcastle Street, the Causeway and Barrack Street Jetty. **Transperth Service Information** (132-213, offers information on public transport, weekdays from 6:30 AM to 9 PM and weekends from 7 AM to 7 PM. For information on country trains phone ((08) 9326-2222.

1872 for children "a thousand years hence to see what the bush was like when Stirling arrived." In spring the park is a mass of beautiful wildflowers, a living example of the wisdom of Forrest's bequest. The best way to see it is on a bicycle hired from **Koala Bicycle Hire** ((08) 9321-3061, located near the rear of Garden Restaurant.

The park overlooks Narrows Bridge and the colony's first flour mill. At the south end of the bridge is the **Old Mill** ((08) 9367-5788, a Perth landmark, which contains relics of the pioneer days. Built in 1835 it is open to the public from 10 AM to 4 PM daily.

St. George's Terrace is Perth's main thoroughfare. Strolling along "the Terrace," you pass a mixture of the city's oldest buildings and the glittering glass towers erected during the last boom. At your feet are more than 150 bronze plaques which have been embedded into the sidewalk. Each one honors a Western Australian who made an outstanding contribution to the life of the state's first 150 years.

At the corner of Hay and Barrack streets is Perth's **Town Hall**, built by convicts in the 1860s in the fashion of an English Jacobean market hall.

Running along the southern side of the Terrace is **Stirling Gardens**, which stretches east from Barrack Street, stopping just short of Victoria Street. These are a popular venue for concerts and art shows. Facing them and opposite Pier Street is **Government House**, the official residence of the Governor built between 1859 and 1864. Described as Jacobean Mansion revival-style, it is set in elegant English-style gardens. Across the road is **The Deanery**, built in the late 1850s and retaining its shingle roof. Walk west up the Terrace and near King Street is the **Old Perth Boys' School** built between 1852 and 1854, Western Australia's first and Australia's second oldest school. If you would like to see it you can enter the fine sandstone building, which contains a café and souvenir shop.

Exhibitions relating to different aspects of the state's history are on display at the **Western Australian Museum** ((08) 9328-4411, in Francis Street, Northbridge. The pride of its collection is the 11-ton Mundrabilla meteorite; opening hours on weekdays and Sunday are from 10:30 AM to 5 PM and on Saturday and public holidays from 1 PM to 5 PM. Admission is free. The museum is part of the **Perth Cultural Centre** that also contains the **Art Gallery of Western Australia** ((08) 9328-7233, with one of the best collections of Aboriginal art in Australia, and the **Perth Institute of Contemporary Art** ((08) 9227-6144.

One of the best ways to see Perth and its environs is from a river cruiser; there is a good selection of trips to choose from, most of which start at the Barrack Street Jetty. The **Transperth Ferry** ((08) 9221-2722, departs daily for tourist destinations near Perth and along the Swan River. One of the more pleasant trips is a short voyage to the **Perth Zoo**,

set in beautifully landscaped gardens. See the world's beasts at rest or at play while they look back bemused at the zoo of humans who visit them every day.

Fremantle

Fremantle, 19 km (12 miles) downstream from Perth, is spread around the mouth of the Swan River. It was once a humble work-a-day seaport.

For years locals valued Fremantle's Old World charm and leisurely pace, which contrasted with Perth. The suburb retains

many buildings dating back to the first half of the nineteenth century, an unpretentious seaside town which was the place to go for an inexpensive meal, a walk along the foreshore or a visit to an art gallery.

"Freo," as it is known to the locals, was thrust into the international limelight when in 1987 the America's Cup defense was held in the waters off Fremantle. A powerful lot of money was spent doing up the town, and some of the eyesores along the foreshore were tastefully renovated. The development included a boardwalk which was built where waterfront restaurants cluster. Several hotels were built to accommodate the yachting crowd and fortunately do not spoil the feel of Freo.

During the day or night, Fremantle is full of people enjoying the sidewalk cafés and pubs or just promenading. There is always something to do.

OPPOSITE: Perth's pedestrian-only shopping center. ABOVE: The Byzantine-style St. Francis Xavier Cathedral at Geraldton.

At the south end, near the river's mouth, is the **Round House** ((08) 9430-7351, built in 1831. This 12-sided building, the oldest in Western Australia, was first used to jail minor offenders. When convicts first arrived in 1850 it accepted more serious offenders. Part of the building is now a café.

Further up High Street, towards the city center, is the **Town Hall**. In 1884 the municipal council put itself in hock for fifteen years to pay for this building, with its ornate façade and elaborately decorated balconies and balustrades. Inaugurated on June 22, 1887, the celebration was spoiled for one councilor when he was shot dead by a gatecrasher.

It is well worth a few hours taken to visit the **Western Australian Maritime Museum** ((08) 9431-8444, on Cliff Street, where admission is by donation. Pride of place is taken by the restored stern section of the Dutch treasure ship *Batavia*, wrecked in 1629 off the Western Australian coast near Geraldton, 330 km (206 miles) north of Perth. The museum is open every day from 10:30 AM to 5 PM.

One of the nicest places in Fremantle is the **Fremantle Arts Centre** ((08) 9335-8244, at One Finnerty Street. The center has three downstairs galleries showing works mainly by Western Australian artists. Exhibitions change every four weeks and works are for sale. The upstairs gallery has a permanent collection of the best from local artists and craftspeople. Through winter this venue is used for Sunday afternoon poetry readings and music is played in the downstairs courtyard from September to April. Daily opening hours are from 10 AM to 5 PM.

The Swan Valley

Vineyards were established in the Swan Valley over a hundred years ago. Not as well known as its counterparts in South Australia, this region produces award-winning Shiraz, Cabernet and Chenin Verdelho wines.

An enjoyable way to tour the Swan Valley is to take a cruise along the Swan River. The **Boat Torque Cruises** ((08) 9221-5844, depart every day for a tour of the wineries — **Houghtons** on Wednesday, Friday and

Sunday, while on the remaining days it visits **Sandalford** where you may meet the vintner, Bill Krapsley, who knows a great deal about Western Australian wines. Phone first because tour schedules change seasonally.

PERTH AFTER DARK

The Swan River is at its prettiest at night, surrounded by the skyline lights of Perth. See it on an evening cruise offered by **Boat Torque Cruises** ((08) 9221-5844, aboard the *Star Flyte* where you can take in the shimmering sights over a meal and then spend the rest of the evening dancing. The dinner cruises depart Friday and Saturday evenings at 7:45 PM.

On the Great Eastern Highway is the AU$300-million **Burswood Resort Casino** ((08) 9362-7777, which incorporates a top-class hotel and 14,000-seat entertainment center. The casino is open until 3 AM, and if you aren't successful at one of its 109 gaming tables and the roulette wheel has been uncharitable, perhaps the cabaret show will cheer you.

When night falls the city is fairly quiet, except for a few clubs such as **Globe Night Club**, at 393 Murray Street, and **Gobbles Nightclub**, at 613 Wellington Street. The main action happens in Northbridge, just north of the city, and in Fremantle. These suburbs are full of people looking for a good time.

In Northbridge, you can party until 3 AM at **Eternity Nightclub and Cabaret** at 78 James Street, or at **James Street Nightclub** at 139 James Street. For some lively jazz drop into the **Hyde Park Hotel** at 331 Bulwer Street, Monday or Tuesday night.

The younger crowd looking for lively music goes to **Metropolis Concert Club** at 58 South Terrace in Fremantle. The **Havana**, at 69 Lake Street in Northbridge, plays disco until 5 AM.

The **Concert Hall** in St. George Terrace features anything from grand opera to folk concerts, and there are also a concert hall and theater at the University of Western Australia campus in Nedlands.

Perth has grown rapidly in the past two decades adding ever taller buildings to its skyline.

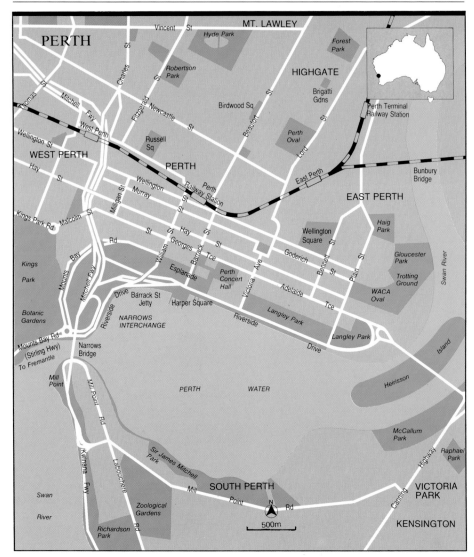

In Fremantle there is no better place to start an evening out than South Terrace, otherwise known as "Cappuccino Strip", where buskers entertain and pavement artists display their latest works. There are also some great pubs in Freo. Drop into the **Sail & Anchor Pub Brewery** at 64 South Terrace, for a drop of one of the local ales, with sprightly names like Redback, Dogbolter, and Iron Brew, some of which are brewed on the premises.

For more information on events in Perth check the entertainment pages of the daily *West Australian*. For a gig guide pick up a free copy of *X Press*.

WHERE TO SHOP

The main shopping areas in Perth are **Hay and Murray Street malls** which are linked by multilevel arcades. These provide shoppers with a wide range of choices, concentrated in a small area. Of the arcades, **London Court** is brimming with character with its mock-Tudor alley of carved woodwork, lattice windows and wrought iron trim.

Perth has good selections of Aboriginal art galleries from which to buy a unique souvenir of Australia. The **Aboriginal Art Gallery** ((08) 9322-3398, at 32 King Street, has a wide selection of authentic items, from bark paintings to modern works by prominent Aboriginal painters. In Fremantle Aboriginal art, craft and artifacts are for sale from **Bellamys Aboriginal Art Gallery** ((08) 9430-7439, at 43 High Street.

Opals are a specialty in quite a few shops. At **Opal Exploration Company** ((08) 9325-2907, at 616 Hay Street, you can watch gemstones being cut and polished. Argyle diamonds from Western Australia's Kimberley region come in a variety of colors including the rare pink or "champagne" diamonds. **Costello's** ((08) 9325-8588, at 1–5 St. Martin's Arcade (downstairs) off London Court, carries a wide selection of jewelry incorporating designs ranging from pendants, earrings, rings and brooches to bracelets, tie bars, cufflinks and watches incorporating Argyle diamonds, pearls or opals.

SPORTS

With such good weather year round, it is no surprise that so many of Perth's attractions are sports or outdoors related. Its climate is perfect for golf and more than 20 courses are close to the city. Forty-five minutes south of Perth, is the Meadow Springs Country Club's **Collier Park Golf Course** ((08) 9581-6360, in Meadow Springs Drive, where you can play 18 holes on a course bounded by a pine plantation and with a couple of lakes to keep the game interesting. If your appetite for golf is not sated, then drive five minutes down the road to the **Secret Harbour** ((08) 9357-0993, a nine-hole course, where you can send little white balls sailing along its fairways between sand dunes and enjoy the ocean views. For details about other courses contact the **Western Australian Golf Association** ((08) 9367-2490.

Few places in the world still have grass tennis courts, but at **Point Walter Grass Courts** ((08) 9330-3262, at the corner of Honor and Point Walter roads, 10 of them are available for hire from 6:30 AM to 5:30 PM weekdays, and from 6 AM to 5:30 PM weekends.

Perth's suburban surf beaches are some of the best in the country. On a fine day those between North Fremantle and Scarborough are crowded with sun seekers.

In the sheltered waters of the Swan River hundreds of yachts and sail boards catch the Fremantle Doctor, a cool breeze that blows most afternoons. You can hire a sailboard from the **Pelican Point Windsurfing Hire** ((08) 9386-1830, at 126 Broadway, Nedlands, or from **Funcat Hire** TOLL-FREE 1800-926-003, in Coode Street Jetty, South Perth.

The waters around Perth are also popular with SCUBA divers. About 25 km (16 miles) from Perth is the **Marion Marine Park** ((08) 9448-5800, accessible from Hil-

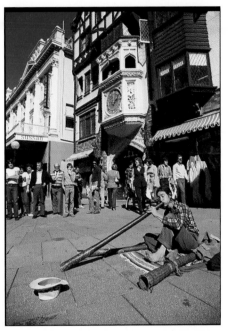

larys Boat Harbour, that features limestone reefs and the wealth of sealife living off them. Off Rottnest Island are eighteenth-century wrecks to explore and some spectacular underwater caves. The **Mindarie Diving Academy** ((08) 9305-7113, in the Mindarie Keys Marina, organizes charter trips to reefs near Perth and runs beginner courses.

Western Australia has recently joined the Australian Football League, and nothing elates them more than beating a Victorian side. In 1992 their team, the West Coast Eagles, won the Australian Football

Showing how it's done with a didgeridoo in Perth's pedestrian-only shopping center.

League's Grand Final, much to the chagrin of Victorians. The Fremantle Dockers are the second team in the west, but not nearly as successful. Usually, one team plays a game in Perth every week at Subiaco Ground ((08) 9381-2187, at 201 Subiaco Road, or the WACA ((08) 9265-7222, in Nelson Crescent, a cricket venue in summer.

WHERE TO STAY

In Perth, hotels are judged good if they are "new" and "large" and few boutique hotels or quaint guesthouses survive. Some of the latter can be found in Fremantle. This and Fremantle's location near Perth make it a good place to be based.

Luxury

In Fremantle, the **Esplanade Hotel** ((08) 9432-4000 TOLL-FREE 1800-998-201 FAX (08) 9430-4539, at the corner of Marine Terrace and Essex Street, is a grand old hotel that was refurbished in 1988 without losing its character; most rooms open out onto a verandah where breakfast can be served in summer.

Overlooking the Indian Ocean and about 20 minutes from the city in Scarborough is the **Radisson Observation City Resort Hotel** ((08) 9245-1000 TOLL-FREE 1800-333-333 FAX (08) 9245-2345, on the Esplanade. The hotel has several bars and two discos.

The **Perth Parmelia Hilton** ((08) 9322-3622 TOLL-FREE 1800-222-255 FAX (08) 9481-0857, in Mill Street, has views of the Swan River. In the center of town is the **Hyatt Regency** ((08) 9225-1234 TOLL-FREE 1800-222-188 FAX (08) 9325-8785, at 99 Adelaide Street.

Moderate

In Perth, **Annabelle Cottage** ((08) 9227-6855, at 246 Lake Street, and in North Fremantle, the **Riverside Bed & Breakfast** ((08) 9336-2209, at 15 John Street, offer some home comforts at a reasonable tariff. A selection of bed-and-breakfast accommodation is offered in and around Fremantle by **Fremantle Homestay** ((08) 9336-4864, at One Norfolk Street.

Inexpensive

The **Cottesloe Beach Hotel** ((08) 9383-1100 FAX (08) 9385-2482, at the corner of Marine Parade and John Street, has one of Perth's best beaches across the road, while just two kilometers (one mile) west of Perth is the **Murray Lodge Motel** ((08) 9321-7441 FAX (08) 9321-7282, at 718 Murray Street. Backpackers can't pass up **Central City North Lodge** ((08) 9227-7588 FAX (08) 9386-9065, at 225 Beaufort Street.

WHERE TO EAT

Dining in Perth is often out of doors, and even the finest restaurants are casual. The emphasis is on having a good time rather than peering through candlelit gloom or being patronized by waiters.

At night, the place to be is Northbridge and Fremantle, where the choice is mind-boggling.

There are quite a few moderately-priced restaurants within a few blocks of one another in Northbridge. **Toledos** ((08) 9227-5282, at 35 Lake Street (moderate), serves a very good range of Spanish tapas to tempt the tastebuds, and with an outside dining terrace popular on summer evenings. There are tables outside the **Fishy Affair** ((08) 9328-6636, at 132 James Street (moderate), whereas the atmosphere inside is more intimate.

Good seafood restaurants abound in Fremantle. With a million dollar view of Fremantle Harbour, **Sails** ((08) 9430-5151, on the first floor 47 Mews Road (moderate), serves the freshest seafoods. Upmarket establishments include **Bridges** ((08) 9430-4433, at 22 Tydeman Road (expensive), and **William's** ((08) 9335-2775, at 82 Stirling Highway (expensive).

There always seems to be a crowd at **Mamma Maria's** ((08) 9328-4532, at the corner of Aberdeen and Lake streets (moderate) — understandable, as this restaurant is popular with locals in the know.

HOW TO GET THERE

Perth is a terminus for one of the world's great train journeys — the transcontinental *Indian-Pacific*. Starting at Sydney the journey takes 64 hours including 482 km (300 miles) of absolutely straight track through the Nullarbor Plain.

There are direct flights every day into Perth from Melbourne, Sydney, Adelaide, Alice Springs, Canberra, Darwin and Brisbane. Traveling time to Melbourne is about four hours. International flights that enter Australia by way of Perth depart from Bangkok, Denpasar, Harare, Los Angeles, Jakarta, Johannesburg, London, Manchester, Singapore, Paris, Stockholm, Tokyo and Zurich.

Background
In the seventeenth century the Dutch explorer, Willem de Vlamingh, landed on a small island off the west coast of Australia. Believing it to be infested with rats, he named it *Rottenest* ("rats nest") Island, quite rightly, because the island is the home of perhaps the least known but most endearing marsupial — the quaintly named quokka. Quokkas, a species of short-tailed wallaby, once roamed the southwest tip of Australia but are now mainly confined to Rottnest and Bald Islands.

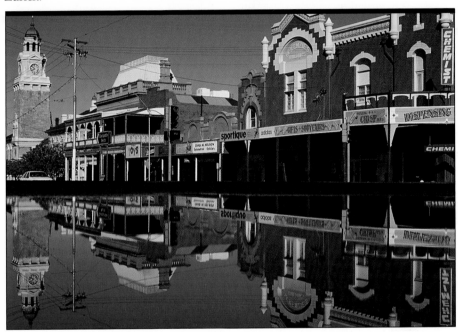

By road Perth is a long way from anywhere: the drive from Adelaide takes about 32 hours, and from Darwin 46 hours. Great care should be exercised if undertaking an automobile journey through the Outback.

DAY TRIPS FROM PERTH

ROTTNEST ISLAND

Rottnest Island, 19 km (12 miles) from Fremantle, provides a range of holiday attractions and is best known for its abundant wildlife. The island is 11 km long and five kilometers wide (seven by three miles) and easily warrants a couple of days' sightseeing.

General Information
There is a **visitor center** ((08) 9372-9752, opposite the ferry terminal in Thomson Bay, and accommodation can be booked by the **Rottnest Island Authority** ((08) 9432-9111.

What to See and Do
There are no private cars on Rottnest Island, so your choices for traveling around are by foot, bike or minibus. A great way to see the island is on a bicycle which you can rent from **Rottnest Bike Hire** ((08) 9372-9722, located behind the **Rottnest Hotel** (also known as the **Quokka Arms**). Most of the terrain is flat but there are some low hills to

Kalgoorlie's historic main street.

ensure that you keep in trim. I give you my personal guarantee that you will come across friendly quokkas after just a few kilometers on the road, who are always more than willing to share a meal with you if invite politely.

Rottnest also has a grim secret. Between 1838 and 1903 the island was used to imprison Aboriginal offenders often under inhumane conditions. The prison, known as the **Quad**, is an octagonal limestone building now transformed into the **Rottnest Lodge**, with its cells converted into tourist

dence of the Governor of Western Australia, and at **Rottnest Lodge Resort (** (08) 9292-5161 FAX (08) 9292-5158. Camping and cabin hire **(** (08) 9372-9737, provide inexpensive alternatives.

How to Get There

Rottnest Island can be reached by a ferry service that runs every day from either Barrack Street Jetty **(** (08) 9211-5844, in Perth; Hillarys Marinas **(** (08) 9246-1039; or off Northport Rous Head **(** (08) 9430-5844, Fremantle. Taking the ferry from Perth

lodging. In the center of the Quad stood the gallows, since removed, perhaps in consideration of the sensibilities of guests who stay there.

The rest of Rottnest Island offers a variety of activities from fishing along its coastline to swimming, SCUBA diving among shipwrecks, and surfing. There are also numerous lakes reflecting a mosaic of colors at sunset and attracting a huge variety of birds.

Where to Stay

Moderately-priced accommodation is available at the **Rottnest Hotel (** (08) 9292-5011 FAX (08) 9292-5188, in Bedford Avenue, which was built in 1864 as the summer resi-

means that you can enjoy a 45-minute trip down the Swan River. The island can also be reached by plane. Rottnest Airlines **(** (08) 9292-5027, flights take 15 minutes from Perth Airport.

THE GOLDEN MILE

Gold found at Coolgardie in 1892 triggered the Western Australian gold rush. Eleven months later, nearly 100 ounces of gold were found at Mt. Charlotte near the Kalgoorlie-Boulder by Paddy Hannan, Tom Flanagan and Daniel Shea. Their discovery set off a rush that was to uncover the richest square mile in the world, hence the area's sobriquet, the Golden Mile.

The Golden Mile is dry and supplies of fresh water had to be trucked in. In 1903 a pipeline was opened supplying water to the gold fields from a dam at Mundaring, 565 km (350 miles) away, pumping across 27,300 cubic meters (35,800 cubic yards) of water every day. It did not, however, fully quench the thirst of everyone — that was left to the 93 pubs and eight breweries which opened in Kalgoorlie for its 30,000 thirsty miners. Coolgardie boasted 23 hotels and three breweries.

To date, a staggering 1,800 tons of gold have been extracted from the Golden Mile, but the days of people picking up gold nuggets off the ground are long gone. Still, there are small-time prospectors in Kalgoorlie, combing the ground with metal detectors and hoping to find another rich lode. These men who spend a lot of time in the bush can be found in town propping up the bar ready to tell a tall tale, if only someone asks.

GENERAL INFORMATION

The **Kalgoorlie-Boulder Tourist Centre** ((08) 9021-1966, at 250 Hannan Street, provides information on Kalgoorlie and will arrange travel booking in the area; it is open Monday to Friday 8:30 AM to 5 PM and on weekends and public holidays from 9 AM to 5 PM.

The **Tourist Bureau** ((08) 9027-1446, is in Irish Mulga Drive, Kambalda, and is open on weekdays from 9 AM to 5 PM.

WHAT TO SEE AND DO

Coolgardie

At its peak, there were about 15,000 people, 23 pubs and six banks in Coolgardie. Today the population has dropped to less than 1,000, making it almost a ghost town. **The Goldfields Exhibition** ((08) 9026-2090, at 62 Bayley Street, in the original Warden Courts building, tells of the rise and fall of Coolgardie. A 35-minute video "Gold Fever" complements the exhibition, open daily from 9 AM to 5 PM; an admission fee is charged.

Another way to appreciate Coolgardie's history is to walk around the town and the surrounding area where traces of workings can still be seen. One hundred and fifty historical markers, illustrated with photographs from the period, help visitors identify the main landmarks. Much of the early transport was provided by camels, and these contrary beasts are available for one-hour rides or for the more hardy, two-day safaris from the **Camel Farm** ((08) 9026-6159, three kilometers (two miles) west of Coolgardie on the Great Eastern Highway. Reservations are essential for treks more than a day long.

Kalgoorlie-Boulder

One of Kalgoorlie's most famous migrant workers was Herbert Hoover, who spent years working there as a mining engineer in 1898 before going on to become the thirty-first President of the United States. He found the place too rough for his taste, describing Kalgoorlie as being only "three yards inside civilization."

The thoroughfares of the twin towns of Kalgoorlie and Boulder still have that rough and ready look they had 100 years ago when Herbert Hoover worked there. Kalgoorlie is still a man's town. The pubs

OPPOSITE: Kalgoorlie gold mine. ABOVE: Statue boldly echoes Kalgoorlie's dominant activity.

are filled with hard drinking men and the entertainment runs between satellite television and topless barmaids. The best known street in Kalgoorlie is **Hay Street** where prostitutes stand outside shacks waiting for their customers. The police politely turn a blind eye to this illegal trade, quietly acknowledging that the street's activity serves a purpose.

The **Palace Hotel** is worth a visit. From the outside it exudes an Edwardian atmosphere, with its wooden verandahs and wrought iron balconies. Inside there is serious drinking going on and the **Shaft Bar** disco is filled with young people ready to rage until dawn.

Seven kilometers (four miles) north of Kalgoorlie is a **Two Up School**, where visitors can play this traditional game of chance. Danny Sheehan tosses pennies in the air in a bush tin shed and punters stand in a circle betting on the fall of the two coins. Two up has been played in Australia for over a hundred years, despite being illegal — that is except at Kalgoorlie where you can enjoy the game from about 4 to 7 PM any day of the year without fear of a run in with the law.

On the **Golden Mile Loopline (** (08) 9093-3055, Boulder City Station, visitors can take an hour's guided journey on a railcar around the Golden Mile; tours depart daily at 10 AM.

On the Eastern By-Pass Road, five kilometers (three miles) north of Kalgoorlie is **Hannans North Tourist Gold Mine (** (08) 9091-4074, which has various displays and demonstrations telling the story of gold mining and extraction. Visitors can go underground to see mining work in progress. There is also a daily bus tour to the "Super Open Pit," a visit which takes around an hour.

Kambalda

There was a short-lived gold rush in Kambalda in 1906 after which the town rested peacefully until nickel was discovered there in 1966.

The town is located on Lake Leroy, and the surrounding countryside can best be viewed from **Red Hill Lookout** on Gordon Adams Road.

WHERE TO STAY

Kalgoorlie-Boulder has a good choice of accommodation and is the best place to base yourself for a tour of the goldfields. **Mercure Hotel Plaza Kalgoorlie (** (08) 9021-4544 TOLL-FREE 1800-090-600 FAX (08) 9091-2195, at 45 Egan Street, and **Sandalwood Motor Inn (** (08) 9021-4455 TOLL-FREE 1800-095-530 FAX (08) 9021-3744, in Hannan Street, provide comfortable accommodation.

There are moderately-priced motels in town but for a bit more character and class try the **Exchange Hotel (** (08) 9021-2833, at 135 Hannan Street, or the **Palace Hotel (** (08) 9021-2788 FAX (08) 9021-1813, at the corner of Hannan and Maritana streets.

Kambalda Motor Hotel ((08) 9027-1333, in Blue Bush Road, is moderately priced, as is the **Coolgardie Motor Inn Motel (** (08) 9026-6002 FAX (08) 9026-6310, on the Great Eastern Highway.

Inexpensive accommodation can be obtained at **Railway Lodge (** (08) 9026-6166, at 75 Baley Street, Coolgardie.

All three towns have caravan parks and vans can be hired quite cheaply.

HOW TO GET THERE

There are Ansett flights to Kalgoorlie-Boulder from Perth and connecting flights from the other states. Qantas flies in direct from Adelaide and Perth.

There are trains from East Perth daily; the *Prospector* and the *Indian–Pacific* run between Adelaide and Perth, with a twice weekly stop at Kalgoorlie.

Australian Coaches and Westliner Coaches run a bus service from Perth twice a week. The Adelaide–Perth Pioneer and Greyhound bus services run daily through Kalgoorlie, Coolgardie and Kambalda.

THE WEST COAST

Heading north along the Western Australian coast there are vast distances between towns. This stretch of coast, however, has some real tourist gems and the effort will be rewarded with unparalleled experiences and sights.

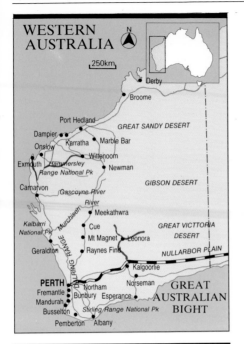

WESTERN AUSTRALIA

250km

Derby
Broome
Port Hedland
Dampier
Onslow
Karratha
Marble Bar
GREAT SANDY DESERT
Wittenoom
Exmouth
Hamersley
Range National Pk
Newman
Camarvon
Gascoyne River
River
GIBSON DESERT
Meekathwra
Kalbarri
National Pk
Cue
Mt Magnet
Leonora
GREAT VICTTORIA
DESERT
Geraldton
Raynes Find
NULLARBOR PLAIN
Kalgoorlie
PERTH
Northam
Norseman
GREAT
Fremantle
Bunbury
Esperance
AUSTRALIAN
Mandurah
Busselton
Stirling Range National Pk
BIGHT
Pemberton
Albany

GENERAL INFORMATION

Information about tours to Monkey Mia can be obtained from the **Denham Tourist Centre and Monkey Mia Information Centre** ((08) 9948-1056, in Knight Terrace, Denham. At Monkey Mia there is a dolphin information center where rangers are available to assist tourists.

Information about the **Ningaloo Marine Park** ((08) 9949-1676, is available from the park ranger or the **Exmouth Cape Tourist Village** ((08) 9949-1101, in Truscott Crescent.

WHAT TO SEE AND DO

Monkey Mia

If you want to meet a dolphin face to face (or more precisely face to beak) then Monkey Mia provides a unique opportunity to see these highly intelligent mammals at close range.

There is just one attraction here; but, seeing the dolphins in the shallows at Monkey Mia is more than sufficient justification for the trip. A family of them comes in most days, weather and other conditions permitting. They speed into the shore and rear out of the water to welcome tourists. They love

being patted and their skin feels a little bit like wet velvet. The best time to see them is between early morning and late afternoon when you can watch them being fed.

Denham

Besides being the access town for Monkey Mia, Denham is popular for both boating and fishing and the bay provides sheltered beaches.

Ningaloo Reef

Because of its remoteness, Ningaloo Reef, running 260 km (160 miles) along the Western Australian coast from Exmouth to Amherst Point is not nearly as well known as the Great Barrier Reef. This is pristine water and because of the small number of visitors, the destructive development that has occurred along the Great Barrier Reef has been avoided at Ningaloo. Access from the coast is easy. This area is home for humpback whales, whalesharks and dugongs, and on its sandy beaches turtles nest. The only way to explore the reef is underwater, and snorkeling and diving gear can be hired from **Coral Coast Dive** ((08) 9949-1004, in Yardie Creek Road, Exmouth, or you can go on an organized dive, with instruction included if needed, with the **Exmouth Dive Centre** ((08) 9949-1201, in Payne Street.

WHERE TO STAY

The best place to stay is the **Monkey Mia Dolphin Resort** ((08) 9948-1320, on Monkey Mia Road, which provides a range of accommodation from inexpensive on-site caravans and cabins to luxury-priced apartments. In Denham there is the moderately-priced **Mala Villas Chalets** ((08) 9948-1323, in Fry Court, and the **Shark Bay Hotel Motel** ((08) 9948-1203, at 43 Knight Terrace.

The **Ningaloo Reef Resort** ((08) 9942-5934, at One Robinson Road in Coral Bay, is moderately priced.

HOW TO GET THERE

Greyhound Pioneer coach service to Exmouth departs Perth Wednesday, Friday and Sunday. There are daily Ansett flights into Exmouth.

The west coast can be explored by car along the North West Coastal Highway which is asphalt-paved all the way.

THE KIMBERLEY RANGES

The Kimberley Ranges are a grouping of mountains and plateaus in the sparsely populated northwest corner of Australia. Rivers which run rapid during the wet season have carved deep gorges into the countryside; the coastline is lined with steep cliffs, some 250 m (800 ft) high, making the Kimberly Ranges's rugged beauty well worth the voyage to this far off part of the continent.

William Dampier visited the Kimberleys in 1688 and made unflattering observations about the infertile land he found. The first European expedition into the Kimberleys was led by Lieutenant George Grey in 1837. On his first day ashore Grey almost came to grief when he tried to swim Prince Regent River, and while he just failed to lose his life he did succeed in losing his trousers in the attempt.

In the 1890s there was effectively a guerrilla war waged by the Bunuba Aborigines under the leadership of Jundumurra, known by the whites as Pigeon because he was shorter than other Bunuba males and fast-footed. He started by spearing the sheep and cattle of the invaders but was captured and taken in chains to Derby. Pigeon's reputation among his people grew after he escaped from custody. When he killed Constable William Richardson in 1894 and freed Bunuba prisoners he became the indisputable leader of the local resistance around Fitzroy River. Capturing a cache of guns he began training his warriors and conducting successful ambushes. Weakened through loss of blood from an earlier wound and hunger, Jundumurra was finally hunted down in 1897 at Tunnel Creek.

Touring the Kimberleys it is possible to see how a skilled bushman could evade superior forces for such a long time. Off the beaten track, few tourists explore this area, rich in wildlife and natural land forms that give the Kimberleys' wide open spaces their majesty.

GENERAL INFORMATION

Broome Tourist Bureau ((08) 9922-2222, is located at the corner of Broome Road and Bagot Street.

The **Tourist Information Centre** ((08) 9191-1426, at Two Clarendon Street in Derby, is open Monday to Saturday.

WHAT TO SEE AND DO

Broome
Broome is a frontier town, with Outback characters galore and a Wild West atmosphere. Don't be surprised to see heavy-drinking macho-types propping up the bar in the town's pubs ready to entertain a crowd with tall tales about bush life.

The region is blessed with shimmering beaches that stretch for miles, endless good weather, boundless blue skies and timeless wilderness that goes on forever. It is a great base for the Kimberleys.

Broome at the turn of the century was the center of a lucrative pearling industry attracting divers and adventurers from many countries. In its heyday a fleet of 300 pearling boats was headquartered here. While the rest of Australia was turning inward and hiding behind the White Australia Policy, this boom town was developing a face as much Asian as European. Faces in the street reflect the high level of intermarriage in the area. There are some nice multicultural architectural touches, too with pagoda-topped public phone booths serving Chinatown.

Pearls are available for sale in a number of shops along **Dampier Terrace**. The dark blue, almost black Harvest pearls are highly prized.

In the **Japanese Cemetery** many Japanese pearl divers lie buried with some 900 headstones marking their graves.

For drive-in buffs, trade in your car seats for deck chairs and enjoy true open-air viewing. **Sun Pictures** is reputed to be the oldest operating picture garden in the world, having operated since 1916. Movies start at 7:55 PM.

A dinosaur footprint thought to be 130 million years old can be seen on the rocks

Sculpted by wind over thousands of years, these limestone pillars, some up to five meters (16 ft) tall, stand in the Pinnacles Desert.

at the beach at low tide at **Gantheaume Point**. These are only visible at spring tides, but cement casts are on display at the tops of the cliffs.

Cable Beach, near Broome, is pristine, clean, and is one of the last opportunities — if you're continuing your travels north — of safely swimming in the sea. Saltwater crocodiles infest coastal waters beyond.

Broome is a good base for visiting the **Bungle Bungle National Park**, with its stripped hive-shaped sandstone domes. Walking in the park is only for the dedicated, but the effort is amply repaid by the scenery. **Broome Aviation** ((08) 9192-1369, has scenic flights on weekdays out of Broome which provide an opportunity to take in the scale of the rock formations from the air.

In the Kimberley's is the world's largest diamond mine. Argyle diamonds are internationally renowned for their brilliance and color. There are tours to the **Argyle Diamond Mine**, a major producer and home of the rare pink diamond.

Derby

The local authorities in Derby once made an unusual use of the area's distinctive baobab tree, the trunk of which is shaped a little like a fat skittle. A thousand-year-old specimen, seven kilometers (four miles) from town, was used as a cell for prisoners and is reputed to have once housed at least twenty Aborigines one night. Directions on how to find the tree can be obtained from Derby Tourist Information Centre.

The area is rich is Aboriginal rock art galleries. It was Wandjina representations of heads with large eyes and "halos" that lead Erick Von Däniken, in *Chariots of the Gods*, to suggest that they were drawings of extraterrestrial beings.

Wyndham

At the northeast edge of the Kimberleys is Wyndham, which has a model of an 18-m (16-ft) crocodile at the entrance to the town. There is a crocodile lookout in town where you can observe these primitive beasts, and while the table manners of these reptiles at feeding time are deplorable, no one seems to have the courage to reprimand them.

WHERE TO STAY

In Broome, accommodation is provided by the luxury **Cable Beach Club** ((08) 9192-0400 TOLL-FREE 1800-095-508 FAX (08) 9192-2249. The resort's bungalows reflect the Chinese and Malaysian heritage of Broome with latticework and verandahs modeled after old pearl masters' homes. They are scattered in lush gardens and the grounds are intersected by canals. The **Quality Tropicana Inn Motel Hotel** ((08) 9192-1204 FAX (08) 9192-2583, at the corner of Saville and Robinson streets, provides motel type accommodation at moderate prices. For a friendly guesthouse atmosphere there is the inexpensive **Broometime Lodge** ((08) 9193-5067 FAX (08) 9192-2429, at 59 Forrest Street.

To the north there is moderately-priced accommodation at the **Derby Boab Inn** ((08) 9191-1044 FAX (08) 9191-1568, in Loch Street, and for real Outback accommodation try **Mt. Elizabeth Station Guest House** ((08) 9191-4644, 370 km (230 miles) north east of Derby; moderately priced.

HOW TO GET THERE

The Greyhound Pioneer and McCafferty's daily service from Perth to Darwin stops at Broome and Derby, and Greyhound's service stops at Broome, Derby and Wyndham.

There are daily Ansett Australia flights to Broome and Derby from Perth and Qantas Airlink operates daily services into Broome from Perth and Darwin.

By road, Broome, Derby and Wyndham can be reached from the Great Northern Highway. Check with the Royal Automobile Club of Western Australia ((08) 9421-4444, about local hazards when crossing from Broome to Wyndham in the wet season.

NATIONAL PARKS

GENERAL INFORMATION

For details of national parks contact the **Western Australia Department of Conservation and Land Management** ((08) 9367-0333 or the **Conservation Council of Western Australia** ((08) 9321-4507.

WHAT TO SEE AND DO

Yanchep ((08) 9561-1661, 51 km (32 miles) north of Perth, features limestone caves, heath, and after rain, a profusion of wildflowers. There is a colony of koalas near the lake of Loch McNess that are worth a visit.

The Pinnacles tower over the landscape of the **Nambung National Park**, 250 km (160 miles) north of Perth off the Geraldton Highway, located 29 km (18 miles) south of Cervantes and two kilometers (one mile)

wildflowers. There are many tracks providing easy access to wildlife and flowers. Alternately the western access via Tourist Drive No. 253 from Cranbrook takes travelers along the Salt River Road, Red Gum Springs Road and into the heart of the national park. Picnic areas with barbecue facilities are located throughout the Park. The Ranges can best be reached Albany and feature rugged mountains with both woodland and heathlands.

Walpole–Nornalup ((08) 9827-9278, 111 km (69 miles) west of Albany has exten-

inland from the beach. Thousands of limestone pillars, some five meters (16 ft) tall, stand in the **Pinnacles Desert** ((08) 9652-7043. These ancient totems have been sculpted by the wind over thousands of years. Dutch sailors saw these limestone outcrops from the sea and thought they were the remains of an ancient city.

Kalbarri Park ((08) 9937-1178, 590 km (366 miles) north of Perth, can best be reached from Geraldton. The national park features spectacular river gorges, mallee and wonderful coastal scenery. The best time to visit is from May to October.

In spring the **Stirling Ranges** ((08) 9827-9278, 322 km (200 miles) south of Perth, comes alive with a richly colored carpet of

sive karri and tingle forest, and secluded inlets.

Cape Range ((08) 9949-1676, 1,700 km (1,000 miles) northwest of Perth, can best be reached from Exmouth. The national park features rugged limestone ridges, scrub and heathland. The best time to visit is from April to September.

Weathered tree in the Pilbara Outback.

Travelers'
Tips

INTERNATIONAL FLIGHTS

More than twenty international airlines fly into Australia. Most enter through Sydney and Melbourne, although others arrive, albeit less frequently, at Hobart, Darwin, Perth, Brisbane and some provincial centers. Airports are generally close to their respective cities; distances are given below:

Adelaide	six kilometers (four miles)
Brisbane	13 km (eight miles)
Canberra	eight kilometers (five miles)
Darwin	15 km (nine miles)
Hobart	22 km (14 miles)
Melbourne	19 km (12 miles)
Perth	12 km (seven miles)
Sydney	seven kilometers (four miles)

In each state capital there are shuttle buses from the airport to the city, and often also to major hotels and the suburbs.

On leaving Australia, don't forget to keep at least AU$20 in your pocket for the departure tax.

The major international carriers can be contacted on:

Air New Zealand (all states) (132-476.
Ansett (all states) (131-777.
British Airways
Adelaide ((08) 8238-2138; Brisbane ((07) 3223-3123; Hobart ((03) 6234-9466; Melbourne ((03) 9603-1133; Perth ((08) 9425-7711; Sydney ((02) 9258-3300.
Cathay Pacific (all states) (131-747.
Japan Airlines
Adelaide ((08) 8212-2555; Brisbane ((07) 3229-9916; Cairns ((07) 4031-2700; Melbourne ((03) 9654-2733; Sydney ((02) 9272-1111.
KLM Royal Dutch Airlines
Melbourne ((03) 9654-5222; other states TOLL-FREE 1800-550-512.
Malaysia Airline (all states) (132-627.
Qantas Australian (all states) (131-313.
Singapore Airlines (all states) (131-011.
United Airlines (all states) (131-777.

INTERNAL FLIGHTS

There are two major internal airlines — Ansett Australia and Qantas Australian — with services to over 100 destinations.

There are around 20 small regional airlines providing services from the main routes as well as flights linking major provincial cities and popular tourist destinations. All these flights are associated with either of the two major carriers — Qantas or Ansett — through which reservations can be made.

For reservations or inquires, both airlines provide single numbers that connect the caller anywhere in Australia with the closest office for the cost of a local call. The numbers are:

Qantas Australian (131-313
Ansett Australia (131-300

Both airlines offer a number of discount fares and both have frequent-flier clubs, which provide free travel and other benefits for accumulated mileage.

Ansett Australia provides a 25 percent discount fare with the See Australia Airpass which is only available to tourists and must be reserved from overseas or within 30 days of arriving in Australia. The Kangaroo Pass provides discounted travel with certain restrictions and costs AU$1,499 for 10,000 km (6,200 miles).

Qantas Australian discounts some fares on advance reservations of 21 days; discounts are usually offered only outside school holiday periods.

There are also special deals, offered from time to time, details of which can be obtained from a travel agent or by contacting the airline directly.

OPPOSITE: Waiting for a bite on the Norman River, which flows into the Gulf of Carpentaria. ABOVE: A local carrier drops off passengers in Darwin.

GETTING AROUND

BY RAIL

In a country with large distances between destinations, trains provide a less expensive alternative to air travel. A long train journey can be an enjoyable experience in itself, and an opportunity to see the countryside at a leisurely pace in comfort.

There are interstate trains connecting all the state capital cities except Hobart, and reservations can be made by at (132-232.

Each state, except Tasmania has its own suburban and country rail network linking its major provincial cities and tourist destinations. Details can be obtained from state rail authorities:

New South Wales (131-500.
Victoria (132-232.
South Australia ((08) 8231-4366.
Queensland (132-232.
Western Australia ((08) 9326-2222.

Trains usually have first- and economy-class carriages, and some interstate routes use XPT trains which travel up to 160 kph (100 mph). This service is offered between Sydney, Melbourne, Brisbane and some provincial cities in New South Wales. On MotoRail services it is possible to take your car with you.

Interstate trains are comfortable, the carriages are air conditioned and overnight trains have sleeping berths. Some have dining cars; in other cars meals are served from a buffet counter.

On the more popular routes, train fares are competitive with long distance coaches, and are faster and more comfortable. Ask about special deals which are offered from time to time.

Overseas visitors can take advantage of an Austrail Pass, which is available for 14, 21, 30 and 90 days, and allows unlimited travel on long distance, inter-capital, provincial and city trains. Prices range from AU$485 to AU$755, and seven-day extensions can be purchased for an additional AU$250. The Austrail Pass can only be purchased by permanent residents of countries other than Australia at railway companies or travel agents.

The main rail line runs down the eastern seaboard from Cairns to Sydney. It then continues, via either Melbourne or Broken Hill to Adelaide and across the Nullarbor Plain to Perth. There is also a rail link between Adelaide and Alice Springs.

There are a few country rail services, but some of these are being closed down and it is necessary to contact the local representative for more information on routes and timetables.

There are several great train journeys in Australia which are an experience in themselves. The *Ghan,* which links Adelaide and Alice Springs, takes its name from the Ghan camel drivers who opened up the Red Center of the country in the late nineteenth century. See the rugged scenery of the Outback from air-conditioned comfort on a journey that takes 20 hours and covers 1,555 km (960 miles).

The *Indian–Pacific* traverses the continent twice weekly from Perth on the Indian Ocean, to Sydney on the Pacific Ocean — a distance of 4,352 km (2,695 miles). From Sydney the train climbs through the Blue Mountains and then into Outback New South Wales to Adelaide. From Adelaide the Nullarbor Plain presents the longest stretch of straight rail line in the world. Passing finally through the goldfields of Western Australia, the *Indian–Pacific* arrives in Perth three days after leaving Sydney.

BY BUS

Bus travel around Australia is fast, relatively comfortable, and a low-cost alternative to train or air travel.

Travelers' Tips

Long distance coaches are air conditioned and have wash rooms and adjustable seats. Some services are introducing videos to keep passengers entertained on long distance journeys, such as the 60-hour trip from Perth to Darwin.

There are two main bus companies which provide regularly scheduled bus services throughout most of the continent. They are:

Greyhound Pioneer (132-030
McCafferty's (131-499
Bus Australia (132-323

There are also a number of regional bus tour companies; details about their packages can be obtained from tourist bureaus or travel agents.

Meals are usually included in package tours and accommodation can be in motels or tents, depending how the tour is organized.

Tour buses don't just keep to the main highways. Getting off the beaten track is possible with packages that use four-wheel drive minibuses. This form of transport allows tourists to experience the remote

All three companies offer the Aussie Pass which allows you to travel on any of their buses, and is based on the number of days traveled. Passes, valid for 21 to 90 days, can be purchased directly from the bus companies or booked through a travel agent. Road-and-Rail Passes and Tassie Passes are also available. There are also a number of regional bus companies that provide services between a limited number of destinations.

There are two major coach companies that organize package tours to specific destinations:

AAT King Melbourne ((03) 9274-7422; (elsewhere) TOLL-FREE 1800-334-009
Australian Pacific (all states) (131-304

Outback and tours may also include interesting diversions such as balloon flights or camel rides.

By Car

Major car rental companies have outlets at airports and in the capital cities. Each region also has at least one local car rental company in competition with the following big four:

Avis TOLL-FREE 1800-225-533.
Hertz (133-039.

Advice for drivers OPPOSITE in the arid Outback. ABOVE : Tourists gaze at the wondrous sandstone monoliths called "The Hidden City of Nathan" in Northern Territory's Nathan River Property.

Thrifty TOLL-FREE 1800-652-008.
Budget (132-727.

Four- and six-cylinder cars are available on request, and some outlets hire four-wheel drive vehicles and caravans.

A deposit must be left when picking up the vehicle. Compulsory third-party insurance is included in the rental price, and comprehensive insurance is available for an additional cost. Drivers are requested to show their license; if it is an international license, a domestic license should also be available for inspection.

should be heeded because a kangaroo may "freeze" in the middle of the road at night, mesmerized, by the headlights. A collision with one can damage the car severely and is usually fatal for the 'roo.

Speed limits are in kilometers per hour, and speed cameras and radar traps are employed by patrollers to catch and fine speeding drivers.

Petrol (gasoline) is sold in liters and most outlets are self-service. Competition exists between petrol stations and large signs displayed outside the station allow consum-

The rental cars need not necessarily be returned to where they were hired, and arrangements can be made to leave them at your final destination.

Traffic in Australia travels on the left-hand side of the road, and right turning cars must give way to cars turning left. Seatbelts must be worn at all times by everyone in the car, and hefty fines for traffic violations apply. The police are particularly hard on drivers who drive under the influence of alcohol.

Pictorial road warnings follow international standards. In additional, yellow diamond-shaped signs with a drawing of a kangaroo or a wombat warn that local wildlife could be crossing the road. These signs

ers to shop around for the best deal. Prices tend to be higher in remote areas.

Each state and territory has its own motoring organization, which may have reciprocal arrangements with overseas equivalents. Check before leaving home. These organizations provide emergency roadside assistance and will help you with information on road conditions. Some also provide general tourist information. The headquarters of these organizations are in the capitals, and lists of local outlets can be obtained from their head offices. They are:

Adelaide Royal Automobile Association of South Australia ((08) 8202-4600, located at 41 Hindmarsh Square.

Brisbane Royal Automobile Club of Queensland (131-905, at 300 St. Paul's Terrace, Fortitude Valley.

Canberra National Road and Motorists' Association ((02) 6458-3341, at 152 Maybe Street, Bombala.

Darwin Automobile Association of Northern Territory ((08) 8981-3837 FAX (08) 8941-2965, at MLC Building, 79–81 Smith Street.

Hobart Royal Automobile Club of Tasmania TOLL-FREE 1800-005-677, at the corner of Murray and Patrick streets.

Melbourne Royal Automobile Club of Victoria ((03) 9607-2137 FAX (03) 790-2844, at 422 Little Collins Street.

Perth Royal Automobile Association of Western Australia ((08) 9421-4444, at 228 Adelaide Terrace, at the corner of Hill Street.

Sydney National Road and Motorists' Association ((02) 9260-9222, at 151 Clarence Street.

Driving from one place to another in Australia can involve substantial distances and every care should be taken to ensure that you remain attentive, particularly in the Outback at night. There are roadside rest areas, and some local organizations encourage drivers to take a break by providing free tea and coffee from vans set up by the road.

TAXIS

Cabs cruising for hire display a lighted "vacant" sign or light on the roof. Taxis can also be hired from ranks located outside major hotels, and bus, train and airline terminals. There is a set initial amount on the meter and then a charge for every kilometer. A higher tariff may apply at night and at weekends. There is a surcharge for cabs booked by telephone, and for luggage. In some states it is possible to share cabs with people going in the same direction, but this is at the discretion of the first person in the queue and fares are discounted by 25 percent for each passenger.

BICYCLES

Most of the capital cities have bike tracks. Alternatively, cyclists can use roads, provided

they obey all the rules for cars. Bikes are banned on some highways and there are signs at access points indicating whether cycling is permitted.

Helmets are compulsory in most states and territories.

Bicycles can be taken on suburban trains, but usually not at peak hours, and there might be additional charges. On country trains accompanied bikes are stowed in the guard's van and prior notice is usually required. Bicycles can also be taken on airplanes as normal luggage but they must be

put into bike boxes, with the pedals removed and the tires deflated. Buses will not take them.

TRAVEL DOCUMENTS

All visitors require a passport and visa to enter Australia, except for New Zealanders who require only a passport. Application should be made before entering the country at the nearest Australian consulate or embassy. The visa will state the permitted length of stay, usually a maximum of six months. Applications for extensions are

OPPOSITE: Cruising up the Hawksbury River, less than an hour's drive north from downtown Sydney. ABOVE: "Baby-packing" in Ormiston.

made through the Department of Immigration and Multicultural Affairs, whose offices are located in most capital cities.

Temporary working visas can usually be obtained by people sponsored by companies or an employer in Australia.

CUSTOM ALLOWANCES

Visitors over 18 years of age may bring into Australia 200 cigarettes or 250 g (9 oz) of cigars or tobacco and one liter (1.75 pints) of alcohol.

Strict prohibitions apply on guns and drugs.

Prescription drugs should be accompanied by a doctor's certificate and should not exceed one month's supply.

Australia is extremely strict about protecting local wildlife from imported pests. It is prudent to declare any foodstuffs, plants and seeds that you have in your luggage. Even products made out of plant material, such as bamboo hats, should be shown to the custom officials.

To prevent the importation of pests all incoming planes are sprayed. The spray used is not harmful to human beings but people with respiratory problems should cover their mouths and noses during this operation.

WHEN TO GO

There are no extremes of cold in Australia, although it can get a bit chilly during winter in the southern states. In summer be prepared for some serious heat, and generally avoid the northern parts of the country in the wet season, which is from November to April, otherwise known as the cyclone season. Further north, monsoons between December and March make traveling uncomfortable, and flooding is an occasional hazard. Reservations must be made well ahead for travel during the school holidays, particularly between the end of December and beginning of February.

WHAT TO BRING

With a wide range of climates in the country at any given time, it is advisable to bring warm and cold weather clothing. Even if you come in the middle of summer there are occasional days in the southeast states when the temperature can drop. In the Outback, scorchingly hot days can be followed by freezing nights. A light jacket or pullover will never go amiss. In winter in the southeast corner of Australia the temperatures can get quite low, but never much below 0°C (32°F); a light overcoat or raincoat and warm clothing are strongly advised.

Australians generally dress fairly casually by overseas standards, and a jacket and tie are usually expressly mentioned if required for a dinner or theater engagement. Otherwise smart casual dress is expected. Even when the weather is hot men

wear a good pair of trousers with long socks and women a light dress.

Australia has one of the highest rates of skin cancer in the world. The sun's rays can be very strong, even on cloudy days. It is essential, when out in the sun, to use 15+ sunscreen which should be reapplied after a swim. Being well tanned is no longer fashionable, and many people are covering up to protect themselves from the sun.

TOURIST INFORMATION

There are tourist bureaus in major cities and many towns. Most states also have tourist bureaus in other state capitals.

The range of services provided by tourist bureaus varies from state to state, but they usually have a good selection of brochures, information on local attractions and addresses of local sporting events and venues. Many tourist information bureaus provide a reservation service for accommodation, package holidays and informal organized tours.

When coming into a small town look for signs with a big white "i" on a blue background, indicating a tourist bureau nearby. Other good sources of information are local councils, branch offices of the state automobile clubs, bus stations and best of all the local residents.

Surfer demonstrates acrobatic skills on a wave crest. A good surf attracts aficionados from hundreds of miles around.

EMBASSIES AND CONSULATES

The telephone numbers for the principal foreign embassies and consulates in Canberra are:

Argentina ((02) 6282-4555
Austria ((02) 6295-1533
Canada ((02) 6273-3844
China ((02) 6273-4780
Czech Republic ((02) 6290-1386
Denmark ((02) 6273-2195
Finland ((02) 6273-3800

Spain ((02) 6273-3555
Sweden ((02) 6273-3033
Switzerland ((02) 6273 3977
Thailand ((02) 6273-1149
United States ((02) 6270-5000

HEALTH

It is wise to arrange health and accident insurance before you leave for Australia. If you sign-up after arrival, there is likely to be a qualifying period of three months; it

France ((02) 6216-0100
Germany ((02) 6270-1911
Great Britain ((02) 6270-6666
Greece ((02) 6273-3011
Hungary ((02) 6282-3226
India ((02) 6273-3999
Indonesia ((02) 6286-2555
Israel ((02) 6273-1309
Italy ((02) 6273-3333
Japan ((02) 6273-3244
Jordan ((02) 6295-9951
Malaysia ((02) 6273-1543
Netherlands ((02) 6273-3111
Norway ((02) 6295-1048
Russia ((02) 6295-9033
Singapore ((02) 6273-3944
South Africa ((02) 6273-2424

may be worth including dental insurance in the policy.

Public hospitals are well equipped and the medical staff highly qualified, but their casualty departments are usually very busy and may require a long wait.

A 20-minute consultation with a doctor runs AU$25 to AU$35. General practitioners are listed in the phone book.

Drug stores, which are called chemists or pharmacies in Australia, are staffed by qualified pharmacists and every city has an all-night roster for medical emergencies. Some pharmaceuticals are sold over the counter, such as headache tablets, while other medication might require a doctor's prescription.

MONEY

Australia uses a decimal system of currency, expressed in dollars and cents. There are silver-colored coins, increasing in size with value — five, 10, 20 and 50 cent denominations. There are two gold-colored coins — the one and two dollar pieces — that are smaller than the 20 cent piece, which can be confusing.

Plastic notes come in different colors and are available in denominations of AU$5, AU$10, AU$20, AU$50 and AU$100.

Travelers' checks present no problems and can easily be cashed at international airports, hotels and motels, money changers, or *bureaux de change*, and banks. Banks are open Monday to Thursday from 9:30 AM to 4 PM and until 5 PM on Friday. Some banks in capital cities are also open Saturday morning. Money can be withdrawn 24 hours a day from automatic tellers, which are located outside banks in most major towns and cities.

A range of international credit cards are accepted in most places; MasterCard and Visa cards are most widely accepted, followed by American Express, Diners Club and Carte Blanche.

At the time of writing the United States dollar to Australian dollar **rate of exchange** was as follows:

AU dollars per US dollars: 1.33; or
US dollars per AU dollars: .75.

WEIGHTS AND MEASURES

All Australian weights and measures are metric.

CONVERSION TABLE

Temperature
Centigrade to Fahrenheit
multiply by 1.8 *and add* 32
Fahrenheit to Centigrade
subtract 32 *and multiply by* ⁵/₉

**Length, Distance
and Area**   *multiply by*
inches to centimeters   2.54
centimeters to inches   .39
feet to meters   .30

meters to feet	3.28
yards to meters	.91
meters to yards	1.09
miles to kilometers	1.61
kilometers to miles	.62

Weight

ounces to grams	28.35
grams to ounces	.035
pounds to kilograms	.45
kilograms to pounds	2.21

Volume

gallons to liters	3.79
liters to gallons	.26

ACCOMMODATION

Australia provides a full range of accommodation choices, from the most exclusive five star resort to a humble country pub or campground. Luxury hotels provide service and facilities at an international standard. At the lower end of the market, such inconveniences as having to share bathrooms can be more than compensated for by an opportunity to meet the locals.

For the purposes of this book, hotels have been divided into three categories

---

OPPOSITE: The Olgas. ABOVE: A precipitous sandstone wall rises out of the plain of the Mount Remarkable National Park near Port Augusta.

according to a range of prices you can expect. At **luxury** hotels you can expect to pay more than AU$130; **moderately-priced** accommodation will range from AU$60 to AU$130; and **inexpensive** lodging will be under (sometimes well under) AU$60. I have taken prices from the high season; if you travel out-of-season prices may be lower than listed here. All price categories assume a double room, double occupancy.

Local tourist bureaus offer hotel brochures. Only a few states provide comprehensive lists of accommodation available and up-to-date rates. This void has been filled by the Australian motoring organizations which have produced *A–Z Australian Accommodation Guide*. The guide covers almost every corner of Australia with comprehensive listings and tariffs. A free accommodation booking service for members is provided by the Royal Automobile Club of Victoria ((03) 9607-2213 TOLL-FREE (outside Melbourne) 1800-337-743. The Royal Automobile Association of South Australia ((08) 8202-4540, provides the same service. For visitors who intend to move around the country a lot, it is worth joining either club just to use this service.

HOTELS

All the capital cities have top-class international hotels, with Hilton and Sheraton Pacific found in most capital cities. Most of the top hotels have toll-free 1800 numbers through which reservations can be made anywhere in Australia. Most offer special weekend packages, and inquires should be made when placing your reservation.

Many top quality private hotels are not part of a chain. These combine the luxury and character unmatched by larger hotels. Smaller hotels, often referred to as "boutique" hotels, combine luxury with intimacy; it makes sense to book well ahead. Some of those recommended throughout this book are also of historic interest.

Two services take reservations for independent hotels around the country. They are: **Country Comfort** TOLL-FREE 1800-065-064, and **Choice Hotels** TOLL-FREE 1800-090-600.

There was once a requirement, as part of their liquor license, for pubs to provide accommodation. Alas, few do so now, but those that still have their no-frills rooms are full of character and pleasant surprises.

MOTELS

Considering Australia's dependence on the car, it is not surprising that the backbone of the accommodation business is the motel. These are dotted along most highways, particularly on the roads into and out of town.

Average motel prices are in the range AU$40 to AU$70 for a double, while a top one should cost no more than AU$140. Special deals can be made if you intend to stay for more than a few days.

An average motel is clean and comfortable, with air conditioning, a television, an electric kettle and everything else you need to make a cup of tea or coffee. Breakfast is usually not included in the tariff, but can be ordered the night before. Menus include juice, toast, cereal and eggs and bacon. Some have a restaurant but these are not necessarily the best places in town to eat. Some, particularly those further north, have a swimming pool. Spas for guests are becoming increasingly popular.

Reservations with the three largest motel chains can be made by calling the following numbers:

Flag (132-400.
Best Western (131-779.
Golden Chain Motor Inns TOLL-FREE 1800-023-966.
Australian Independent Motels TOLL-FREE 1800-066-835

The **Budget Motel Chain** does not have a central booking number, but a booklet with contact numbers for its motels can be obtained on ((03) 5143-1077.

BED AND BREAKFAST AND FARM STAYS

The tradition of bed-and-breakfast accommodation is new to Australia, but growing as increasing numbers of tourists are looking for intimate places to stay that provide an opportunity to meet locals and fellow travelers. This industry is not well organized and while the occasional book listing bed-and-breakfast places has been published, a second edition seldom appears. One association still promoting this type of accommodation is **Bed & Breakfast Australia** ((02) 9498-5344 FAX (02) 9498-6438. Tasmania is strong on colonial accommodation, and the Tasmanian Tourist Bureau can furnish you with an up-to-date list.

Bed-and-breakfast accommodation is also offered on farms, an arrangement which helps farm families make ends meet and provides them with an opportunity for some company in what can otherwise be an isolated lifestyle. Accommodation ranges from self-contained cottages on the prop-

erty to a room in the main homestead. Lists of farm stays can be obtained from state tourist organizations.

TIPPING

There is no obligation to tip in Australia. Wages are generally good, and tipping should only be done if the standard of service is exceptional.

In restaurants and hotels there are no service charges, and tips up to about 10 percent are customary but not necessarily expected. When buying drinks in pubs it is acceptable to leave the change behind for the bartender; rounding the fare to the nearest dollar in taxis is also common.

NATIONAL PARKS

Australian national parks are areas of conservation, not always beautiful in a conventional sense but invariably unique in their own way; frequently of great scientific interest, they reflect a sense of responsibility on the part of the authorities to ensure the survival of untouched, primeval antiquity.

The Royal National Park in Sydney was declared in 1879, making it the second such institution, after Yellowstone, to be established in the world. This precedent was followed by the creation of the Belair Recreational Park, South Australia in 1891, Kuring-gai Chase National Park, New South Wales in 1892 and Wilson's Promontory, Victoria in 1898.

As Australians began to appreciate the wild beauty and variety of their country's landscape, more and more areas were declared reserves. Today, national parks cover over 40 million hectares (100 million acres) or about five and a half percent of Australia's land area. About 38 million hectares (95 million acres) has been reserved as Marine and Estuarine Protected Areas,

Gold rush ostentation of a Kalgoorlie hotel.

including three on the World Heritage List of natural and cultural significance. They are Kakadu, Willandra and Western Tasmania.

Most parks provide camping facilities, usually near the main access road, and huts. The main camping site usually includes fireplaces, wood, fresh water and toilets. Camping away from the main camping sites may require permission from the park ranger.

Often there area information booths in the main camping area which can provide

Australian bush can be dangerous. Organized walking tours are available in several parks and details obtained from the park ranger or local tourist bureau. It is standard procedure, when walking into a national park, to leave details with the ranger of your route and when you expect to complete the walk.

Another thing to keep in mind when traveling around the bush is that Australia is dangerously susceptible to bush fires, and every care should be taken. (I recall traveling with one bushman who would always

you with maps, details of their walking tracks (and their grading) and fact sheets on what to see and do. Some parks provide numbered markings which indicate natural features, unique habitats and points of interest that can be cross-referenced with their fact sheets. To cover the cost of maintaining services to visitors there is a modest charge for entering some national parks.

Touring parks can be done by coach, self-drive in a four-wheel drive vehicle or walking. Parks generally have few access roads, and seeing them from a car or bus is extremely limited. Only walking provides the opportunity for (literally) getting off the beaten track, but long treks should not be attempted by inexperienced hikers as the

extinguish his cigarette in the palm of his hand to ensure that it was out before throwing it away!)

Sufficient water should be taken for the trip and all rubbish should be removed from the park. Rangers frown on hikers who pick native flowers or plants.

There may seem to be a lot of "don'ts" on entering a national park, but these rules are designed for the safety of visitors and to ensure that the park can be enjoyed in its natural state by all.

WOMEN ALONE

Australia was once a male-dominated society, and some vestiges of this history have persisted over the years. Even into recent decades, parties usually divided into the men around the barbecue and women in the kitchen preparing the salads or fussing over the children. In pubs it was unheard of for women to enter the public bar; instead there were ladies' lounges where they could enjoy a gin and tonic or shandy (beer and lemonade).

These attitudes are changing, although in the Outback women are still likely to suffer some discrimination such as not being served quickly in a public bar.

Out of the 110 varieties of snakes in Australia eight can inflict a fatal bite.

In unprotected, open waters around Australia **sharks** have been known to attack people. However, the chances of being attacked are remote, and most city beaches have mesh barriers erected offshore to keep sharks out.

The **blue-ringed octopus** can give you a fatal bite if disturbed. Don't try it. This species is found all around the continent and can be recognized by its irregular blue markings.

Hitchhikers have been known to disappear, and women should certainly not travel alone on the road.

DANGEROUS ANIMALS

Aside from sea creatures, most of Australia's dangerous creatures are small, with the singular exception of crocodiles. Estuarine or saltwater **crocodiles**, which can grow to seven-meters (23-ft) long, have been known to attack people. The freshwater crocodile generally is not dangerous unless provoked.

There are several venomous **snakes** slithering around the bush and its spiders are among the most poisonous in the world.

There are now antivenins for the deadly **funnel-web spider**, found within about 160 km (100 miles) of Sydney, and the **redback spider** which is much more widespread.

The **box jellyfish** lives and stings in tropical northern waters. Other aquatic hazards are the **stonefish** and **cone shell** which live in waters between Brisbane and Geraldton. **Stingrays** and **puffer fish** are widely found in coastal waters.

It is best to ask locals what hazards to watch out for. Despite this seemingly

Gorge country. OPPOSITE: Red Bluff LEFT and Old mine RIGHT in Wittenoom Gorge. ABOVE: Dales Gorge LEFT in Hamersley Range National Park and Windjana Gorge RIGHT.

alarming list, few deaths are caused in Australia by any of these creatures.

SHOPPING

Foreign visitors are allowed duty-free concessions on a variety of goods, including cameras, electrical equipment and jewelry. A number of shops at the airports, popular tourist destinations and capital cities specialize in duty-free goods. It is worth shopping around for the best deals, which are seldom at shops at the airport. A list of duty-free

COMMUNICATIONS

Post

Post offices are open from 9 AM to 5 PM on weekdays, and will hold mail *poste restante* for visitors. Outside of these hours, the capital cities have post office shops open on Saturday morning and some news agents also sell stamps.

Mail posted from anywhere in Australia costs AU$.45 for a standard letter while

shops is listed in the *Yellow Pages* phone book under "Duty Free."

To make a purchase you will require your passport and airline ticket. Retain all the paperwork, which may be required at your destination to meet local customs requirements.

Opals, "champagne" diamonds and jewelry made from Australian gemstones are widely admired. There are also high-quality crafts and handmade woolen goods which make good presents.

Aboriginal art is just being discovered by visitors, and many galleries will arrange for purchases to be posted safely back to your home. These are better bought at reputable galleries than shops catering for tourists.

aerograms cost AU$.60. The rate for postcards is less than airmailed letters, and these vary depending on their destination.

Telephones

Local calls cost AU$.40 from pay phones and AU$.25 from home telephones and are not timed. Some hotels charge an additional fee for outgoing calls.

Pay phones can be found in most hotels and motel rooms, and public call boxes are spread around populated areas. Public phones take 10-, 20-, 50-cent and one-dollar coins. It is possible to pay in advance for calls by purchasing a phone card from a news agent in AU$2, AU$5, AU$10, AU$20 and AU$50 denominations. Many public phones have been converted to take them; when inserted, the display on the telephone shows the residual value on the card. They are particularly useful for making long distance calls.

The prefix for telephone numbers listed throughout this book in parentheses is the STD district code, and should be omitted for local calls. When phoning into Australia omit the 0 in the STD code. Within Australia the full STD code must be used when phoning long distance.

It is possible to make long-distance (STD) calls in Australia and overseas calls (ISD) from most public phones. The rates vary according to the time of day and how far away you are calling. The rates are cheaper after 6 PM and cheaper yet after 10 PM, Monday to Saturday, and on Sunday. For example, a three-minute call to Brisbane from Melbourne will cost AU$1.35 during a weekday, but just AU$.63 after 10 PM or on Sunday.

If the prefix is 1800, the call is free anywhere in Australia. Such numbers may not be used for local calls, and a second number may be listed for use in that district. Long distance calls made on six-digit phone numbers beginning with 13, are charged at a local call rate.

Few telephone boxes have phone books so if you need assistance dial 013 for a local number, 0175 for an STD number and 0103 for international inquiries. There is no charge but the operator will only give you one telephone number at a time and does not provide addresses. For operator-connected calls within Australia dial 0176, and for an overseas number dial 0107.

To telephone overseas on ISD dial 0011, the country code, city code and then the number.

For life threatening emergencies, the police, fire brigade and ambulance service can be contacted on 000, a free call.

NEWSPAPERS

Australia has three national newspapers. *The Australian* and *Australian Financial Review* appear Monday to Friday, and *The Australian* has a bumper issue on Saturday. *The*

Bulletin, which provides news analysis of purportedly high quality is published every week.

Each state and territory has at least one daily newspaper, many of which contain an entertainment guide on Thursday or Friday and run a lift-out magazine on Saturday and Sunday. On other days there are sections on dining out and television guides.

Certain foreign journals such as *Time* and *Newsweek* are widely available from newsstands, and a variety of others in foreign languages at major hotels and in the central

districts of larger cities. Some high-circulation foreign newspapers are available in the larger news agencies.

TELEVISION

Five channels are screened in the major cities — two of which are financed, fully or partially, by the government. The government stations are the Australian Broadcasting Commission (ABC) which serves locally produced shows, good quality British and American programs and documentaries.

OPPOSITE: The fierce appearance of the thorny devil belies its timid nature. ABOVE: Aboriginal boy in ceremonial paint. OVERLEAF: Koalas

The Special Broadcasting Service (SBS) shows subtitled foreign language programs, films and sporting events from abroad.

Programming on the three commercial networks is virtually indistinguishable, with insipid American serials, telemovies and some truly awful homegrown soaps. Program details are available in the daily newspapers.

There are several cable stations now operating, and some motels and hotels subscribe and provide the service to customers.

OPENING HOURS

There used to be restricted shopping hours in Australia, but this has been abolished in most states, and shoppers can now do their thing seven days a week. Bars and pubs are open to all hours.

RELIGION

The main Christian religions are well represented in Australia, with Roman Catholi-

BASICS

CRIME

There is very little street crime in Australia compared to other Westernized countries. Pickpockets usually only work large, crowded events and purse snatchers are rare. There is, however, a high incidence of house break-ins, mostly involving drug addicts looking for ways to finance their habits. Be certain to lock motel or hotel doors and windows when you are out. Always lock your car and don't leave valuables such as cameras in a vehicle or anywhere they can be clearly seen, as this could invite a break-in.

cism and Anglicanism making up the majority, and there is usually a church for your denomination nearby. There are sizable Jewish and Moslem communities in the capital cities, and mosques and synagogues are located where the communities are concentrated.

Details of services for Christian denominations can be found listed in Saturday newspapers across the country. *The Australian Jewish Times* and *Moslem Times* have several pages on services for their respective religions.

At the end of a long hot day, bushmen like nothing better than to brew a billy of strong tea over the campfire.

EASY STRINE: AUSTRALIAN SLANG AND USEFUL WORDS

arvo afternoon
the Alice Alice Springs
back o' Bourke in the remote Outback
bang on precise or correct
Banana-bender Queenslander
barbie barbecue
bathroom a bathroom; not used as a euphemism for toilet
beaut excellent
belt up keep quiet
bikkie a biscuit or cookie
billy can for boiling water for tea over an open fire
bloke man
bloody universal oath; the great Australian adjective
bludger scrounger
blue fight
bookie bookmaker
bugs short for Moreton Bay Bugs which are a native crab-like crustacean found off the coast of Queensland.
bush anywhere which isn't in the cities or towns
Captain Cook rhyming slang for "take a look"
cackle berries eggs
chemist pharmacist or druggist
chips French fries
chook chicken
crook unwell
Crow-eater South Australian
damper bush bread cooked on coals of an open fire
deli delicatessen
dingo wild native dog; also serves as an insult
dinkum the truth
dinky di genuine
dunny toilet
fag cigarette
fair go plea to be reasonable
flog sell
footy football
g'day good day or hello
galah idiot
grog alcohol
heart starter first drink for the day
icy poles popsicles

jackaroo cowboy
jam jelly
jelly gelatine
jillaroo cowgirl
jumper sweater or pullover
Kiwi New Zealander
knocker a critic
knuckle sandwich a punch
lurk a racket
mate a friend or acquaintance
milk bars corner stores that sell milk, bread, newspapers and foodstuffs
mozzie mosquito
mug fool; a person who has been tricked
nappy diaper
ocker hick Australian
O/S overseas
one-armed bandits slot machines
Oz Australia
parka ski jacket
plonk cheap wine
pokie slot machine
Pom Englishman
ratbag an idiot, eccentric or loudmouthed political agitator
ripper terrific
'roo kangaroo
Sandgroper Western Australian
she's sweet everything is fine
sheila young woman
shoot through leave in a hurry
silvertail rich establishment figure
stockman cowboy
stubby small bottle of beer
supper late evening snack or light meal
ta thank you
TAB legal betting shop
tea evening meal, dinner
togs swim suit or bathers
tube can of beer
tucker food
two-pot screamer someone who gets drunk easily
up the creek in trouble
ute pickup truck
wowser killjoy
yabbie a native freshwater lobster, about 15 cm (six inches) in length

Further Reading

ASTLEY, THEA. *It's Raining in Mango*. Penguin, Melbourne 1989.

AUSTRALIAN INFO INTERNATIONAL. *Australian Aboriginal Culture*. Australian Government Publishing Service, Canberra 1993

BAIL, MURRAY. *Contemporary Short Stories*. Faber and Faber, London 1988.

BERNDT, RONALD and CATHERINE. *The Speaking Land*. Penguin, Melbourne 1988.

BLAINEY, GEOFFERY. *The Tyranny of Distance: How Distance shaped Australia's History*. Melbourne 1966.

CAREY, PETER. *Oscar and Lucinda*. University of Queensland Press, St. Lucia 1988.

CHATWIN, BRUCE. *The Songlines*. Picador, London 1987.

FIGGIS, PENNY (ED.) *Rainforests of Australia*. Ure Smith, Sydney 1985.

HUGHES, ROBERT. *The Fatal Shore: The Epic of Australia's Founding*. Pan Books, London 1988.

JACOBSON, HOWARD. *In the Land of Oz*. Penguin Books, London 1987.

JOLLY, ELIZABETH. *Mr. Scobie's Riddle*. Penguin, Melbourne 1983.

KNIGHT, STEPHEN. *The Selling of the Australian Mind: From the First Fleet to Third Mercedes*. William Heinemann, Australia 1990.

LAWSON, HENRY. *Best Stories of Henry Lawson*. Australian Literary Heritage Series, Sydney 1990.

LOW, TIM. *Bush Tucker*. Angus & Robertson, Sydney 1992.

LUCK, PETER. *This Fabulous Century*. Lansdowne Press, Sydney 1980.

MALOUF, DAVID. *Johnno*. University of Queensland Press, St. Lucia 1975.

MORCIMBE, MICHAEL and IRENE. *Discover Australia's National Parks and Naturelands*. Ure Smith, Sydney.

RANKIN, ROBERT. *Classic Wild Walks of Australia*. Rankin Publishers, Brisbane 1989.

RAYMOND, ROBERT. *Discover Australia's National Parks*. Ure Smith, Sydney 1985

STEWART, DAVID. *Burnum Burnum's Aboriginal Australia: A Traveller's Guide*. Angus & Robertson, Sydney 1988.

WHITE, PATRICK. *The Tree of Man*. Penguin, Melbourne 1961.

WINTON, TIM. *Cloudstreet*. McPhee Gribble, Melbourne 1991.

Photo Credits

Adina Amsel: pages 105, 263, 265, 279, 285.

Australian Tourist Commision: pages 10, 11, 12, 13, 14, 15, 16, 17, 19 *(top and bottom)*, 21, 22, 24, 25, 27, 29, 30, 31, 35, 38, 41, 43, 44, 45, 46 *(top and bottom)*, 47, 51, 52, 56, 57, 58 *(top and bottom)*, 62, 64 *(top and bottom)*, 65, 67, 68, 69, 71, 72–73, 75, 103, 117, 127, 152, 153, 159, 161, 170, 176–177, 188, 190, 193, 194–195, 196, 199, 202–203, 213, 217 *(top and bottom)*, 231, 248–249, 288, 290–291, 292.

David Austens: pages 165, 282.

Douglas Baglin: pages 79, 164, 178, 179.

Bob Davis: pages 116, 136, 141, 224, 225, 278.

Terry Duckham: page 108.

Alain Evrard: pages 90, 96, 99, 106–107, 134–135, 187, 209, 210, 211, 214–215, 230, 232–233, 236–237, 258–259.

Robert Gale: pages 113, 155.

S.T. Gill: page 87 (illustration).

Globe Press: page 85 (illustration).

Manfred Gottschalk (Globe Press): cover, pages 77, 84, 174, 277, 295.

Dallas & John Heaton (Globe Press): pages 80 *(top and bottom)*, 83, 101, 157 *(top)*, 175.

Dallas & John Heaton: pages 5 *(left)*, 109, 115, 150, 169, 173, 235, 256.

Geoff Higgins: pages 7 *(right)*, 33, 48–49, 60, 61, 78, 94 *(top and bottom)*, 95, 98, 100, 104, 110, 111, 114, 121 *(left and right)*, 123, 124, 125, 131, 138, 139, 142, 144, 145, 147 *(top and bottom)* 157 *(top and bottom)*, 162, 163, 171 *(left)*, 180, 181, 184, 185, 189, 192, 197, 201 *(top and bottom)*, 204, 205, 206, 221, 223, 227, 228, 229, 242–243, 246, 247, 250, 251, 252, 254, 255, 257, 264, 272, 272, 273, 274, 276, 283, 286 *(left and right)*, 287 *(left and right)*, 289.

P. J. Mackay: pages 140, 219.

Tony Nolan (Globe Press): pages 280–281.

David Ryan (Globe Press): page 275.

Paul Steel (Globe Press): pages 82, 88–89, 97, 148–149, 268–269.

R. Talmont (Globe Press): page 32.

Robert Wilson: page 171 *(right)*.

Carl Wolinsky: pages 253, 261.

This amazing array of chimney-like sandstone monoliths, known as the "Hidden City of Nathan", is part of the Abner Range on the Nathan River Property in the Gulf of Carpentaria.

Quick Reference A–Z Guide
to Places and Topics of Interest with
Listed Accommodation, Restaurants and
Useful Telephone Numbers